W9-DCU-509

Praise for *The Science of Enlightenment*

"Not since the Buddha himself has a clear, intelligent, and practical guide to mindfulness and awakening been available. *The Science of Enlightenment* brings a modern, technological, and scientific approach to the Buddha's teachings. Polymath and polyglot Shinzen is not shy to explain the nature of the Universe and our place within it as we expand and contract. Anyone who reads this book, embraces the recommended practices, and commits to the wisdom provided will catapult themselves towards an enlightened life. In short, *The Science of Enlightenment* will blow your mind!"

ARNIE KOZAK, PHD, author of *Mindfulness A to Z*
and *The Awakened Introvert*

"This is Shinzen Young at his best—spiritual mentor, guide, scholar of Asian languages, Dharma teacher, scientist, and spiritual adept. Shinzen is my teacher, and this book is his master work. It is a gift to those of us who follow the Dharma and want to deepen and expand our meditation practice. This slender book offers an extraordinary range of knowledge and wisdom. We are lucky to have it!"

POLLY YOUNG-EISENDRATH, PHD, author of
The Present Heart: A Memoir of Love, Loss and Discovery

"At long last, beloved meditation teacher Shinzen Young lays out his unique meditative vision for us all. This comprehensive manual, peppered with his personal experience and his vast interdisciplinary knowledge, is a testament to his many years of deep exploration and teaching of this terrain. This is sure to appeal to meditators of all levels for the development of wisdom, peace, and freedom."

DIANA WINSTON, director of mindfulness education,
UCLA Mindful Awareness Research Center,
and coauthor, with Susan L. Smalley, of *Fully Present*

"The most respected man in Western dharma has published his master-piece. I've been looking forward to Shinzen Young's book for 25 years. It's here now. And it's fantastic. A tour de force and an instant classic."

KENNETH FOLK

"What a joy it is to see this work! Shinzen Young is one of the great meditation teachers alive today. He has a profound understanding of tradition while also innovating for today's world. His rigorous experimentation reminds us that contemplative traditions aren't bound to dusty, tired ways of expression but are living and dynamic forces that still speak to us. The original *Science of Enlightenment* deeply influenced how I experienced my life and what I should do with it. I'm thrilled that another generation can learn from this master's ever-fresh voice."

JEREMY HUNTER, PHD, founding director, Executive Mind Leadership Institute, and associate professor of practice, Peter F. Drucker Graduate School of Management

"With warmth, wisdom, and stunning precision, Shinzen Young maps out his unique path through and out of the realms of suffering; a towering work by one of the great teachers of our time."

LEONARD COHEN, Grammy® Award-winning singer/songwriter and poet

"I am not a big fan of the language of 'special meditative states' or 'enlightenment' as the most skillful ways to think about or broadly cultivate access to the full range of our intrinsic wisdom and warm-heartedness. Nevertheless, Shinzen's brilliant, wide ranging, deeply passionate, and very clear developmental approach here can give anyone who cares about wisdom and compassion a precise and compelling perspective—both scientifically rigorous and culturally inclusive—on what it might mean to be fully who and what we already are, in other words, fully human, and how to realize it and let it ripen us through the systematic lifetime cultivation and application of mindfulness/heartfulness writ both seemingly small and inwardly, and seemingly large and outwardly. The fate of the world hangs in the balance, so Shinzen's highly disciplined methods and message are best taken seriously, and yet at the same time, approached with a light touch and a sense of humor, as he himself emphasizes, so we do not take ourselves and the possibility of our attaining 'special states' too seriously, especially since they are already here in this moment and there is no one to take them seriously anyway. Seriously."

JON KABAT-ZINN, author of *Mindfulness for Beginners* and co-editor, with Mark Williams, of *Mindfulness: Diverse Perspectives on its Meaning, Origins, and Applications*

"This is a beautifully rich, integrative work for students of meditation in our time. Shinzen Young speaks with clarity and authority grounded deep in contemplative experience, and informed by serious, modern scientific inquiry. This book will engage and guide anyone interested in the scholarship, the practice, and the science of meditation."

DIANE MUSHO HAMILTON, author of *Everything is Workable: A Zen Approach to Conflict Resolution*

"Shinzen's writing, like his embodied teaching style, is direct, lucid, and insightful. Through his practice, teachings, and ways of transmitting his teachings, he is able to connect with the seeker and the scientist alike in profound ways. *The Science of Enlightenment* is a must-read for those interested in how meditation works in everyday, practical terms; as well as in logical, scientific terms."

ROBERT W. ROESER, PHD, professor of psychology, Portland State University

"Shinzen's wisdom shines forth in this practical and helpful guide."

JUDSON BREWER, MD, PHD, director of research, Center for Mindfulness

"This book meets the most critical test of science excellence in that Shinzen's Unified Mindfulness strategies are both simple and therefore readily learnable, yet deeply transformative. Learning and practicing Unified Mindfulness has the potential to radically facilitate the reader's 'happiness for no particular reason.' Equally important is its potential to reduce suffering in the delivery of human and health services. Our team at The Centre for Conscious Care Canada, together with

Shinzen's guidance, has developed a revolutionary improved way to support individuals who have autism and other developmental disabilities to be all that they can be. Shinzen's unique qualities of competence and compassion—a perfect balance of science and heart—is woven into the fabric of this sacred gift."

PETER MARKS, executive director of The Centre for Care Canada and coauthor, with Gareth Marks, of *Conscious Care and Support*

"Cutting to the heart of the matter, this book explores the essence of meditation across all spiritual traditions, and in wonderfully practical ways, shows readers how to reap the rewards of greater mindfulness, concentration, and emotional balance. Shinzen is deeply trained and wise, and I've personally benefited from his instruction. His book is grounded in science, friendly, clear, relentlessly helpful—and highly recommended."

RICK HANSON, PHD, author of *Buddha's Brain: The Practical Neuroscience of Happiness, Love, and Wisdom*

"*The Science of Enlightenment* is a highly practical distillation of the key elements of many contemplative traditions, presented as a balanced, practical, and precise method. Shinzen's personal story will resonate with many and his wry humor peeks out of many sections. This book creates the ability to inquire deeply into oneself and learn the skill of responding skillfully to life, as opposed to reacting. In the words of Victor Frankl, 'Between stimulus and response there is a space. In that space is our power to choose our response. In our response lies our growth and our freedom.'"

BILL DUANE, superintendent of well-being and sustainable performance, Google

"Shinzen Young offers a map of meditation that has the incisiveness of good science, and is fully engaging and refreshing. Whether you are seeking an approachable entry, or wanting to deepen on your spiritual path, this book is a brilliant guide, full of insight and inspiration."

TARA BRACH, PHD, author of *Radical Acceptance* and *True Refuge*

"Shinzen Young's *The Science of Enlightenment* is a wonderful and informative book for anyone interested in meditation. Beginners will find clear explanations of what meditation is and how it works to support one's evolution; experienced meditators will find new perspectives that will enhance their practices; and 'ShinHeads' will rejoice at having so much of Shinzen's teaching readily at hand. Highly recommended for anyone who practices meditation."

LEIGH BRASINGTON, author of *Right Concentration:*
A Practical Guide to the Jhanas

"Shinzen Young's approach to mindfulness is both poetic and rigorous. He has already benefitted countless people with his innovative techniques. In *The Science of Enlightenment*, he demystifies the process of practice and makes it easily accessible, which will undoubtedly benefit both new and experienced meditators."

MARIA (MYOSHIN) GONZALEZ, bestselling author of
Mindful Leadership: The 9 Ways to Self-Awareness,
Transforming Yourself, and Inspiring Others

"In this fascinating, clearly written, and easy-to-read book, Shinzen takes us on a journey that combines autobiographical anecdote with correlations between many different mystical traditions, all leading to a set of principles upon which a science of meditation can be founded. This is an important and groundbreaking addition to world literature on Awakening."

CULADASA, author of *The Mind Illuminated: A Complete Meditation*
Guide Integrating Buddhist Wisdom and Brain Science

"The best book I have read on the full process of Buddhist insight meditation, from the muddy beginnings to the strange and beautiful deep end of practice. Young's primary interest is in making contemplative development more rigorous—to disambiguate the confusions, define the terms, and tease out the fundamental dynamics. Between the two great Magisteria of science and spirit, he explores a middle ground of direct experience. There is simply no teacher alive today who can do this with Young's level of experience and precision. The man has the perceptual acuity of a high-powered microscope, with enough actual scientific discipline to clearly describe what he's seeing without falling into premature conclusions or half-baked interpretive conjectures (the pitfall of too many spiritual books that seek the imprimatur of science). The effect is thrillingly provocative, a dramatic validation of the deepest aspects of what it means to be human. The text is also gracefully written, filled with fascinating personal stories and rich cultural and historical context. Simply wonderful. A must-read for anyone curious about both meditation and the future of science."

JEFF WARREN, author of *The Head Trip: Adventures on the Wheel of Consciousness* (i.e., student number 762)

"Shinzen Young is a genius in making meditation more comprehensible and practical for modern people, writing both from widespread and deep intellectual understanding and from deep personal experience and accomplishment! I give it my strongest recommendations both for those beginning meditation and for those expert in the practice."

CHARLES T. TART, professor emeritus of psychology, UC-Davis, and author of *Altered States of Consciousness* and *The End of Materialism*

"Shinzen says that 'to teach about enlightenment is to mislead people,' but that 'to fail to teach about enlightenment is also to mislead people.' It's impossible to perfectly describe and guide others on this paradoxical path. That said, it's a rare thing to have a guide that fails quite so as well as Shinzen does."

VINCENT HORN, cofounder of buddhistgeeks.com and meditate.io

"Only a broadly trained and practiced dharma-farer like Shinzen Young could have pulled off this remarkable blend of Zen's nonconceptual immediacy, Vipassana's precision, and the Western scientific perspective, along with numerous other helpful perspectives, into something so readable and practical while yet plunging the depths of practice and awakening. In short, Shinzen has totally rocked it!"

DR. DANIEL M. INGRAM, MD, MSPH, author of *Mastering the Core Teachings of the Buddha: An Unusually Hardcore Dharma Book*

"Shinzen is one of the very best meditation teachers I have ever worked with. His openness to feedback and continuous improvement embodies the essence of science: precision, depth, power, simplicity, and universality. This book is a gift from a unique visionary, presenting ancient wisdom in a manner that exemplifies the contemporary zeitgeist."

CHADE-MENG TAN, bestselling author of
Search Inside Yourself

"In this remarkable book, Shinzen shares both his personal story and the knowledge of Buddhist practice that he has accumulated over a lifetime. With his unique approach he synthesizes teachings from multiple traditions and presents them in a clear and accessible way. An accomplishment as impressive as it is inspiring."

SUSAN KAISER GREENLAND, author of *The Mindful Child*
and creator of the Inner Kids program

"Shinzen is a genuine meditation master and spiritual teacher, among other talents and abilities far beyond those of mortal monks. His grand vision furthering the unification of science with spirit, as exemplified in this tremendous new work, will help further the integrated science of enlightenment for wise living in this next century."

LAMA SURYA DAS, author of *Awakening the Buddha Within*
and founder of the Dzogchen Meditation Center

"Shinzen is my teacher, my mentor, and my friend. I was a skeptic who came to mindfulness desperately looking for relief, and Shinzen's pragmatic voice, his sheer logic, leveled my distrust. Now, as one of his senior facilitators, I'm grateful and honored to share his brilliantly wrought, unifying system of mindfulness, which has had such a radically positive effect in my life. This book speaks to your ultimate thriving as a human being."

JULIANNA RAYE, senior Shinzen Young facilitator and founder
of Unified Mindfulness training programs

The
Science of
Enlightenment

The
Science of
Enlightenment

HOW MEDITATION WORKS

SHINZEN YOUNG

sounds true
BOULDER, COLORADO

Sounds True
Boulder, CO 80306

© 2016, 2018 Shinzen Young
Foreword © 2016, 2018 Michael W. Taft

Sounds True is a trademark of Sounds True, Inc.
All rights reserved. No part of this book may be used or reproduced in any manner
without written permission from the author(s) and publisher.

Published 2016, 2018

Cover design by Lisa Kerans
Book design by Beth Skelley

Excerpts from "Four Quartets" by T.S. Eliot. Copyright 1936 by Houghton
Mifflin Harcourt Publishing Company; Copyright © renewed 1964 by T.S. Eliot.
Copyright 1940 by T.S. Eliot; Copyright © renewed 1970 by Esme Valerie Eliot.
Reprinted by permission of Houghton Mifflin Harcourt Publishing Company and
Faber and Faber Ltd. All Rights Reserved.

Printed in Canada

ISBN 978-1-68364-212-1 (paperback)

The Library of Congress has cataloged the hardcover edition as follows:
Names: Young, Shinzen, author.
Title: The science of enlightenment : how meditation works / Shinzen Young.
Description: Boulder, CO : Sounds True, 2016. | Includes index.
Identifiers: LCCN 2016003516 | ISBN 9781591794608 (hardcover)
Subjects: LCSH: Meditation—Buddhism.
Classification: LCC BQ5612 .Y68 2016 | DDC 294.3/4435—dc23
LC record available at http://lccn.loc.gov/2016003516

Ebook ISBN 978-1-62203-748-3

10 9 8 7 6 5 4 3 2 1

To my teachers

We shall not cease from exploration
And the end of all our exploring
Will be to arrive where we started
And know the place for the first time.

T. S. ELIOT, "LITTLE GIDDING"

Contents

Editor's Foreword

first encountered Shinzen Young while working as an editor at Sounds True almost twenty-five years ago. We put out a couple of audio programs with him, and as part of that, I helped create the tiny cassette-sized booklet that went with his *Break Through Pain* recording. That meant working with him quite a bit, going over the text, making edits, and so forth.

Sounds True was a dream job for me because of moments like this. Getting to see the world through the eyes of advanced practitioners, talking with them one-on-one about their understanding of their teachings and tradition, observing how they solved problems, and so on. I was a gung-ho spiritual seeker at the time, back from several trips to India, often paying good money to buy a book, hear a recording, or sit at the feet of a spiritual teacher. The fact that I was *getting paid* to work with them was almost too good to be true. It was like being a student at a real-life Hogwarts or going to meditation college. Given that meditation and spiritual practice was both my all-consuming personal interest as well as my job, I thought I had seen it all, so to speak. But Shinzen was something quite different.

This impression was confirmed a year or two later, when I was given the assignment of editing a much larger audio program by him. He had come into our new, spacious studio with five or six students who sat on the floor while he spent a solid week talking to and meditating with them. I had sat in on several of the recording sessions, and had been quite intrigued by what I heard. Tami Simon had asked Shinzen to deliver a "brain dump of everything he knew about meditation," and it was fascinating. When the time came to edit this magnum opus, the computer hard drive contained almost fifty hours of his talks. (We edited digitally even though the program would be published on cassette.) My job then was to sit in a small, dark, very silent room and edit this enormous pile of material into a twelve-part cassette tape series to be entitled, "The Science of Enlightenment." The process of editing reminded me of some of the retreat practices I had done.

The next couple of weeks were a revelation. Shinzen's guidance, his concepts, his outlook were those of the kind of meditation teacher that I had sensed must be out there. He had a comprehensive grasp of Asian languages—the original tongues of the books, scriptures, and terms that compose the bedrock of many of the meditative traditions. He had a scholar's grasp of the philosophy of spiritual practice and was comfortable talking about not only the upsides of various viewpoints, but also their potential downsides in a frank and knowledgeable manner.

But he wasn't just some dry theoretician either. He had done extensive retreat practices in all three vehicles (i.e., types) of Buddhism, including three years as a robed Shingon monk in Japan and decades of hardcore traditional Zen retreats in both Asia and the United States. He had sat with vipassana teachers in India. And he had done numerous sweat lodges and sun dances with the Lakota Sioux in a fully traditional Native American context. He was even willing—unlike so many American dharma teachers—to talk about enlightenment as a serious goal of meditation practice, as something that a regular human being could aim for and achieve.

But there was more. Shinzen is a classic nerd, the kind of guy who wants to talk about arcane minutiae of word etymologies, and is highly conversant in science and math. A dharma talk with Shinzen is as likely to include a discussion of tensor calculus, the physics of fluid dynamics, or an unpacking of how the Japanese word "Zen" and the English word "theory" sprang from the same Indo-European root as it is to include an explication of meditation practice or aspects of the spiritual path. What's more, he relates such topics to each other, interweaves them, and shows them to be interconnected facets of greater and deeper ideas and teachings.

On top of it all, Shinzen is a compelling storyteller. He has the most amazing tales, ranging from the often-shocking extremes of monastic practice in Asia to hilarious and insightful anecdotes about meditation centers in America.

In short, I was hooked. He was exactly the kind of teacher I had been looking for: brilliant, funny, learned, and steeped in a lifetime of serious practice. It took me about two weeks of heavy engagement to edit the tape series into its final form. The hardest part about it was the upper limit on the size of our tape sets, which meant that I had to leave so much valuable material on the (virtual) cutting room floor.

A decade later, I had left Sounds True, and that box of twelve audio-cassettes had become something of a cult classic. Never a bestseller, it "had legs" as they say. *The Science of Enlightenment* was one of those rare programs about which listeners were likely to say, "It changed my life." Particularly, long-time meditators who felt like their practice had become stale, or who had lost momentum, were benefitting from it. This unassuming program from a nerdy meditation teacher nobody had ever heard of had the secret sauce that could transform a solid but lackluster meditation practice into something truly alive, power-ful, and life altering. Around that time, Tami approached me with a question: Would I be interested in editing the audio series into a book for Sounds True?

My answer was an instant and unequivocal "Yes." We guessed it might take a few months to complete. (Can you hear the Fates gig-gling in the background?) Shinzen, Tami, and I were all excited about the possibilities of the book, and I got going right away.

Initially, the idea had been to simply make the tape set into a book, but I felt that here was a chance to rescue all that excellent material that I had had to cut out of the audio. So I obtained a tran-scription of the entire raw recording and worked from that. Making spoken word audio read well as text is not as easy as you might assume. There are a lot of differences between the spoken and writ-ten word, and sometimes things that make sense when said become ambiguous when the context, tone, and emphasis of the speaker are lost. Furthermore, the spontaneous wandering of live talks doesn't translate well into the linear logic we expect of books. It's an arduous process, but for me it's also fun and fascinating. Within a few short months, just as we predicted, I had produced a rough draft of a large portion of the book.

It was a decent first shot, but there were several things I wasn't happy about. First, during the intervening years, I had spent many hours in meditation retreats with Shinzen, and I realized that while *The Science of Enlightenment* was a large and comprehensive program, it was actually missing a great deal of Shinzen's vast storehouse of knowledge. I furthermore realized that Shinzen's teachings had themselves evolved and been refined since the set was recorded. He is a very creative teacher, always refining and reworking his lessons. Thus, I felt compelled to supplement the original material by both adding to it and reworking it to fit his new formulations.

Little did I know the rabbit hole this would lead me down. Shinzen had a lot of other recordings, some of which I thought would be helpful to add in, and which I dutifully transcribed. I also interviewed Shinzen endlessly on the telephone, asking him clarifying questions on a multitude of topics. This produced many more hours of fascinating content, which also needed to be transcribed. Then there were the hundreds of hours of dharma talks. And as the years passed, dozens of hours of video also appeared. The project assumed a Sorcerer's Apprentice quality; it seemed that the more questions I asked, the larger and deeper the scope of Shinzen's answers became, and the bigger the task grew. There was always another facet, and another story, and another unexpected jewel.

Eventually all this raw material became so huge and unwieldy that it was necessary to break up many hours of dharma talk recordings into pieces, and distribute them to a veritable army of volunteer transcribers who transformed them into text files. (A heartfelt thank-you to you all!) The physical stack of paper printouts was about a yard tall. All of which I read, evaluated, organized, vetted, reshuffled, ranked, and then actually edited into something which reads like a book. This process ended up not taking months, but years.

But it wasn't just the size of the project that was challenging. Shinzen had not been standing still while I was attempting to wrangle this book together. He had continued to grow, change, and improve his teachings. His overarching metaphors, the themes, organizing principles, labels, and even the ways he talked about the basics of meditation shifted in ways great and small. As helpful as these changes and additions were, they made writing the book an exercise in what software programmers call "feature creep," which means that the features of the thing you're supposed to make change before you're done making it. Chapters were written, only to become obsolete and require complete rewriting as later chapters were completed. Tears of frustration were shed. Deadlines were missed, and new deadlines passed away. All told, instead of a few months, it took almost ten years to complete.

But as the years passed, something else was occurring also. I was attending long retreat after retreat with Shinzen, dozens of them. I got a lot out of that personally; my practice deepened, and my life improved dramatically. And my understanding of his teachings, as well as the stories he liked to tell, and the ideas that most deeply underpinned his work, grew clearer and more precise. During dharma talks at retreats, I made notes about particularly interesting or illuminating topics, often noticing how these fit together in ways not apparent on the surface. Slowly, I assembled a list of what I considered to be Shinzen's "greatest hits"—the themes, stories, and concepts which he returned to most often, which had the most impact, and which were the most uniquely his. And these became the basis and organizing principle of the book you are holding in your hands now.

This is a unique text in many ways. First of all, it's not intended as a beginner's guide to practice. It's probably the most relevant to those who have at least some level of ongoing practice and meditative insight. Shinzen is a teacher who can work well even with children if need be, but whose finest expression (at least in my opinion) is when he's expounding upon the deeper aspects of serious practice.

Furthermore, many of the chapters of this book are adaptations of talks, given in the context of a long retreat, to students who had been sitting with him for years. As editor, I have arranged the talks in an order that allows each one to build upon the context of the earlier ones, brick-upon-brick fashion. Since he was assuming a shared knowledge of many of the underlying concepts with the audience, I have also inserted or expanded explanations of some ideas to help the reader.

Editing this text has been one of the biggest challenges and greatest honors of my life. It has caused me to dig down into these profound teachings much more deeply than I may have otherwise. Shinzen has proven himself to be infinitely patient, as well as generous and giving beyond all bounds. Any mistakes or distortions you find in this book are mine, not his. All the magic and brilliance, on the other hand, is uniquely his own. It is my deepest wish that the material in this book give you as much joy, depth, and insight into life, yourself, other people, and the world as it has me.

MICHAEL W. TAFT
BERKELEY, CALIFORNIA, 2014

Author's Preface

I t took me quite a while to get the point of publishing this book—many years actually. That may seem like a strange statement. How can someone not get the point of publishing something they themselves wrote? Let me explain.

A central notion of Buddhism is that there's not a thing inside us called a self. One way to express that is to say that we are a colony of sub-personalities and each of those sub-personalities is in fact not a noun but a verb—a doing.

One of my doings is Shinzen the researcher. Shinzen the researcher is on a mission to "take the mist out of mysticism." Contrary to what is often claimed, he believes that mystical experience can be described with the same rigor, precision, and quantified language that one would find in a successful scientific theory. In his opinion, formulating a clear description of mystical experience is a required prenuptial for the Marriage of the Millennium: the union of quantified science and contemplative spirituality. He hopes that eventually this odd couple will exuberantly make love, spawning a generation of offspring that precipitously improves the human condition.

Shinzen the researcher also believes that many meditation masters, current and past, have formulated their teachings with "less than full rigor" by making unwarranted, sweeping philosophical claims about the nature of objective reality based on their subjective experiences—claims that tend to offend scientists and, hence, impede the science-spirituality courtship.

Shinzen the researcher has a natural voice. It's the style you would find in a graduate text on mathematics: definition, lemma, theorem, example, corollary, postulate, theorem. Here's a sample of that voice:

It may be possible to model certain global patterns of brain physiology in ways that feel familiar to any trained scientist, i.e., equations in differential operators on scalar, vector, or tensor fields whose dependent variables can be quantified in terms of SI units and whose independent variables are time and space (where space equals ordinary space or some more esoteric differentiable manifold). It is perhaps even possible to derive those equations from first principles the way Navier-Stokes is derived from Cauchy continuity. In such fields, distinctive "flow regimes" are typically associated with relations on the parameters of the equations, i.e., $F(P_j) \rightarrow Q$, where Q is qualitative change in field behavior. By qualitative change in field behavior, I mean things like the appearance of solitons or the disappearance of turbulence, etc. Through inverse methods, it may be possible to establish a correspondence between the presence of a certain parameter relation in the equations modeling a field in a brain and the presence of classical enlightenment in the owner of that brain. This would provide a way to physically quantify and mathematically describe (or perhaps even explain) various dimensions of spiritual enlightenment in a way that any trained scientist would feel comfortable with.

That's not the voice you'll be hearing in this book. This book is a record of a different Shinzen, Shinzen the dharma teacher, as he talks to students engaged in meditation practice. Shinzen the dharma teacher has no resistance at all to speaking with less than full rigor. He's quite comfortable with words like God, Source, Spirit, or phrases like "the nature of nature." In fact, *his* natural voice loves spouting the kind of stuff that makes scientists wince. Here's an example of that voice:

The same cosmic forces that mold galaxies, stars, and atoms also mold each moment of self and world. The inner self and the outer scene are born in the cleft between expansion and contraction. By giving yourself to those forces, you become those forces, and through that, you experience a kind of immortality—you live in the breath and pulse of every animal, in the polarization of electrons and protons, in the interplay of the thermal expansion and self-gravity that molds stars, in the interplay of dark matter that holds galaxies together and dark energy that stretches space apart. Don't be afraid to let expansion and contraction tear you apart, scattering you in many directions while ripping away the solid ground beneath you. Behind that seeming disorder is an ordering principle so primordial that it can never be disordered: father-God effortlessly expands while mother-God effortlessly contracts. The ultimate act of faith is to give yourself back to those forces, give yourself back to the Source of the world, and through that, become the kind of person who can optimally contribute to the Mending of the world.

Shinzen the hard-nosed researcher and Shinzen the poetic dharma teacher get along just fine. After all, they're both just waves. Particles may bang together. Waves automatically integrate. Just one problem though. The researcher is a fussy perfectionist. He is very resistant to the notion of publishing anything that lacks full rigor. Spoken words return to silence from where they come. Printed text sits around for centuries waiting for every tiny imprecision and incompleteness to be exposed.

So it took a while for me to see value in allowing my talks to be published in something close to their original spoken form.

Deep gratitude to my editor Michael W. Taft; Tami Simon, founder and publisher of Sounds True; Todd Mertz, my business development manager; and my genius assistant, Emily Barrett, for their encouragement, support, probing, and astounding levels of patience over the many years that it took for this book to see the light of day. I would like to thank Danny Cohen, Martin Hoy, Har-Prakash Khalsa, Don

McCormick, Chade-Meng Tan, Chris Trani, and Jeff Warren for their comments and suggestions. I sincerely hope that you, the reader, find the book fun and useful.

Furthermore, let me express my appreciation (in no particular order) for: Bill Koratos, my friend and business partner, who supported me in so many ways through the long process of developing this material; Ann Buck for her warm friendship and generosity of spirit; Choshin Blackburn for her impeccable grace in organizing my retreats and creating such a welcoming atmosphere; Charley Tart for his constant encouragement and thoughtful as well as thought-provoking dialogue; Shelly Young, Stephanie Nash, Soryu Forall, Julianna Raye, and Peter Marks, among others, for helping me create my system; Magdalena Naylor, Dave Vago, David Creswell, and Emily Lindsay for their interest in applying the rigors of scientific research to this work; Markell Brooks, Bob Stiller, Dave Stiller, Christian Stiller, Greg Smith, and Judith Smith for all they have done to support my work. If I forgot to mention anyone, it is due to the limitations of memory, not appreciation.

Lastly, I'd also like to thank all my students for their enthusiastic collaboration in all the meditation experiments I've tried over the years.

One final note about the terminology in this book. I like experimenting with language. Over the years, I've created an idiosyncratic jargon for describing both ordinary sensory experience and certain special phenomena that can occur in the course of practice. Often but not always, I'll employ capitalization to alert you to the fact that I'm using language idiosyncratically. For example: "See" refers to any and all visual experience, "Hear" refers to any and all auditory experience, "Feel" refers to any and all body experience, "Gone" refers to the instant when a sensory experience vanishes, "Flow" refers generically to change in a sensory experience, and "Source" refers to the deepest level of consciousness.

I should also mention something about how I use the word "space" as it can refer to several rather different things. There is physical space, which Einstein showed is inextricably mixed with time. Then there is formal space, which refers to various mathematical abstractions:

Euclidian spaces, projective spaces, topological spaces, and so forth. Then there's the sensory experience of space.

If you observe carefully, you'll notice that everything you see, hear, and feel has width, depth, and height. It's spatial by nature. Even the mind is spatial. The mind has a front part, which I call the center of image space (for many people this is located in front of and/or behind their eyes). And the mind has a back part, which I call mental talk space (for many people this is located in their head and at their ears). Some people refer to the center of image space as their mental screen, which is a two-dimensional paradigm, but for other people, the center of image space is more like a stage; that is, it has width, height, *and* depth. Similarly, mental talk space has width, height, and depth, although for most people, those parameters are rather ill-defined. So mental experience is spatial: image space + talk space = mind space.

Physical and emotional experiences are also spatial. Physical sights appear in front of our eyes, and they obviously have width, depth, and height. External sounds can be localized: right, left, front, back, above, below. Physical-type body sensations occupy regions within or around the body. The same holds for emotional-type body sensations.

Being aware of the size, shape, and location of sensory events represents clarity with regard to the *spatial* nature of experience. As your focus skills grow, you increasingly appreciate the spatial nature of experience. But at some point, a qualitative shift may occur. You begin to notice the *spacious* nature of sensory experience. Sensory events seem to arise within a vast openness and are pervaded by a feathery thinness. It's as though the inner self and the outer world are literally made of space.

To sum it up, the word "space" can mean four different things depending on the context. There's what the physicist means by space, there's what the mathematician means by space, there's the ordinary experience of space (i.e., the spatiality of the senses), and then there is the extraordinary experience of space (i.e., the spaciousness of the senses).

Throughout this book, the word "space" usually refers to experiential space, the third and fourth meanings described above. I'm not claiming that those necessarily have any link to what physicists or mathematicians mean by space. That's a philosophical question above my pay grade.

Appreciating the *spatial* nature of sensory experience has great practical value. It makes sensory experience trackable and, therefore, tractable. Appreciating the *spacious* nature of sensory experience goes beyond that. Taken to the deepest level, it's synonymous with enlightenment itself.

SHINZEN YOUNG
BURLINGTON, VERMONT, 2015

CHAPTER ONE

My Journey

I have practiced, taught, and researched meditation for almost fifty years. If you were to ask me how that has had an impact on my soul, I'd have to say it's been bittersweet. Don't get me wrong; the sweet part totally trumps the bitter. Meditation has been very good to me. It has vastly deepened my sensual fulfillment and allowed me to see that my happiness need not depend on conditions. It has given me a new way to view myself and provided me with a set of tools for refining my behaviors and improving my relationships. Yes, sweet. But the icing on the cake is that every day I get to see people's lives change as the result of things I share with them. Often those changes are dramatic. People get to live their lives on a scale two or three times bigger than they otherwise would have been. That's a large claim, but the mechanism is quite simple: meditation elevates a person's base level of focus. By focus, I mean the ability to attend to what's relevant in a given situation. By base level, I mean how focused you automatically get in daily life when you're not making an effort to be focused. If you're consistently two or three times more focused in each moment of life, then you're living two or three times bigger, two or three times richer. Five decades ago, some very kind people in Japan slipped me the secret: you can dramatically extend life—not by multiplying the number of your years, but by expanding the fullness of your moments. Knowing that I have lived with such richness makes the visage of my inevitable death less problematic. That's the sweet part.

So what's the bitter part? It is that most people will, in the end, not allocate the modest amount of time and energy required to do that. I live with the knowledge that most people will never have what they so easily could achieve. I know that the demands of daily life will convince them that they cannot set aside even a few moments to develop the one skill that will make it possible for them to optimally respond to those demands. The phrase "what's wrong with this picture?" comes to mind. But once again, don't get me wrong. I'm not bummed out. In fact, I'm rather optimistic about the future. I explain why in the last chapter of this book.

Although we may never meet in person, I feel subtly connected to you through these pages. Whether you have a meditation practice or not, the mere fact that you're interested in a book like this means that you've come a long way. Welcome.

∽

I call what I present here a "science of enlightenment." By science, I mean an experiment that is reproducible by anyone. Meditation is something that human beings all over the world have been doing for a long time. Done properly, under the guidance of a qualified teacher, the results are—to a certain extent—predictable. Science can also refer to a structured body of knowledge, which the path of meditation definitely represents.

The other noun in the title is "enlightenment." Defining enlightenment is notoriously tricky. Almost anything you say about it, no matter how true, may also be misleading. Having said that, here's a place to start: you can think of enlightenment as a kind of permanent shift in perspective that comes about through direct realization that there is no *thing* called "self" inside you.

This is a very rough and ready definition. We might call it the "executive summary." Notice that I'm not saying that there is no self, but rather no *thing* called a self. Of course, there is certainly an *activity* inside you called personality, an *activity* of the self. But that is different from a *thing* called the self. Meditation changes your relationship to sensory experience, including your thoughts and body sensations. It allows you to experience thoughts and body sensations in a clear and unblocked way. When the sensory experience of the mind-body becomes sufficiently clear and uninhibited, it ceases to be a rigid thing that imprisons your identity. The sensory self becomes a comfortable home, not a jail cell. That's why enlightenment is sometimes referred to as liberation. You realize that the thingness of self is an artifact caused by habitual nebulosity and viscosity around your mind-body experience.

Confusingly, the experience of no self can also be described as the experience of true self or deepest soul. You can call it no self, true self, big self, elastic self, liberation, nature, or true love—you can call it whatever you want. The important thing is not so much what you call it but to know why it's relevant to your life and how you can feasibly get there. That's the purpose of this book.

Sometimes this realization happens suddenly. You can read about that sudden version in books like Philip Kapleau's classic *The Three Pillars of Zen,* which contains numerous testimonials from people who experienced enlightenment quite suddenly. But in my experience as a teacher, enlightenment usually sneaks up on people. Sometimes they don't quite realize how enlightened they've become over time because they have gradually acclimatized to it.

So the perception of self—what it is, and how it arises—is central to the science of enlightenment. We'll be looking at this in detail in the course of this book. But for now, I'd like to make a few disclaimers about my definition of enlightenment.

First, my definition represents the low bar. That is, it describes the *minimum* change needed to qualify. However, that doesn't mean it's the end of the journey. In point of fact, it is merely the beginning of the unfolding of the "wisdom function" within you.

Second, there are some people who claim that enlightenment is fictional, an exaggeration, or a celestial height that mere mortals can never approach. Let me be clear: enlightenment is real. Not only is it real, but it is something that can be achieved by normal human beings through the systematic practice of meditation. Can people get to that place without practicing meditation? Yes, but meditation makes it more probable that they'll get to that place, and meditation makes it more probable that they'll continue to grow optimally after they get there.

In the course of this text, we'll look at some of the signposts along the path as well as some of the potential pitfalls and how to avoid them. I hope to sensitize you to the issues that can arise and give you a practical understanding of how to proceed. Of course, none of this can substitute for getting personal guidance from a qualified teacher, but it will hopefully function as an inspiration, a supplement, and a guidebook.

Third, I'm fully aware that "enlightenment" is a term with the potential to cause misunderstandings and even contention. There is some dispute in spiritual circles about whether enlightenment is something a teacher should even explicitly talk about, and whether it's a goal to be achieved or something that already exists, or both.

I'm familiar with these various viewpoints and am sensitive to the concerns they represent. Philosophically, I'm fully prepared to argue for either side of such questions. But as a teacher, I feel it is my duty to take a stand and to teach from a certain perspective. Each perspective has its own characteristic hazards. The perspective I've chosen is to explicitly describe enlightenment and present it as a feasible goal for ordinary people.

Spiritual practice is often described as a kind of path with recognizable stages. But such a practice-as-path paradigm can involve some pitfalls. In colloquial usage, the word "path" implies a starting point, a destination, and a distance separating the two. But if enlightenment means realizing where you've always been, then the distance between the starting point and the destination must be zero, contradicting the very concept of a path.

Moreover, when we describe spirituality as a path, it immediately sets up all kinds of craving, aversion, confusion, and unhelpful comparisons. People wish they were at some other place on the path, and they struggle to get there. When we think about spirituality as a path, we create the idea of enlightenment as an object out there in the future, separate from ourselves.

As teachers, we're damned if we do and damned if we don't. If we describe a path to enlightenment, it leads to the aforementioned problems. If we fail to describe a path, people won't have motivation or direction, and they won't be sensitive to the benchmarks. They won't know how to make optimal use of signs of progress. They won't know how to recognize windows of opportunity when nature presents them.

portab

Thus to teach about enlightenment is to mislead people. On the other hand, to fail to teach about enlightenment is also to mislead people. You might say that to be a teacher means being willing to take on some bad karma in the service of greater good karma.

There is a Zen story about an enlightened teacher who was climbing a tree. He slipped and fell in such a way that he was able to bite onto a branch, but he couldn't reach it with his hands or feet. He was literally hanging by his teeth. Then, from under the tree, a student asked him the question, "What is the essence of enlightenment?"

The teacher knew the answer to the question, but in order to give it, he would have to open his mouth, in which case he would fall to his death. On the other hand, if he failed to give the answer, he would be shirking his duty to aid his fellow beings.

This story is the basis of a *koan,* or Zen question: "If that were *you* hanging from the tree, what would you do?" The koan is intended for advanced students who are in the position of teaching. It deals with a central paradox that comes up whenever we attempt to describe a path to enlightenment. If you teach that there is a path, you subtly mislead people, so you're dead. If you don't teach a path, you fail to inform and encourage people, so you're dead. Either way, you're dead. What would *you* do?

So to write a book like this represents a choice on my part—a choice to die in the line of duty. But how did I get involved in all this to begin with?

Growing Up

I was born in Los Angeles, California, in 1944. My mother tells me that I was a difficult baby—whiny, fussy, agitated, high maintenance. Many of my earliest memories center around three themes: great difficulty dealing with physical discomfort, utter inability to be around others who were in emotional discomfort, and a constant sense of agitation and impatience. If I physically hurt myself in any way, or if the room was too hot or too cold, or if I was ill, I would literally freak out. I can remember devising elaborate strategies to put off for as long as possible visits to the doctor (shots!) and visits to the dentist (drilling!). I simply could not abide pain of any sort.

I was also inordinately impatient in school. I would watch the clock all day, longing for the hands to reach 3:00 p.m., when I could leave. I felt frightened and uncomfortable in social situations and had to leave the room if any adult was going through difficult emotions. A girl I knew in school, whose parents were close to mine, died suddenly. My parents went to visit the family, but I refused to accompany them. I simply had no idea what to do around people who were grieving.

I did very poorly in school, which was a source of great consternation for my parents. If the concept of attention deficit hyperactivity disorder had existed in those days, I probably would have been diagnosed as having a severe case and been heavily medicated.

To sum it all up, my genes and early conditioning predisposed me to be "antimeditative."

At the age of fourteen, I developed a passionate fascination with Asian languages and the traditional cultures of the East. As a result, I began attending a Japanese ethnic school in addition to American public school. In 1962, I graduated from Venice High School where I was a nerdy social outcast. In the same week, I graduated from Sawtelle Japanese Language Institute, where I was the class valedictorian. The institute wanted to showcase the Japanese-speaking white guy. My high school grades were not good enough to get me into college, but my uncle Jack found out that, even if you had bad grades, if you did well on tests that measured your potential for success in college, you could get admitted to the University of California system. I took the tests, did quite well, and was admitted to UCLA as a potentially gifted student.

At UCLA, I majored in Asian languages and took my senior year in Japan as an exchange student. That year was one of the happiest times in my life. I was in paradise. In those days, it was uncommon for a foreigner to speak Japanese, but I could speak, read, and write like a native. I could open any door just by opening my mouth. I hardly attended my university classes at all. Instead, I spent most of my time exploring the culture. One of the things I got involved with was the *sencha* tea ceremony. I was horrible at it, being by nature klutzy, antsy, and unfocused, but it was still a lot of fun because almost all the other students were young, cute, kimono-clad girls. I felt like the sole thorn in a rose garden. My tea teacher must have sensed that I needed some remedial training in being an adult, so she suggested that I go to Manpuku-ji, a Zen temple in Kyoto, with which she had some connections.

I spent a month at the temple. I didn't do any meditation, but I did hang out with the monks, talking with them and learning about Buddhist culture. They made a profound impression on me. I sensed that they knew about some sort of "secret sauce," a way to be deeply happy regardless of conditions. And I sensed that they would willingly share it with me but would never force it upon me. I would have to take the initiative if I wanted to experience it for myself. But I was not ready yet, given my intrinsically antimeditative personality.

Still, hanging out with the monks of Manpuku-ji did change me. I became fascinated with Buddhist ideas and culture, albeit from an academic perspective. Upon my return to the United States and my graduation from UCLA, I entered a PhD course in Buddhist studies at the University of Wisconsin. In the late 1960s, Madison was a wild scene, and I loved it. I participated in the riotous antiwar protests, got tear-gassed and clubbed by the city police, vastly improved my Sanskrit, studied Tibetan and Pali, and read the Buddhist classics in their original, canonical languages. I spent my summer breaks in San Francisco, learning about pot and LSD. I was able to complete all my PhD coursework in just two years and was sent back to Japan to do research on my doctoral thesis.

At that time, the University of Wisconsin had the largest academic program in Buddhist studies in the Western Hemisphere. The chairman of the program, Richard Robinson, was my mentor, idol, and role model. He was an awesome polymath who could pun in Sanskrit and Japanese in the same sentence. His specialty was Buddhist logic—the syllogistic forms used by Indian and Tibetan philosophers to refute the "thingness" of things based on reasoning similar to Zeno's paradoxes.

During this time, two events occurred that profoundly altered the course of my life, one just before my departure to Japan and the other about a year after.

The Brownie Epiphany

As I mentioned, during my two years of graduate school, I spent my summers in San Francisco, being initiated into the drug-centered zeitgeist of Haight-Ashbury. One afternoon, my friends and I dropped acid and went to the movie *Yellow Submarine*. The next day, I was alone in a friend's apartment and decided to smoke some hashish. Then I got the munchies, and began eating a delicious, chewy chocolate brownie.

I *really* got into that brownie. For a few minutes, I entered a state of *samadhi* (extraordinary concentration) centered on the taste and tactile sensation of the brownie. I became so focused on the act of eating the brownie that everything else fell away. There was just the brownie.

It was sweet and yummy, but I also noticed that it had interesting textural properties. There were holes in the brownie caused by gas bubbles, and around those holes, the cake was harder and more dense than in its other parts. As I bit into the brownie, I could clearly detect the diffuse texture of the cake, the dense envelope around the holes, and the nothingness inside the hole. I remember thinking, "The holes taste as good as the cake." *At that instant, the duality of existence versus nonexistence passed away, and for a moment, I was thrust into a world of oneness.* Something had shifted—dramatically.

That shift did not immediately go away, even after I had completely come down from the drugs. For about two weeks, I walked around in a magic world. Prior to that, the things I had read about in my Buddhist studies seemed to me to be nothing but mythological ruminations and philosophical conjectures, elaborated by scholars with too much time on their hands. Now, for the first time, I realized that they were not just concocting speculations. They were trying to describe something that human beings actually experience. After a couple of weeks, the experience faded into a pleasant memory, but it left me with a permanent intellectual shift. I now knew that certain parts of the Buddhist tradition, which I had been studying as philosophical concepts, were in fact direct descriptions of actual experience. At the time, I had no way to get back to that experience, but at least I knew for sure that there was something in Buddhism besides quaint culture, scholastic speculation, and superstition.

Looking back now, with decades of experience under my belt, I understand exactly what occurred that day in the Haight. Such spontaneous, transient, micro-tastes of enlightenment are not uncommon. I suspect that they occur for many, perhaps even most, people. Typically, the experience happens without warning and without previous practice, and passes after a few minutes, or hours, or days. In my present capacity as a meditation teacher, I am frequently approached by people who have had such spontaneous experiences—unfortunately often well after those experiences have already faded for them. I do not understand exactly why such spontaneous experiences occur when they do, to whom they do. In my case, the drugs may have facilitated it, but they were not the central factor, because drug-based epiphanies vanish as soon as the drugs are metabolized, and my experience definitely did not vanish immediately. I'd give anything to know what occurs neurophysiologically when people have such spontaneous quasi-enlightenment experiences. The fact that unitive no-self experiences happen to people who have no meditative training or spiritual perspective indicates to me that enlightenment is in some sense natural and just waiting to happen. When we finally learn why they happen spontaneously, albeit transiently, to some people under certain circumstances, we will probably be able to foster an enlightened age on this planet. That's why I said that I'd give anything to know, from a scientific point of view, what happens in cases like my brownie epiphany.

On the other hand, although I don't know why such experiences occur spontaneously for some people, I definitely know why they fail to last for most people. There are several reasons for this. The first is that, in general, people who do not meditate do not have high habitual levels of concentration power. When a unitive, or no-self/big-self, state arises, they lack the concentration power to zero in on it and maintain it in the center of their awareness. Second, even if people have some concentration power, they usually lack the sensory clarity to track how selfhood arises and passes in real time. Third, most people do not have high levels of habitual equanimity. Equanimity is the ability to allow sensory experience to well up without suppression and to pass away without identifying with it. After a glimpse of no self, the old habitual "self-self" will rearise. Without tracking skills and equanimity, people quickly re-identify with their former habitually patterned identity and, consequently, the unitive perspective fades.

By way of contrast, if some level of cultivated concentration power, sensory clarity, and equanimity precedes a spontaneous insight into oneness, that insight can be held centrally in awareness through concentration, and when the old habitual self reemerges, there need not be a reidentification with it. This is the difference between peak experiences, such as my brownie epiphany, and actual enlightenment. Enlightenment is not a peak from which you descend over time. It is a plateau from which you ascend, further and further as the months, years, and decades pass.

Learning to Pay Attention

Once I completed my PhD coursework, all I needed to do to get my academic degree was write my dissertation. As my thesis topic, I decided to study the Shingon school of Japanese Buddhism. Shingon is a Japanese version of Vajrayana, similar in many ways to the practices that are central to Tibetan Buddhism. However, Shingon is not a direct import from Tibet to Japan; rather, the Tibetan Vajrayana and the Japanese Vajrayana share a common ancestor in late Indian Buddhism. Interest in Tibetan Vajrayana practice was beginning to burgeon in the late 1960s, but virtually no Westerner had studied the tradition's Japanese version. It occurred to me that Shingon studies would be a perfect subject to make my academic specialty. The topic required familiarity with a wide range of languages—modern Japanese, classical Japanese, classical Chinese, Sanskrit, and Tibetan—all of which

I had studied. My plan was to go to Japan, study Shingon for a year or so, write my dissertation based on that study, and come back to the United States and find an academic position as the foremost Western scholar of Japanese Vajrayana. But as we shall see, things didn't work out that way.

I arrived at Mount Koya, the center of Shingon Buddhism, with letters of introduction and a command of both the canonical languages and the doctrinal framework of Shingon. But when I asked to be taught more, I was literally turned away at the gate. The master with whom I wanted to study, Abbot Nakagawa, told me in no uncertain terms that Shingon practice was not an intellectual curio, but a path for transforming a person's consciousness and life. If I wanted to actually practice it, then I would first have to live in the temple doing menial tasks. After a while, if he felt that I was worthy, I could then be ordained as a monk. But he offered no guarantee that would ever happen. And even if he did ordain me, I would have to live as a monk for a time while he determined if I was worthy to receive the Shingon initiations. He also couldn't guarantee that would ever happen.

The message was clear: it was his way or the highway. I would have to either pick some other topic for my dissertation or jump through Abbot Nakagawa's hoops. I had been told that he was "the last fully traditional" Shingon master, and to learn from anyone else was to miss out on what old-school Shingon training was really about.

I waffled back and forth on this. As you'll remember, I am by nature an agitated, impatient, and wimpy sort of guy. The prospect of the severe training involved in being a Buddhist monk in Japan was utterly daunting to me. But in the end, I decided to take up the abbot's challenge because, although I was still primarily interested in Shingon as an academic specialty, the brownie epiphany had convinced me that there was something valid and personally meaningful to be found in Buddhist practice. I made a momentous, life-altering decision. I moved into the abbot's temple, Shinno-in.

Every morning the monks would do a long chant, and I would join in. I set myself the task of memorizing the entire liturgy. After the chanting, I spent most of the day doing simple jobs around the temple, such as cleaning, washing dishes, raking the garden, and serving meals to guests. I found this regimen extremely difficult. Previous to this, I had spent my days in studying and reading. Doing menial labor was torture for me. I was bored and agitated, my attention constantly wandering into memory, planning, fantasizing—always thinking about how I could be understanding Buddhism better by studying. Why was I wasting my time washing floors and cleaning toilets?

After a few months, I was at my wit's end, and probably would have bailed had it not been for a stroke of good luck. One day, I was watching a group of monks practice sumo wrestling, and they asked me if I wanted to try it myself. I stripped down and put on the distinctive loincloth of the sumo wrestler and started to fool around with them. They were all much bigger and heavier than I was; I felt like a Chihuahua among German shepherds. Not only was I skinny and weak, but I was poorly coordinated to boot. The whole thing was pretty comical: skinny white boy in a loincloth being pushed around by Japanese giants.

We were all laughing and having a great time. Then I noticed an older monk watching us from the sidelines and laughing too. His name was Okamura Keishin, and he was the coach of the sumo club. We struck up a conversation, and I found out that, although he was a Shingon monk by lineage, he was connected with the so-called Kyoto School of Zen philosophy. He told me that he had a weekly Zen sitting group there on Mount Koya and suggested that I attend.

When I started to sit with his group, he gave me the traditional, initial Zen concentration practice of breath counting. He insisted that I sit in full lotus for the full hour of the practice, which was hugely painful. But after a few months, I started to notice something interesting toward the end of my sit. My breath would slow down spontaneously, my body would relax despite the pain, and—miracle of miracles—the voice in my head would stop frantically screaming. It was still there, but more like an undercurrent, a whisper.

I went to Okamura sensei and said, "My meditation is becoming interesting." He said, "Oh, is that so? Interesting in what way?" I described to him the slowing of the breath, the relaxing into the pain, and the semi-quieting of the self-talk. He said that that was good, and that I was beginning to experience the very first stages of *zammai* (which is the Japanese pronunciation of samadhi). Of course, as a scholar of Buddhism, I was very familiar with the term, a generic one for "concentration." I could tell you how to say it in a half-dozen languages, although I had never *experienced* it. But now, I knew firsthand what the term meant! Okamura sensei told me that this experience would become deeper and deeper as I continued my practice, but then he said something that totally blew my mind: "You must try to be in this state at all times, even as you go about ordinary activity." I thought to myself, "I can barely get a little taste of it after an hour of busting my buns, trying to count my breath. How can I possibly be in this state in day-to-day life?"

He then said something even more mind-boggling. "As a general principle, any positive state that you experience within the context of silent sitting practice, you must try to attain in the midst of ordinary life." He explained to me that there is a natural progression of challenges to attain this: The first is to experience some degree of samadhi during formal sitting. The next is to experience it during simple tasks like cleaning, then to maintain it during more complex tasks like cooking meals, serving guests at the temple, and so forth. The next level of challenge would be to stay in samadhi during small talk. The ultimate challenge would be to stay in samadhi while having important, emotionally charged, social interactions with others.

Finally, I got it! The menial tasks I had been assigned to around the temple were meant to be an exercise in meditation. Whether washing dishes or cleaning toilets, my job was to try to stay in samadhi. When my attention wandered from the activity, I was to bring it back over and over again to my task. By doing that, I should eventually be able to enter that same pleasant, focused state that I experienced while sitting.

Suddenly it all made sense. I stopped thinking of my jobs in the temple as a meaningless waste of time and began to see them as fascinating challenges. Everything shifted: "How deep can I get this morning as I wash these dishes?" "How deep can I stay as I rake the sand?" I also began to notice that it was relatively easy to enter samadhi during the morning chanting. It was natural to let the external sound of the chant replace the internal sound of my self-talk.

A Different Kind of Life

Eventually, I was assigned to teach some of the young monks English. Needless to say, it was very difficult to maintain the taste of samadhi during the complex activity of teaching, but I would still attempt to do so. During the break periods between the monks' English lessons, I would go off by myself for ten or fifteen minutes and attempt to reconnect to the concentrated state by doing a short sit. Then I would come back and see if I could maintain the taste of the concentrated state during the class. Usually I was unsuccessful, but just making the effort seemed meaningful.

One day before break time, a monk handed me an envelope, saying, "This letter came to the temple for you." The letter was from one of my fellow graduate students in the Buddhist studies program at the University of Wisconsin. I went off by myself, opened the letter, and read it.

Its contents shook me to the core. My friend informed me that our mutual idol and my personal role model, Dr. Robinson, had suffered a horrific accident in his home. A fuse had burnt out in his basement, and when he went down to change it, he had struck a match for illumination. He didn't know that a pipe was leaking and the basement was filled with gas. When he lit the match, the gas ignited, turning him into a fireball. He suffered severe burns over most of his body, including his eyes, which were destroyed. He was hovering between life and death; they didn't know which way it would go. Even if he lived, he would be horribly disfigured and blind. In the end, he lived for about a month in agonizing pain and then died.

This turned my life upside down. Up to this point, I had devoted myself to the acquisition of information and the honing of my intellect. But so what if you know a dozen languages and possess an intellect the size of Wisconsin? It won't help a bit when you're facing such intensities of pain, terror, and grief. *Dukkha,* "suffering"—the first noble truth of Buddhism—hit me like a ton of bricks. Being in horrible physical and emotional pain could happen to me, in fact probably *will* happen to me, if only toward the end of my life. And it can also happen to everyone I love or am invested in. Indeed, it already had happened to Richard.

You'll recall that my earliest memories center around an absolute need to avoid physical discomfort and an inability to deal with negative emotions, such as fear or grief, within myself and especially within others. I imagined what it would have been like had I not been in Japan but back in Madison, dealing with the emotions that my friends and colleagues were going through. I realized that I would simply have had to avoid the whole situation. I wouldn't have been able to visit Richard in the hospital or be with his significant others because I simply wouldn't have known what to do with the emotions.

Then I imagined what it would have been like to be in his body, writhing in pain day after day. I would have been in abject hell. Between reading that letter and receiving the news of his death a month later, a deep shift occurred in my value system. My academic study of Buddhism, my transient glimpse of enlightenment in San Francisco, and the beginnings of tasting samadhi had intellectually convinced me that it was, in theory, possible to experience physical and emotional pain without suffering. My idol's horrific death convinced me, emotionally, that I must pursue this goal. That's how I transformed from an armchair academic to a committed monastic.

Richard's accident and death occurred in the summer. That fall, Abbot Nakagawa approached me with a piece of paper upon which were written two Chinese characters: 真 (shin) and 善 (zen). This *shin* means "truth," and *zen* means "goodness." The abbot asked me if Shinzen (真善) would be an acceptable monk name for me. I was stunned. He was agreeing to ordain me, and giving me a very heavy name. The name spanned the totality of spiritual practice: shin or truth being the liberating wisdom piece, and zen or goodness being the compassionate service piece. Moreover, the name spanned the history of the temple where I had been living. The temple was founded by Prince Shinnyo over one thousand years ago. Famous in Japanese history, Prince Shinnyo was the first Japanese person to attempt to visit the "Western world," which in his age meant India. He wanted to study Vajrayana directly under Indian masters as opposed to indirectly through Chinese converts. The Shin of my name is the first *kanji* (character) in Shinnyo's name and the Zen is the first kanji in the abbot's name, Zenkyo. In essence, the abbot was saying, "There's a lineage of masters who have lived here for a thousand years. Take it back with you when you return to the U.S." I told the abbot that I didn't think I could live up to the name. He said, "I know that, but is it acceptable to you?" I stuttered, "Yes."

∞

Several months later, as winter approached, and it was getting cold and uncomfortable, Abbot Nakagawa told me that if I wanted to be trained in traditional Shingon practice, he would allow it—but I would have to do it the old-fashioned way. I would have to do a solo retreat of one hundred days in winter, most of the time with no source of heat, in complete silence other than occasional instruction from him, and with no meal after noon.

With all that had happened, I felt that I was now ready for such an ordeal. My training began on December 22, the day of the winter solstice. The abbot had warned me that part of the old-fashioned way involved certain ascetical practices derived not from Buddhism, but from the shamanic tradition of Shinto, Japan's pre-Buddhist tribal religion. One of the most common methods that tribal cultures use to obtain visions of gods or spirits is through prolonged exposure to extreme hot or cold. In India, Hindus have the "five fires" practice; in North America, Native Americans have the sweat lodge and the sun dance. These involve heat. The traditional Shinto shamanic practice goes in the other direction. It involves cold—squatting under freezing waterfalls in winter, or standing in cold springs, or dousing your body with ice water, and so forth.

Because Shingon is Vajrayana, the main meditation practice involves working with visualizations, mantras, and *mudra* gestures. You replace your self-image with that of an archetype, you replace your usual mental talk with the mantra of that archetype, and you take on the physical and emotional body experience of that archetype through making mudras—ritual hand gestures. If your concentration is good enough, your identity briefly shifts. You *become* that archetype. This gives you insight into the arbitrary nature of self-identity. The technical term for this practice is *deity yoga* because you experience merging (yoga, i.e., "yoking") with a mythic archetype. My current way of teaching mindfulness is, in part, informed by this early Shingon training. I have people observe self in terms of inner mental images, mental talk, and emotional body sensation, the three sensory elements used in the Vajrayana deity yoga practice. I've created a hybrid approach. *What* I have people observe is derived from the Japanese Vajrayana paradigm: self = mental image + mental talk + body. But *how* I have people observe is derived from mindfulness, which has its origin in Southeast Asian Theravada practice. So, in a sense, I have brought the abbot's lineage back, although probably not quite in the form that he was expecting.

The visualizations, mantras, and mudras are woven together into the framework of a ritual invocation. The traditional basic training (known as *kegyo*) involves doing three such invocations daily, with the abbot privately initiating you into how to do the ceremonies. The Shinto shamanic piece comes prior to each of the three ritual invocations, when the practitioner is required to do cold-water purification. You have to go to a cistern filled with half-frozen water, break the ice on top, fill a huge wooden bucket, and then squat and dump the bone-chilling liquid over your naked body. It's so cold that the water freezes the moment it touches the floor, and your towel freezes in your hand, so you are sliding around barefoot on ice, trying to dry your body with a frozen hand towel.

For me, this cold-water purification was a horrific ordeal. Maybe being a thin-skinned Californian had something to do with it. I did notice, however, that if I stayed in a state of high concentration while I did it, my distress was noticeably lessened. On the other hand, as soon as my attention wandered, the suffering became unbearable. I could see that this whole training situation was a giant biofeedback device designed to keep a person in some degree of samadhi at all times.

On the third day of this training, as I was about to pour the water over myself, I had an epiphany. It hit me with crystal clarity. I was faced with a trichotomy; the future forked into three branches. I could spend the next ninety-seven days in a state of high concentration all my waking hours, spend them in abject misery, or give up and fail to complete my commitment. The choice was obvious.

When I completed the hundred-day training, it was the spring of a new year, and I had a new self. I had entered the crucible (or should I say cryostat?) of the traditional Shingon training and had come out a different person. From that time on, I was able to consciously experience the taste of high concentration whenever I wanted to. One hundred days subtracted from my life were really a very small price to pay in order to live a totally different kind of life.

Turned on to Science by a Jesuit Priest

I often say that my life's passion lies in exploring what may arise from the cross-fertilization of the best of the East with the best of the West. Meditation is the systematic exploration of nature from the *inside,* and the East has done better than anyone else. Science is systematic exploration of nature from the *outside.* It's what the West did best—at least between the sixteenth and nineteenth centuries.

In point of fact, science does not, in general, belong to any specific human culture. Yet it is also true that the foundations of current science were formed during four centuries of explosive growth that began in Europe with the Renaissance. So it's fair to say that modern science had its origins in the West and is Europe's great gift to the world. How to develop meditative states, systematically and reliably, is India's great gift to the world.

I've talked a bit about how I got involved in meditation; now I'd like to say a few words about how I got involved in science.

Like my interest in meditation, my interest in science was ignited during my years in Japan. After having lived as a monk there for several years, when I was about to return to the United States, I got together with my friend Father William Johnston, a priest living in Japan who was responsible for vastly broadening my intellectual horizons.

As soon as we met, Father Bill began talking about an exciting discovery he had made. At the time, scientists were beginning to study brain wave changes and other physiological parameters associated with contemplative practice. Father Bill was a Jesuit, a religious order that has traditionally drawn its members from the intellectual elite of the Roman Catholic world. As a Jesuit scholar, the notion of using science to study mystical experience, the deepest and most important sort of spiritual experience, was utterly fascinating to him.

Specifically, he was excited by two facets of this research. First, the research seemed to show that while the conceptual systems of the various religions (and specifically those of Buddhism versus Christianity) are very different, the underlying neurological correlates of contemplative adepts in those traditions are often rather similar. This lent credibility to the notion that the world's contemplative traditions can be viewed as a unity, an idea that I had already wholeheartedly embraced and which I'll discuss more in chapter 3.

Even more exciting to Father Bill was the prospect that science could actually lend credibility to the reports of contemplatives. He was particularly interested in the results published by two researchers at Tokyo University, Japan's most prestigious academic institution. Their paper seemed to prove that some of the subjective experiences reported by meditators had a clear basis in objective physiology.

Father Bill's spark of excitement ignited a bonfire in my mind. If science could provide evidence to confirm one effect of meditation, perhaps it could confirm other effects. More importantly perhaps, it could discover *new things* about enlightenment that none of the greatest masters in the past had known. Deep, fundamental, important things. Perhaps science could even discover things about enlightenment that would make enlightenment attainable by large masses of human beings. Perhaps science could *democratize* enlightenment as it had democratized other aspects of power, comfort, and convenience.

This concept utterly changed my world. What had initially brought me to Japan was a fascination with the cultures of the East. In learning how to meditate, I felt I had discovered the pinnacle, the highest thing that Asia could give me. Having directly experienced Asia's unique offering to the world, I asked myself, "What next?"

Surveying the achievements of all world cultures, I saw one other pinnacle as high as the subjective science of the East, and that was the *objective* science of the West. Then and there, I decided what was next for me. I knew I would be spending the rest of my life in the practice and teaching of meditation. In parallel with that, I resolved I would study science so that perhaps, at some future time, when my Buddhist practice had deepened, I would be able to intelligently dialogue and collaborate with scientists, helping them to understand meditative states and perhaps even how enlightenment comes about. That meeting with Father Bill changed the course of my life.

And indeed, my intuitions in this regard have been dramatically confirmed. At the present time in major universities all over the world, vigorous research programs exist aimed at turning the lens of science toward the experience of contemplative adepts. Much of this research involves an active collaboration between the adept and the researcher. Even more significant is the fact that many young neuroscience students are taking on a meditative practice, meaning that soon the research designer and the research subject may often be the same person!

Discovering Mindfulness

After returning to the United States, I lived for many years at the International Buddhist Meditation Center (IBMC) in Los Angeles. True to its name, each of the main historical forms of Buddhist practice is represented there: mindfulness (Theravada), Zen (Mahayana), Tantra (Vajrayana). My ordination had been in Shingon, and I had some experience with Zen through Okamura sensei, but now I currently prefer to teach within the framework of mindfulness. That shift occurred through interacting with mindfulness teachers who were living at the IBMC—specifically a young, mellow Californian named Bhante Rahula. Later, I sought out a number of prominent mindfulness teachers, such as U Silananda and U Pandita from Burma, Bhante Punnaji from Sri Lanka, Ajahn Sobin from Thailand, and Bill Hamilton, an American with broad experience in the Mahasi tradition. I also attended numerous retreats conducted through the Goenka organization. Through these teachers, I became familiar with the two major lineages of contemporary mindfulness (or *vipassana* as it is often referred to in Asia): the Mahasi lineage and the U Ba Khin lineage. From the Mahasi tradition, I learned the power of the noting method. From the U Ba Khin tradition, I came to appreciate the importance of body sensation in the process of psychospiritual growth.

There are two reasons why I currently teach within the framework of mindfulness. The first is that mindfulness is the least culture-bound of the three Buddhist practice traditions. It is relatively easy to extract it from the cultural and doctrinal matrix within which it arose and to present it as an evidence-based, secular, and culturally neutral process. The second reason is that the general method of mindfulness shares some features with the general method of modern science.

I like to describe mindfulness as a threefold attentional skill set: concentration power, sensory clarity, and equanimity working together. These three components in some way parallel three important facets of the scientific method. A scientist makes progress through focused investigation of an important question for as long as required. Although it's not quite the same as a meditator's real-time focus, there is perhaps a loose analogy here.

One aspect of clarity that is developed in mindfulness is the ability to detect and resolve the subtle details of our sensory states. This parallels how scientists use high resolution, awareness-extending tools (microscope, X-ray diffraction, and so forth) to reveal the subtle infrastructure of the physical world. Another aspect of clarity developed in mindfulness is deconstruction, or component analysis. We take a complex sensory event (such as selfhood) and break it down into its natural components, its atoms, so to speak. This parallels the way a scientist or mathematician would break down a complex system into manageable parts—atoms, primes, basis vectors, and so forth.

Finally, in mindfulness we practice "equanimity"—a gentle matter of fact-ness with whatever comes up in experience. In a similar way, a scientist is trained to maintain the detached viewpoint of a neutral observer.

For many years, I maintained a two-pronged learning regimen, studying mindfulness with Asian and Western teachers while simultaneously studying science on my own. My goal was to deeply integrate the power of those two worlds within one person, but I still felt a lack. I longed for contact with a teacher whose experience was vastly senior to my own.

Zen Again

On Mount Baldy near Los Angeles was a Zen master named Joshu Sasaki Roshi. He was without a doubt the senior Zen master living in the United States, and arguably the senior living Buddhist master in the world at that time. He started his practice in a monastery at the age of thirteen and died at the age of 107. You do the math.

I studied with Sasaki Roshi for many years. I don't think I have the personality type to be a very good Zen student. I am much more attracted to the systematic, if somewhat prosaic, style that characterizes vipassana (mindfulness meditation). I did, however, learn several hugely important things from Sasaki Roshi, some of which I might not have learned if I had practiced solely within the mindfulness context.

For one thing, I learned that impermanence is not merely something that you experience in your sensory circuits. It also informs your motor circuits. It's a kind of effortless energy that you can "ride on" in daily life. It imparts a bounce to your step, a flow to your voice, and a vibrancy to your creative thought. I also learned about the expansion-contraction paradigm for how consciousness works. That paradigm, described in chapter 10, informs the core of the way I teach. Moreover, through contact with Roshi, I learned the importance of not suppressing the arising of self. I describe this insight in chapter 8. Finally, he provided me with a role model around devotion to teaching—an example of seemingly endless availability and service to students. For all of that, I'm eternally grateful.

On the other hand, a few years ago, I was shocked to discover that Sasaki Roshi had engaged in some questionable behaviors. People have been terribly confused and understandably upset by those revelations. How could a highly enlightened person do such things?

We would like to think that enlightenment is a unity that grows in a uniform way. But actually, it is a many-dimensional process. Usually growth in one dimension facilitates growth in the others, but not inevitably. Sometimes a person can become stunningly proficient with regard to certain dimensions of spiritual empowerment while underemphasizing other aspects. In my way of thinking, the ultimate reason to experience liberation is to better serve others. And a sine qua non for effectively serving others is to be a decent person by the ordinary canons of society, or as my father would have put it, a *mensch*. Freedom should be manifested within clear ethical guidelines and an egalitarian feedback structure.

Informed by the Spirit of Science

I currently divide my time between teaching meditation and designing research related to meditation. I characterize my approach to teaching meditation as informed by the spirit of science. One aspect of that is my use of metaphors. As you will find in this book, I derive great joy from discovering parallels between situations that come up in math and science and situations that come up in meditative experience. Another aspect of "informed by the spirit of science" comes out in how my students and I use language. I attempt to define things very carefully and insist that language be used precisely and rigorously.

One of the things that you learn if you delve into the physical sciences or mathematics is a habit of precision in expression and thinking. For example, in ordinary colloquial English the words "energy," "potential," "power," and "force" sound sort of similar. We might use them interchangeably on occasion. But in physics, each one of these words means something completely different and distinct. Each one is defined very carefully, and in many cases, it took centuries for that precision of language to be honed and perfected.

An example from mathematics, which you would learn in a beginning calculus course, is the definition of "derivative of a function." Initially, the definition seems quite complicated and subtle, and you have to read it over and over until it finally registers. I had to read it dozens of times before it appeared natural and obvious. (If you're interested, you'll find a reader-friendly definition in Wikipedia under "derivative [mathematics].")

What they don't tell you in your beginning calculus book, and what would have helped me a lot had they told me, is that the modern textbook definition of the derivative is not the one that Newton—the inventor of calculus—used. The modern definition is the result of contributions from generations of the finest mathematical minds in the world. Two and a half centuries of confusion, discussion, and contention on the topic separate Newton's first formulation from what appears in the modern textbook. No wonder it seems subtle and you have to read it over and over again until it finally registers.

So in math you get used to speaking in a precise, careful way. You realize that you are going to really have to think about the definitions, and that you are going to have to read and reread. But it's going to be totally worth it. An ordinary high school student who is willing to come back to the definitions and read them over and over again will be able to understand calculus more clearly than its inventors, because the wisdom of many generations of mathematicians is stored in the current pithy definition. That spirit of precision informs the way I teach. My system requires people to master some carefully defined technical vocabulary and to acquire the ability to "say what you mean."

I like to think of myself as being on a mission to "take the mist out of mysticism." I have a good general knowledge of science and math, but I have a professional, academically trained knowledge of comparative mysticism and Buddhist studies. The scientific exposure causes me to be somewhat fussy with regard to how my students use language. Some people find this aspect of my teaching difficult at the beginning, but it saves them a lot of time in the end. It allows people to conceptualize and communicate the entire path to classical enlightenment, using a precisely defined technical vocabulary. That's what I mean by taking the mist out of mysticism.

Another influence from mathematics and science involves the notion of generality. You are probably familiar with the term *general relativity.* Within the context of math and science, "general" means broad or universal. Mathematicians and scientists usually try to discover the broadest possible unifying vision. General relativity covers more cases than special relativity. I have applied that principle to the teaching of meditation by creating a universal grid for classifying meditation techniques. Each of the major innovations within the history of world meditation has a natural place on that grid. Furthermore, I have reformulated each of those innovations in modern, secular language and expressed it within the unifying framework of mindfulness.

I've used that framework to design mindfulness research projects at numerous institutions, such as Harvard Medical School, Carnegie Mellon University, and University of Vermont. One result that I'm particularly pleased with is a breakthrough piece of research that Dr. David Vago and I have been conducting at Harvard Medical School since 2010. The research for our first publication, "Neurobiological Substrates Underlying Varieties of Restful Experience," utilized my distinctive periodic table of sensory events.

At Harvard, we are currently investigating automated mindfulness software as an aid to psychotherapy. This is based on an app that was developed by me, David Creswell, and Emily Lindsay at Carnegie Mellon University. In this clinical study, therapists prescribe an app-based interactive mindfulness tutorial that systematically trains their clients in attentional skills—concentration power, sensory clarity, and equanimity. We're testing the hypothesis that this might dramatically potentiate positive therapeutic outcomes. Interesting times!

CHAPTER TWO

The Most Fundamental Skill

Have you ever been in a situation of extreme danger, where time slowed down, everything got very peaceful, and you felt extremely focused, without fear, and able to respond in a remarkably effective way? When I ask this question to any large group, several people will always raise their hands and say, "Yes." One woman described going into a state like this when she almost drowned in California's Kern River. As a result of being so tranquil and present, she avoided panicking and was able to survive the incident. She added an interesting comment: "If I could only have bottled that state, I could have addicted the world to it."

People who have experienced this spontaneous state of extraordinary focus often say that it was the most meaningful moment of their life, and that it changed them forever. Sometimes, it happens under conditions of exceptional stress—in sports, combat, terminal illness, accident, or assault. But it can also occur at the opposite end of the spectrum, when you feel extremely safe and connected—say, while walking in the forest alone, or during a particularly profound experience of making love. In these circumstances, you again find that time slows down, your mind becomes very peaceful, you are very present, focused, and unified with what is going on.

What few people realize is that such states of presence and focus are *trainable*. You don't have to wait for unusual or extreme conditions in order to experience them. And the experience does not have to be sporadic or short-lived. It can be a permanent abode. Indeed, any person can live their day-to-day life with that level of focus. In other words, *a person's baseline of focus can be elevated through systematic practice.* The discovery that extraordinary focus can be intentionally cultivated is one of the most significant findings the human species has made and has enormous ramifications for both our personal lives and our world. The systematic training in focus is called meditation practice; it is the basic tool in the science of enlightenment.

Benefits of Meditation

Cultivating focus is very much like doing a physical exercise. To begin, you have to learn the procedure or form of the exercise. Then you have to make the exercise part of your daily regimen and continue to put some effort into it for a long period of time. As a result, your muscles get stronger, and you can utilize those improved muscles for many activities in your life.

Your focus muscle can be strengthened by much the same process. To do so, you need instruction in certain procedures that increase concentration power. Then you need to put some work into them on a regular basis and keep it up for the long term. And as a result, your concentration muscle becomes permanently stronger.

When you enlarge physical muscles through exercise, added strength is available to you all day long, enhancing all your activities. The same is true of concentration power. When you strengthen your concentration muscle, added focus power is available to you all day long, enhancing all your activities. Concentration power impacts every aspect of your day because there is no part of human experience that is not affected by our degree of presence and focus.

So concentration power is trainable, and by developing it, you can greatly improve your life. In this sense, meditation is the most fundamental study that any human being can undertake, because concentration power is at the base of the pyramid of all human endeavors.

In science, there are pyramids of power and universality. Here's what I mean: certain sciences are broader and deeper than others. By broader, I mean more universally applicable; by deeper, I mean more powerful.

For example, if you want to be the best possible botanist, you have to be really good at biochemistry. And if you want to be really good at biochemistry, you have to be good at physics. But if you want to be really good at physics, you have to be good at mathematics. Biochemistry is broader in its application than botany, and it's also, in a sense, deeper. Most people would find Botany 101 quite easy to pass, but many people would find Biochemistry 101 to be a significantly greater challenge. Biochemistry is a particular form of chemistry, but chemistry at the deepest level is a consequence of physics, specifically quantum physics. Physics is broader than chemistry. It attempts to explain *all* forces in the natural world, not just those associated with chemical bonding. But to understand physics, you need a good grounding in math—calculus and differential equations at the very least.

As you can see, each of these sciences is broader and deeper than its predecessor. Taken together, they create a kind of hierarchy or pyramid. At the base of the pyramid lies mathematics. For many people, math is hard and takes time and patience to learn. But if you're really interested in science, you're willing to put in the time and the effort. That's because, if you hone your math skills, you can usually ace most science courses. On the other hand, if you never master basic algebra, you'll struggle a lot in science classes, even elementary ones.

Is there some skill even deeper and broader than mathematics? Yes, and the good news is, unlike mathematics, just about anyone can become proficient in it. The skill I'm referring to is *concentration ability*.

The training of concentration power lies at the base of the pyramid of *all* human training. You can use concentration power to get good at math, and therefore to get good at physics, and therefore get good at biochemistry, and therefore become a master botanist.

I flunked all my math courses in high school—which caused a lot of static with my parents. Later, after practicing meditation for many years, I tried to learn math again. I discovered that as a result of my meditation practice, I had concentration skills that I didn't have before. Not only was I able to learn math, I actually got quite good at it—good enough to teach it at the college level.

လ

What's the relationship between meditation and concentration? There are many forms of meditation. Different systems have been developed in different ages and in different cultures based on different philosophical assumptions and employing different techniques. However, there is a common thread, a defining characteristic that will allow us to determine unambiguously whether a practice can legitimately be called a form of meditation: every legitimate form of meditation will elevate a person's base level of concentration power. By base level of concentration, I mean how concentrated you are in daily life when you're not particularly trying to be concentrated.

Naturally, a given form of meditation might develop other things in addition to concentration power. For example, the kind of meditation I like to teach—mindfulness—explicitly develops two other skills: sensory clarity and equanimity. But within the triad of mindfulness skills—concentration power, sensory clarity, and equanimity—concentration is the easiest to understand. It's also the most universal because it's the common thread shared by all forms of meditation. So let's start with it.

You can apply concentration skill to learning mathematics or any other intellectual endeavor. But it doesn't stop there. You can also apply your concentration power to physical endeavors like sports. In the sports world, sporadic states of high concentration which happen occasionally to athletes are considered to be the peak of the athletic experience. Athletes even have a locker room term for this state—they call it being "in the zone." What most athletes don't realize is that being in the zone with their sport doesn't have to be something that happens only on a good day. Using the systematic practice of meditation, you can train yourself to be in the zone whenever you are doing your sport—indeed, whenever you are doing *anything*.

Because meditation elevates your base level of concentration power and because concentration power facilitates all human endeavors, the question "what's meditation good for?" has a simple answer: meditation is good for *everything*. It will allow you to be more present in your interactions with other people. It will allow you to understand yourself better. And it will allow you to pursue a spiritual path more effectively.

It will allow you to reduce the suffering you experience when you go through physical or emotional pain. It will allow you to increase the fulfillment you derive from physical or emotional pleasure. It can help you make positive behavior changes and live more ethically. It can improve your professional life as well as your sex life.

All this might seem to be too good to be true. Is meditation really that valuable? Yes it is, because a person's base level of concentration is, in a sense, the most valuable thing that they have. Anything a person may want will be more easily attained if they are functioning from a high level of effortless focus. The entire range of human endeavors relies on concentration, and if your base level of concentration is elevated through practice, it means that you can function from a continuous state of extraordinary focus every day.

Many cultures have been fascinated by the idea of life extension. For example, the dream of the Fountain of Youth intrigued Western civilization for centuries. Alexander the Great searched Asia for magical waters that would keep a person forever young, and Juan Ponce de Leon discovered Florida while looking for the same thing in the New World. In both classical Indian civilization and classical Chinese civilization, the practice of alchemy centered around the theme of creating substances that would extend the human lifespan. In India and China, the search for the elixir of immortality involved ingesting compounds of mercury.

The fabled Fountain of Youth turned out to be a myth, and imbibing mercurial compounds is hardly a recipe for health. It's possible, indeed probable, that in the future, medical science will dramatically extend the length of human life. But what about right now? If I told you that there's a process that would require ten minutes of your time each day for the rest of your life, and if you do this process, it is likely to add sixty years to your lifespan, you would probably say that that was a good deal. Now imagine that you will live just a normal number of years, but that your experience of each moment will be *twice as full* as it currently is; that is, the scale at which you live each moment will be doubled. If you only lived for sixty years, but lived each moment twice as fully as the ordinary person lives it, that would be the equivalent of one hundred twenty years of richesse. Not a bad deal.

The first process, which doubles the actual length of your life, is mythical—like the Fountain of Youth. There is currently no such process in the real world. However, the second process—the expansion of the *scale* of life—is real and available to anybody.

Meditation is the key to this kind of nonmythical life extension. The central feature of any meditation system from anywhere around the world is that, by developing an extraordinary degree of focus and presence, it allows you to live your life two or three hundred percent "bigger."

Physiological Effects of Meditation

So meditation is a sort of exercise for consciousness. But meditation also affects the body wherein that consciousness resides.

First of all, meditation changes the breathing pattern, allowing people to breathe more slowly and deeply due to a reduction in oxygen hunger. This reduction probably has to do with the fact that when we are in a meditative state, we process everything more efficiently; therefore, our metabolic needs are reduced—we are doing more with less. Most people breathe about fifteen times a minute, but a person in a midlevel state of meditation may breathe four or five times a minute, and someone in a really deep state of meditation may breathe only once or twice a minute.

You may think that I'm exaggerating about the breath, but let me tell you a story. I once lived with a Chinese master who attempted not to lose consciousness at night. His name was Wuguang. Every night, he would sit in meditation for four hours, then lie down for four hours. But while he was lying down, he would attempt not to go unconscious. Then for the rest of the day, he would receive a train of people who would come in to his office with their problems. He would try to help them with spiritual counseling and the special powers that he had cultivated. He was what Buddhists would call a functioning Bodhisattva; that is, someone who practices meditation primarily so they can better serve others.

He was also quite eccentric; for example, he rode a motorcycle, which was unusual for Chinese Buddhist monks at the time. One day

I met him at the temple gate as he was returning on his motorcycle. He said he'd just been to the doctor for a physical check-up, and the doctor had told him: "You're not alive!" In other words, even after driving on a motorcycle through a Taiwanese traffic jam, when he arrived to the doctor's office, his heart rate and breathing were so slow, that the doctor could hardly detect vital signs. This is an extreme example of the impact that meditation can have on a person's metabolic efficiency.

Another physiological concomitant of meditation is a decrease in the electrical conductivity of the skin. Scientists have found that when people are nervous, their skin becomes more conductive. So reduction in skin conductivity is associated with increased relaxation. Not surprisingly, meditation causes reduction in skin conductivity.

Perhaps the most interesting physiological change associated with meditation occurs in the brain wave patterns. We have four basic patterns of brain waves: delta, theta, alpha, and beta. Delta is associated with dreamless sleep. Theta is associated with the state just leading to sleep—called the hypnogogic state—when you see vivid dreamlike images in a kind of twilight zone. Beta is often associated with activity. It's the normal state of most people during the daytime.

From the viewpoint of a meditator's physiology, changes in alpha brain waves are the most noticeable. Alpha is associated with being both alert *and* relaxed at the same time. Being very alert and, at the same time, deeply relaxed could be taken as the definition of a meditative state. Everybody knows what it is like to be alert: you drink some coffee and bop around town and are quite awake, but also possibly frenetic and agitated. Everybody also knows what it is like to be relaxed: you deeply rest in sleep, but you aren't consciously present to appreciate it. Now imagine a state that contains the good part of both without the bad part of either. A state in which we are *alert and relaxed* at the same time. This is what happens in meditation. A person's growth in meditation is a progression: your alertness gets brighter and sharper while your relaxation gets deeper and broader.

During meditation, there is a measurable increase in alpha wave activity in the brain. There's nothing remarkable about that. It's what we would expect; alpha is the physiological signature of alert restfulness. However, there is another aspect of meditators' brain wave activity that is unexpected. Most people can only maintain a state of high alpha if their eyes are closed. If they open their eyes, alpha tends to go away. Standard textbooks on physiology had always assumed that this correlation of alpha with closed eyes is part of basic human physiology. So researchers were quite surprised to discover that meditators have very high alpha wave activity even with their eyes wide open. That makes the electrophysiology of meditators somewhat different from that of other human beings.

Another physiological feature of the meditative state relates to the electrical activity in the muscles. If we use an electromyograph to measure the activity in the back muscles of an experienced meditator who has been sitting bolt upright for many hours, the muscles will appear to be as relaxed as those of someone who's lying down asleep. Clearly, a profound change is taking place in the physiology of the muscles to allow them to do a rather demanding activity yet at the same time to be as relaxed as though you were asleep. I believe this again points to meditation creating a more efficient metabolism.

We might guess that these desirable physiological changes due to meditation would have an impact on health. And indeed, hundreds of recent studies seem to support that conclusion. However, it is important to remember that meditating *just* for the health effects would be a limited perspective on the benefits that meditation can deliver. Health is a facet of happiness that is dependent on conditions. Happiness dependent on conditions is certainly an important goal for humans, but as we shall see, meditation is capable of delivering something even more fundamental: happiness *independent* of conditions.

The Meditative State

There are a lot of misconceptions and stereotypes around what meditation is and what it is not. People who have not practiced it may think that there is a single meditative state. But there is a continuum of meditative states, starting from a light focus that almost everybody has experienced and proceeding to profound states of physiological trance that very few people have experienced. So one dimension of growth in meditation involves depth. As a general tendency, as the months and years pass, our ability to achieve deeper states improves.

A second misconception about meditation is that it is something that can only be done sitting cross-legged on the floor in a quiet room. By definition, meditation is any practice that significantly elevates a person's base level of focus, and a meditative state is any state wherein you are extraordinarily focused. So any situation wherein you're consciously cultivating focus is, by definition, a meditation.

For example, you can practice meditation while talking to someone. In fact, you could do that in a number of different ways. You can do that by intently focusing on the sights and sounds of that person—so intently focusing on those sights and sounds that you enter into what Martin Buber calls an "I-Thou" relationship with them. I call that approach Focus Out. But that's just one way that you could meditate while talking to a person. Another way would be to monitor, in a state of high concentration, your mental and emotional reactions to that person. I call that approach Focus In. Yet another way to meditate while talking to a person would be to intentionally create loving-kindness emotion in your body and then taste an expansive flavor of concentration by spreading that pleasant body sensation out into the room, enveloping your interlocutor with love. I call that approach Nurture Positivity. Although the specific strategies vary, in each of these circumstances, there's a conscious tasting of a concentrated state.

You can also meditate while washing the dishes. You anchor yourself in the physical touch of the water and dishes, along with the sights and sounds of washing, the motion of the water, and the clacking of the dishware. You get into a zone state and become one with the water and the dishes—yet another instance of Focus Out.

The Focus Out approach makes it possible to enter a meditative state while driving through traffic. You put all your attention on what's relevant to driving, such as the sights of the road, the sounds of the other cars, and the physical body sensations of driving, the touch of the steering wheel, the touch of the seat, the physical linkage to the car. That way you can enter a deep state and still be driving safely—indeed more safely than most people. In this case, your meditation practice is the way that you drive. You're fully focused on the seeing, hearing, and feeling of the drive.

Rigorous research by people in the positive psychology movement has shown that a concentrated state is intrinsically rewarding, and that reward is independent of the *content* of one's experience. Boring, even painful, experiences can become interesting and pleasant when experienced in a state of intense concentration. This intrinsic high associated with meditation is sometimes colloquially referred to as a "flow state" or a "zone state." (Although in the way I formulate meditation, the word "flow" has a different meaning.)

As your experience grows, you eventually come to a point where you are so present that there is a kind of merging of inside and outside. When that happens, focus becomes more than an extremely interesting and pleasant experience; it becomes a spiritually transformative experience. You begin to get an insight into the nature of oneness. You begin to break through one of the most fundamental illusions, that of the separateness of inside and outside. Hopefully at some point, something as mundane as dishwashing will become a vehicle for cultivating spiritual transformation and expressing that transformation.

So meditation is not just something that is practiced on a special cushion or in a special posture; a meditative state can be entered during any ordinary activity.

With the combination of formal practice in stillness, formal practice in motion, and informal practice in daily life, your meditative skills grow in two dimensions. On one hand, deeper and deeper meditative states become available. On the other, you are able to maintain those states throughout more and more complex activities of life. We might refer to the first dimension of growth as depth and the second dimension of growth as breadth.

Eventually, a delicious figure-ground reversal takes place. In the beginning, meditation is something that happens within your day. Eventually, the day becomes something that happens within your meditation. At advanced levels of practice, the dimensions of depth and breadth come together. Profoundly deep experiences occur continuously throughout your daily activities. Or, put more accurately, your daily activities continuously arise from and return to the Profound.

For most people, it takes time to get to that level. Learning to meditate is in some ways analogous to learning how to drive a car. You have to start in an empty parking lot where everything is simple, and there are no pressures on you. Formal practice in stillness, such as sitting meditation, is analogous to the empty parking lot. Over time, however, you internalize the skills of driving and are able to drive on a quiet country road. Formal practice in motion, such as walking meditation, is the quiet country road. Eventually, driving becomes second nature. It requires little thinking or effort. You simply get in a car and driving happens.

At first, meditation requires a lot of effort. You have to think about what you're doing, and you can only get in a meditative state while sitting still, perhaps with your eyes closed. But at some point, the skill becomes second nature. You can attend to the business of life and still be in a meditative state just like you can listen to the radio while driving on a freeway at rush hour.

So, as your meditation gets deeper, you're able to achieve more and more profound states of concentration and tranquility. As it gets broader, you are able to maintain those states throughout more and more challenging and complex activities of life. When depth and breadth pass a certain critical point, you find yourself living an enlightened life.

Common Misconceptions about Concentration

I like to describe concentration as the ability to focus on what you deem relevant. In terms of space, concentration can be narrow or broad. An example of narrow: you are able to focus on the tiny sensations of breath at your nostrils. An example of broad: you are able to hold your whole body in awareness at once.

In terms of time, it's good to be able to focus on one thing for an extended duration, but it's also good to learn how to taste "momentary concentration." With momentary concentration, you let your attention be pulled from thing to thing, but you *consciously* taste a few seconds of high concentration with each of those things. So there are actually four subskills to concentration: learning how to restrict attention to small sensory events, learning how to evenly cover large sensory events, learning how to sustain concentration on one thing for an extended period of time, and learning how to taste a momentary state of concentration with whatever randomly calls your attention.

In the early twentieth century, the Burmese master Mahasi Sayadaw realized that momentary concentration (*khanikasamadhi*) on whatever spontaneously comes or calls could be as powerful as sustained concentration on one thing. This insight allowed him to develop a distinctive way to do mindfulness practice. At the time, this method was referred to as "the Burmese method of *satipatthana*," but nowadays, it is simply called "noting." Noting is currently perhaps the most popular approach to mindfulness both in the East and the West. But when Mahasi first started teaching it, it generated considerable controversy. Some masters from Thailand and Sri Lanka claimed that "noting whatever arises" is indistinguishable from a scattered, wandering state of mind. Mahasi pointed out (and quite correctly in my opinion) that momentary concentration is key. To "note" an experience entails more than just labeling it. Whether you use labels or not, to note a sensory event implies that you attempt to tangibly taste a momentary state of high focus upon that sensory event. This skill is especially useful for staying deep during complex daily activities.

One sometimes encounters contention regarding the role of concentration in psychospiritual growth. This comes about because people fail to appreciate all four dimensions of concentration power. For example, I sometimes hear statements like "concentration is not needed for mindfulness." What they're trying to say is that the ability to maintain a spatially restricted focus for an extended period of time is not necessarily needed for mindfulness practice. That statement is true. But some concentration (if only of a momentary kind) is always involved in mindfulness practice. Moreover, all four dimensions of concentration skill are potentially useful for mindfulness. I like to describe concentration in a way that's both broad and nuanced. In my way of thinking, mindfulness without concentration is analogous to water without wetness.

To sum it up, concentration power could be described as the ability to focus on what you deem relevant. If what's relevant at a given time is fully experiencing the external world, then concentration power allows you to focus out and do that. If what's relevant is to understand yourself, solve a problem, or be creative, then concentration power allows you to attend to your inner world and access your creative resources without being disturbed by ambient distractions.

Is Meditation Self-Centered?

People sometimes criticize meditation as being self-centered. Let's consider that issue.

Imagery is very powerful, and the archetypal image of meditation is of someone sitting on the floor in a funny posture with eyes closed, burning incense, and chanting "*om.*" So it's easy to understand why people might view meditation as a kind of self-centered, narcissistic activity. Formal practice in stillness *looks* like a withdrawal from life and other people.

My personal image of meditation is quite different. When I think of meditation, I think of someone in a gym having a good, sweaty workout. If you do a physical workout with regularity, you elevate the base level of body strength. If you do meditation with regularity, you elevate the base level of your focus strength.

When I hear people say that meditation is self-centered and selfish, I don't know whether to laugh or cry. If you think about it, virtually every moment of just about everybody's life is self-centered. In general, people's experience of life involves a sequence of moments of identification with self. Meditation equips us with the skills needed to break that identification. So the long-term effect of meditation is the *opposite* of what the archetypal image seems to convey. People who are successful with meditation experience an elastic identity. They are able to better take care of themselves but can also extend their identity out to include a oneness with others. That ability naturally evolves into a desire to serve others.

This concept leads us to another way to think about meditation. Meditation is something that a person does for themselves, but it's also something a person does to make the world a better place and to be of service to others. This fundamental polarity is reflected in the vocabulary of traditions from around the world. In Hinduism, one speaks of *sadhana* (work done on yourself for yourself), which is coupled with *seva* (service to others). In Theravada Buddhism there's *vipassana* (observation) coupled with *metta* (lovingkindness). In Mahayana Buddhism, *prajna* (wisdom) is coupled with *karuna* (compassion), and in Vajrayana Buddhism, one speaks of *prajna* (wisdom) and *upaya* (outreach). An example from Christianity would be the motto of the Dominican order: "Meditate and give to others the fruits of your meditation."

Meditation for Ourselves

Let's look at how meditation is something we do for ourselves. Since meditation enhances any life activity, we meditate for ourselves so that we can gain a special kind of strength. We can work more joyously and effectively, we can perform better, we can enjoy our meal more fully, we can enjoy music more, and there is a general elevation of pleasure in life.

For example, when we eat a meal in a meditative way, it is going to be much more pleasant to us. This means that there are two ways to experience good dining: one is to eat in gourmet restaurants, the other is to learn to be fully focused with whatever food happens to be available. We could even eat in gourmet restaurants *and* be fully focused, and thereby have the best of both worlds. So our entire life is magnified by our meditative abilities, and that is something we do for ourselves.

Meditation can also help us to experience life's unavoidable physical and emotional pain with less suffering, less bother. And meditation can give us an internal microscope, so to speak, with which we can explore our infrastructure at a very deep level, a level unavailable to the naked eye.

The ultimate personal goal of meditation is to achieve happiness independent of conditions. That's a pretty audacious claim.

Happiness independent of conditions? It might seem that just about everything in life is dependent upon conditions. Your health is a condition, your reputation is a condition, your financial situation is a condition, having food to eat is a condition, having air to breathe is a condition, the ability to think is a condition. When we make the claim that meditation can bring a person to a happiness that is not dependent on conditions, it is quite a bold assertion.

The greatest favor we can do for ourselves is to come to a state where our happiness is no longer dependent on conditions. You can lose your health, you can lose your wealth, you can lose your reputation, you can even lose your ability to think, and still be deeply happy.

How could that possibly be? That's what we'll be looking into in depth in this book. But the quick explanation is that happiness independent of conditions occurs whenever we have a *complete sensory experience*.

To have a complete experience means to experience something in a state of extraordinary concentration, sensory clarity, and equanimity. Any ordinary sensory event, when experienced completely, becomes extraordinary and paradoxical: its richness is maximal but its somethingness is minimal. A complete experience of pleasure delivers pure satisfaction but has little substance. A complete experience of pain is deeply poignant but not problematic. A complete experience of desire is desireless. A complete experience of mental confusion nurtures intuitive wisdom. A complete experience of self convinces you there never was a self.

Here it is in a nutshell. The only way we know of a condition is through sensory experience—what we see, hear, and feel on the inside and the outside. Desirable conditions create pleasant sensory experiences. Undesirable conditions create unpleasant sensory experiences. Neutral conditions create neutral sensory experiences. But *any* sensory experience can, in theory, be a complete experience. And when we're having complete experiences, we're happy regardless of the content of the experience. Complete experience is a kind of metapleasure, a pleasure that both unifies and transcends pleasure and pain.

But is happiness independent of conditions really a good thing? If your happiness becomes less dependent on objective circumstances, does that mean that you will tend to be indifferent to objective circumstances? In theory that could happen, but a good teacher won't let you go down that path. No, no, no . . . *hell no!* The substance of enlightenment may be emptiness, but its function is to provide a place outside yourself—a place from which you can *optimally* refine your personhood and joyously improve your world.

The ultimate state of meditation dawns when we start to have moments of complete experience during the day. Inside a complete experience, time, space, self, and world are enfolded into the Still Point. Creation and the Source of creation are united. I realize that this may sound a bit far out, but it's something that is a daily reality for tens of thousands of ordinary people.

So meditation is partially something you do to help yourself at many levels, including the ultimate level, which is to transcend your self. People usually identify with their thoughts and feelings, their minds and their bodies. The thinking mind and the feeling body thus become a prison within which most people spend their lives. Meditation makes it possible to transcend that limited identity, so that the mind and body become a home that you can go in and out of, rather than a prison that you are stuck in. And how do you free your mind-body? By having a complete experience of your mind-body! This is one possible way of viewing the path to enlightenment.

Meditation for Others

So meditation is something that we do for ourselves for many legitimate reasons. It helps us mentally, it helps us emotionally, it helps us physically, and eventually it helps us to experience an identity larger than our thoughts and feelings. Ultimately, it lets us taste happiness independent of conditions. But meditation is also something that we do for others.

In what way is meditation something that we do for others? For one thing, as you personally become happier and more fulfilled, the people close to you reap the benefits of that. And as you become happier and more fulfilled, it becomes easier and more natural to care for others. Furthermore, if you are really successful with your meditation practice, you will be able to have a complete experience of other people. When you experience another person completely, they are no longer "other." There is a shift in perspective. You go from an I-It paradigm to an I-Thou paradigm. This naturally leads to a spontaneous sense of caring.

Most people who stay the course of meditation will have to face challenges—wandering mind, sleepiness, confusion, physical discomfort, emotional intensity, and so forth. The struggles and failures you experience early on in your practice imbue you with a poignant sense of the reality and ubiquity of suffering. This in turn plants the seeds for compassionate service and engagement with others later on.

Meditation Helps the World

Everyone who develops meditation skills contributes to correcting a basic evolutionary flaw that is responsible for enormous unnecessary suffering in this world. This fundamental flaw infects all scales of human life, from the interpersonal level to the international level. It's so universal and pervasive that people fail to recognize its ubiquity. As the proverbial expression goes, they can't see the forest for the trees and so forget that most human problems are merely special cases of this general pattern.

Here's the general pattern I'm referring to: An objective situation presents itself. That objective situation affects our subjective thoughts and feelings, and then we make an objective response—we take action in one way or another.

The objective situation could be anything. Should I stay in my current relationship or leave? What should we do about this social inequity or that political issue? What should I do about my personal enemies, or what should we do about our collective enemies?

Most people don't maintain a continuous mindful relationship with their subjective thoughts and feelings, so most people do not have the ability to experience anger, fear, sadness, shame, and confusion without suffering. When an objective problem presents itself, it produces uncomfortable subjective mental and emotional states, and you suffer. *A salient feature of suffering is that it distorts behavior.* You cannot perform the delicate act of threading a needle while somebody is holding a flame to your body. Your whole body shakes; the objective functioning is distorted because of the internal suffering. In the same way, the delicate act of human interaction is frequently subject to the distorting influences of (perhaps subliminal) suffering. Because of this subjective suffering, our objective responses to objective situations are often less than optimal, and sometimes horribly distorted.

When objective responses are nonoptimal, they sow the seeds for new problems—new objective situations that cause distress. Then we respond suboptimally to that new situation. This can create a feedback loop that has the potential to spin out of control at any time.

Even in situations where the suffering appears to be quite small, the distorting influences can add up. For example, a current cultural norm in the United States is to go from passionate love to acrimonious divorce in just five or ten short years. How does this happen? It happens in dozens and dozens of small daily interactions, some of them a little bit emotionally charged and a few of them charged in big ways. When interactions that are unpleasantly charged are not experienced completely in the moment, they are not metabolized. They leave a ghost, a remnant suffering that haunts the cellar of our own mind. That remnant suffering sinks into the subconscious and distorts our subsequent responses. We make cutting remarks when we merely need to reply. We yell when we merely need to be emphatic. We bite when we merely need to bark.

The same cycle destroys a relationship here, a career there; leads to a war here, a rampage there; a repressive dictatorship here, an ethnic cleansing there. That is the basic pattern on this planet: People do not understand how to experience pain fully, that is, without suffering. Suffering distorts their response to the source of the pain, and this distorted response can easily lead to more pain and, hence, more suffering.

Here's a diagram that sums up the problem.

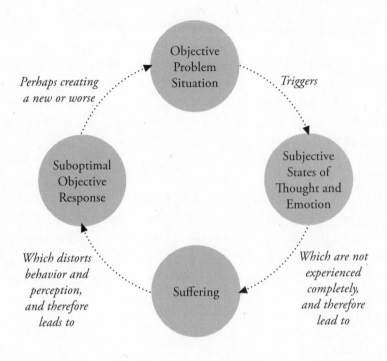

Perhaps creating a new or worse

Triggers

Objective Problem Situation

Subjective States of Thought and Emotion

Suboptimal Objective Response

Suffering

Which distorts behavior and perception, and therefore leads to

Which are not experienced completely, and therefore lead to

Figure 1

So where does meditation come in? Meditation allows us to experience pain without suffering and pleasure without neediness. The difference between pain and suffering may seem subtle, but it is highly significant. Let's go over it again. When physical or emotional pain is experienced in a state of concentration, clarity, and equanimity, it still hurts but in a way that bothers you less. You actually feel it more deeply. It's more poignant but, at the same time, less problematic. More poignant means it motivates and directs action. Less problematic means it stops driving and distorting actions. I appreciate that merely hearing these words may not be enough to clarify the concept. But look back; perhaps you've experienced something like this in the past. If not, having read these words here will help you know what to look for in the future.

I started to meditate back in the 1960s, when a catch phrase said that you were "either part of the problem or part of the solution." It is a very good expression, although perhaps the current understanding of it—an exhortation to political correctness—may be somewhat limiting. There is a fundamental way for *anyone* to become part of the solution on this planet, regardless of their political perspective, and that is to snip the cycle of suffering and distortion. This cycle has a name: the law of karma. Meditation makes it possible to break the cycle of karma.

Imagine a woodcutter whose job it is to cut down many trees, year after year, yet who refuses to spend twenty minutes each day to sharpen his ax. Then he wonders why he can't cut as much wood as he needs to, and why it is such hard work. He never realizes that he is using a dull ax, a less than optimal tool. If we look at the big picture, this is the general human condition. Meditation sharpens the ax of awareness, allowing one to cut the karmic cycle, the cycle of pain propagating pain.

You might think that the compelling goals of action in the world demand that we bypass allocating time and energy to meditation. Why sit alone in a room staring at your navel when you could be feeding the homeless? Direct action is good, but it alone is not necessarily the optimal way to approach the goal. When we are involved in the path of love and service, we need self-care, a resource to avoid what I call the "three outs": Burn-Out, when we lose energy and motivation to help; Bum-Out, when we suffer deeply when our efforts to help don't work; and Freak-Out, when we respond in a distorted, perhaps even abusive way.

A good example of how well-intentioned people may end up distorted by the three outs can be found in the history of religion. A religion starts out as a noble ideal, a path of love, but somewhere along the line, it ends up creating inquisitions, crusades, persecutions, jihads, and pogroms—all in the name of God's love. This is obviously perverse, so why do things like this happen over and over? Because of the general mechanism illustrated in figure 1. It is just a bigger version of the same pattern, extended over longer periods of time and involving more people. It covers whole centuries, whole civilizations, yet it is exactly the same pattern. People start out with a religion of love, but become outraged that anyone would reject God's freely given love, frightened that the nonbelievers may impede the religion of love, and emotionally wounded when the basis of their belief is directly challenged. Their inability to experience rage, fear, and hurt in a concentrated, clear, and equanimous state causes those emotions to distort perception and behavior, leading to hate in the name of love.

Often terrible things are done by people who started out honestly wanting to help. So it's not enough to simply and sincerely want to help. We have to become skillful at dealing with our emotions so that we can help in an optimal way. Meditation is a tool that can help us avoid the three outs, optimally serve others for our whole lives, and die fulfilled.

∞

So meditation gives us the ability to be less bothered when we experience physical or emotional pain and more fulfilled when we experience physical or emotional pleasure. This, in turn, affects our behavior, allowing us to act in more skillful ways. Pain that doesn't turn into bother ceases to drive us but continues to motivate us. In a similar way, pleasure that brings fulfillment ceases to drive us but continues to motivate us. Actions that are motivated by pleasure and pain but not driven by suffering and frustration tend to be more skillful actions, and skillful actions tend to create desirable circumstances, leading to more pleasure and less pain for one's self and for others. Thus, meditation reverses the deep, vicious cycle that is responsible for so much misery on this planet. The effect of an individual's meditation on the course of the world may seem small—smaller than the proverbial drop in the bucket. Quantitatively, that may be true, but qualitatively, in terms of depth, meditators know that each day they are part of the fundamental solution to the problems of this planet. As more and more people become interested in meditation, the impact of that deep effect could gradually improve the quality of life globally. Subtle can be significant.

CHAPTER THREE

Mysticism in World Culture

Several themes dominated my life from a very early age. One was that I hated the idea of wasting time. My idea of hell was standing in line, or being trapped at an airport, or any other unproductive use of time. But after learning to meditate, I realized I would never waste time again, because, even if I was just waiting in a line, I could use that time to work on deepening my samadhi. I could literally make use of every waking moment, because during the dead moments when I wasn't engaged in something specific, I could use the time to cultivate my concentration.

Because I was part of the 1960s, another theme in my life was that I liked getting high. Samadhi became for me an amazing kind of high. It's legal, doesn't cost anything, deepens over time, it's good for the mind and body, and replaces the need for a drug-induced high. And it was available any time I wanted it.

Learning to bring the samadhi experience into my daily activities totally revolutionized how I thought about my day. The day was now a sequence of opportunities to go deeper. More complex activities were challenges. "How deep can I stay when I am cooking, shopping, talking with someone?" I wanted to spend more time deepening my concentration. I marveled at how the Buddhist tradition had created a methodology which anyone could use to systematically improve their concentration and live their lives consciously enjoying a highly focused state. Because I had experienced this totally within the context of Buddhism in Asia, through Asian languages, I originally thought that such states were to be found only in Buddhism.

What happened next was interesting. I went to a *sesshin,* or Zen retreat. In Japan, such retreats are notoriously tough. I call them

Thoreau — live deliberately

"samurai boot camps." As we were all sitting down to begin the week of intensive training, I noticed that there was another foreigner present. Not just any foreigner, but a Roman Catholic priest. I thought it was pretty unusual and interesting that a Catholic priest would come to a Zen retreat. I also thought that this poor guy must have no idea what he was getting himself into.

He shocked me right away, however, by sitting down in perfect lotus posture and entering samadhi. You can tell the depth of someone's meditation by the way they sit, and he was sitting like a veteran Zen monk. During a break, I introduced myself and discovered that he was an Irish Jesuit. That's how I met Father Bill, mentioned previously in chapter 1. Father Bill spent his life as a missionary in Japan. But he was a very unusual missionary, a sort of "bidirectional" missionary. He had originally come to Japan to propagate Christianity, but he felt that he would never be able to do that unless he understood the soul of the Japanese people. And he felt that he could only gain that understanding by having the Zen meditation experience. He had already had at least a decade of Zen training by the time I met him, and had also written several books, including the now classic *Christian Zen*. Through those books, he rekindled an interest in systematic focus techniques throughout the Christian world.

Father Bill and I became friends, and I learned that he no longer saw his Zen practice as a mere aid to cultural understanding. It had become a way for him to reconnect with something that had been almost lost within the Christian tradition. He explained to me that a rich tradition of concentrative meditation had existed for centuries in the Christian West. The same state of high concentration that we were experiencing through Zen practice had been a central feature of Christianity until just a few centuries ago. This was mind-boggling for me because I had no idea that any system for cultivating that state existed anywhere outside of Buddhism, let alone in the West!

Father Bill's personal library at his residence in Tokyo opened my eyes even further. There were books on meditation and mysticism from many different cultures. It dawned on me that techniques for attaining states of high concentration were central to *all* the religious traditions of the world. *All the world's religions have a meditative core,* which is sometimes referred to as the mystical or contemplative side of that religion. Suddenly, I realized my own personal experience in Buddhism was part of a phenomenon that is universal for human beings.

Three Types of Spiritual Experience

Very broadly, there are three aspects to religious or spiritual experience around the world. The first is what I call the *spirituality of thought.* The vast majority of people have their religious experience centered around concepts, belief systems, prayer, dogmas, faiths, credos, and so on. This is the most common form of spiritual experience because adult human beings are very centered in their thinking process. Word-centered spirituality reaches its extreme in fundamentalism. This form of rigid relationship to concepts is found in every country and religion around the world. Sometimes fundamentalists within a religion end up persecuting the contemplatives within that religion. This is not just something in the distant past. It has happened in our time—jihadis tend to persecute Sufis.

Many aspects of human spirituality have a good side and a not-so-good side. The not-so-good side of fundamentalism is that it can bring out the worst in people, but it's also an easy and natural way to bring out the best in people. I wouldn't want you to think that I'm wholly condemning it here. In fact, it's a natural tendency for humans and, as such, should be appreciated, although probably not encouraged. I've taken to heart the words of the Roman playwright Terence: *homo sum humani a me nihil alienum puto.* I am human, so nothing human should be alien to me.

The second type of religious experience, I call the *spirituality of feeling.* It is characterized by devotion, piety, and what we might call the heart. We human beings are after all not just thinking creatures, we're also feeling creatures. People have always felt a sense of what the Romans called the *numen,* the mystery—that which is awesome, awe-inspiring. We experience feelings of love, awe, and devotion with respect to the spiritual Source. We feel love and devotion for Jesus or

Krishna. A spirituality centered in feeling is called pietism in the West or *bhakti* in the East. Currently on planet Earth, most religion is either based in feeling, based in thinking, or a mixture of the two.

But there is a third kind of spirituality, which is the one that I find most interesting. The technical term for it is *mysticism*. Unfortunately, in everyday, colloquial English, the word usually implies something occult, weird, airheaded, New Age, impractical, or obscure. However, this is not at all what scholars of religion understand by mysticism, a term they have borrowed from Christianity. In Christianity, spirituality centered on states of high concentration was referred to as "mystical theology." Scholars then generalized the term to cover the worldwide phenomenon. We might also call this kind of spirituality "cosmic consciousness" or the "spirituality of enlightenment," although these terms can also lead to misunderstandings.

What sets mysticism apart from the spirituality of thought or feeling is that it involves the cultivation of high concentration. In terms of organized religions at this point in history, this third type of spirituality is definitely in the minority. However, just because something is in the minority doesn't mean that it is not extremely important. Relatively few people master the equations of quantum physics, but that doesn't mean that quantum physics lacks relevance.

I read everything in Father Bill's library that I could about spirituality as practiced by the meditators and the contemplatives of the world. It was quite astonishing for me to discover that all over the world and in every historical period there had been people who lived their lives in the state of high concentration that I was just beginning to explore. I began to feel a link to them all. It was fascinating to feel that I shared something deep and important with people living centuries ago and having customs and beliefs completely different from mine. I realized that when we practice meditation, we are engaging in a quintessentially human endeavor. The science of enlightenment doesn't belong to any particular religion or culture or period, rather it belongs to humanity as a whole and helps us to connect to our basic humanness.

One way to trace the theme of meditation in world spirituality is through vocabulary. Most of the world's contemplative traditions have a generic technical term that designates any concentrated state. In addition, there are often specific technical terms used to describe different depths or levels of concentration. When we take the systems and put them side by side, we notice some broad parallels between the Christian, Jewish, Islamic, Taoist, Buddhist, and Hindu systems of contemplation.

Meditation Traditions in the Abrahamic Religions

Let's start in the West. Most westerners, whether Jews, Christians, or Muslims, don't have a clue that members of their religious tradition actively cultivated meditative states at some point in the past. If you were to ask even well-informed Jews, Christians, or Muslims the technical term within their religion for a state wherein the mind becomes highly focused, most wouldn't know what to tell you. But these terms do exist and reflect what was once a rich tradition of cultivated concentration.

According to the Catholic Church, there are two kinds of prayer. The first type of prayer is what most people today usually think about when they hear the word "prayer": creating words and images in the mind, and feelings in the body about God. We talk to God, we think about God, we feel an emotional connection to God. This type of prayer is known technically as *discursive prayer,* meaning prayer in the nature of a discourse or a conversation. The second type of prayer is called nondiscursive prayer or the *prayer of quiet.* In this type of prayer, we go into a state of very deep peace and high concentration that is without words. Prayer of quiet (*hesychia* in Greek) is, roughly speaking, the Christian term for samadhi.

Another term for high concentration in Christianity is *recollection.* This word does not mean "to remember" as it does in modern English. Rather, it means "to gather back together," in other words, to become concentrated. We gather the scattered mind; we "re-collect" it. In fact, a Catholic priest is required to become recollected for at least one moment, even if he can't be recollected in his daily life. That moment is when he consecrates the host. In former times, great numbers of

Christians wanted not just sporadic moments of recollection but to be able to live their entire lives in the recollected state. That led to the development of monasteries.

If you're familiar with European history, you probably know that at one time monasteries dominated the landscape of Europe. Only a fraction of those have survived. Most were destroyed by wars and revolutions. What were those monasteries used for? In essence, they were the meditation centers of the medieval world. The monastic system of Europe was founded by Saint Benedict. According to the Benedictine tradition, the main reason for entering the monastery is to attain a habitually concentrated state (*recollectio*) and to use that to radically transform one's self (*conversio*). A monastery is like a giant feedback mechanism where a person's life is simplified, and there is nothing to do but concentration-building activities like simple physical labor, chanting, prayer, and so on. Before the Counter-Reformation (in the sixteenth century), obtaining the prayer of quiet was deemed central to European Christian life. It's still central in the Eastern Orthodox form of Christianity.

There are perhaps three works that best exemplify the Christian meditative tradition. *The Interior Castle* of Saint Teresa of Avila, who was a Spanish Carmelite nun, is useful because she analyzes the prayer of quiet into a series of well-defined levels. It makes it easy to see the different benchmarks along that continuum and how they rather roughly line up with the standard Buddhist system of eight or nine "absorptions." Another book is called the *Cloud of Unknowing*, by an anonymous fourteenth-century English author, which gives a very beautiful poetic description of the meditative process. Finally, there are the writings of Meister Eckhart, a thirteenth-century Dominican. Eckhart's writings went unnoticed for many centuries, but he is now appreciated as among the greatest Christian mystics.

∽

Within the Jewish tradition, the general Hebrew term for the state of high concentration is *kavanah,* which literally means "maintaining one's direction." The eleventh-century rabbi Bahya Ibn Pakudah famously said, "Prayer without kavanah is like a body without a soul." In other words, if you attend all the services and say all the prayers, but you're not in a recollected state, then you've missed a basic point of Judaism.

The Jewish meditative tradition is found within a body of literature known as the Kabbalah. Unfortunately, much of what you'll find in the Kabbalah is nothing more than superstition and manipulative magic, that is, mysticism in the sense of New Age fluff. On the other hand, if you dig deep and know what to look for, there are some real gems. Of particular importance is the notion of *bittul ha-yesh,* "the annihilation of the somethingness within you." According to the Kabbalah, if we are willing to go through this annihilation of somethingness, we can have a direct experience of what in Hebrew is known as *bri'ah yesh me-ayin*—how the Source creates things from nothing, continuously, moment by moment. As you'll see later in this book, this is a central theme in my formulation of enlightenment.

∞

In the Islamic tradition, the main way of cultivating the state of high concentration is by chanting and dancing, and the people who practice it are called Sufis. This way of developing high concentration is called *zikr* in Arabic, which literally means "remembrance." Like all paths of deepening concentration, zikr eventually culminates in a state of concentration so great that we start merging with things, a state which is sometimes referred to as "unitive experience." In the Muslim tradition, this unitive experience is called *fana'* (annihilation). There are two kinds of fana'. The first is called *fana' filsheikh. Sheikh* means "teacher" or "elder" in Arabic. As Sufi students dance and chant, the first kind of merging they experience is with their teacher. I'll describe the mechanism that allows for that a little later in this chapter. Sufis eventually go beyond that to experience the second kind of fana', which is called *fana' fillah,* dissolution into Allah, into the Source, into a oneness with God. So technical terms for levels of high concentration and mystical experience are also present in Islam. Famous Sufis include Rumi, Al-Hallaj, and Al-Ghazali.

As you can see, there exists a rich vocabulary of technical terms in the Western traditions describing states of concentration and their impact on one's life. Now let's move to the East.

Meditation Traditions in the East

In classical Taoism, the state of high concentration is called *shouyi,* which means "to hold to the one," or *zuowang,* "to vanish where you're sitting." The Taoist meditative tradition developed in several stages. First came the philosophy of oneness exemplified in the teachings of Lao Tzu and Chuang Tzu. In this system, the mystical "one" was called the Tao. We achieve the Tao through surrendering to the fundamental forces of the universe, expansion (*yang*) and contraction (*yin*). Later masters developed an elaborate technology of physical exercises involving three steps to facilitate this process. First essence (*jing*) is transmuted into energy (*qi*). Then energy is transmuted into spirit (*shen*).

But what the hell is "essence"? Well, it sometimes means sexual sensation, but more broadly, it can refer to any "distilled" sensory experience, that is, any sensory flavor you concentrate fully on—for example, pure emotional joy or pure physical pain or pure breath pleasure. Put another way, the essence of a given sensory category is achieved when there's only that flavor, and it pervades your entire being. We tend to be afraid of letting a single sensory quality distill into its essence, even if it's something pleasant like sexual sensation. We're afraid to let just one sensory essence pervade our entire being for a significant period of time because we think that we will be utterly overwhelmed. But we need not fear because very quickly, essence transmutes into energy (qi), and then energy transmutes into spirit (shen).

Although the words sound quite different, the Taoist experience of qi and shen is related to the Buddhist experience of *anicca* (impermanence). Qi and shen represent two stages in the process of contacting the impermanent nature of a given sensory event. After you have held a single sensory quality in a concentrated state long enough (essence, jing), you start to notice subtle waves and vibrations in that event. Those waves and vibrations are qi. At a deeper level, that sensory event polarizes into pure yang and pure yin. Pure yang is a kind of efflux—space effortlessly spreading out. Pure yin is a kind of reflux—space effortlessly pulling in. Space itself is simultaneously expanding and contracting. That's shen. This roughly parallels something that happens in the material world: a frozen substance may melt into liquid (jing), then vaporizes into gas (qi), and finally polarizes into a plasma (shen). In other words, what the Buddhists call impermanence, the Taoists view as an energy flowing in patterns, a practice called *neidan,* which means internal alchemy.

The term *neidan* has an interesting history. For hundreds of years, the Taoists pursued physical immortality through physical alchemy. They felt that certain substances such as mercury could be transformed into pills that would give immortality. This elixir of immortality turned out to be impossible, of course. When they realized that there was nothing in the outside world that would give them immortality, they got the idea that perhaps there might be an internal alchemy, an elixir of immortality that could be found within sensory experience.

And, indeed, it's true. Within each of us is a sort of eternal fountain of youth that constantly gushes and gathers.

ɔ☯ɔ

Now let's visit India. When it comes to systematic, principled approaches for developing concentration power, India is without peer. We can see this quite clearly in Patanjali's *Yoga Sutras,* which has been a source text in the yogic tradition since the fourth century. Today we think of the word "yoga" as meaning a certain type of physical exercise, but yoga is a generic term referring to many kinds of practices, including spiritual exercises.

Patanjali's system of cultivating high concentration is called *Raja* (royal) yoga. The Raja yoga system contains an early and very clear description of states of concentration. Raja yoga is also sometimes referred to as *ashtanga* ("eight-limbed") yoga because it describes a spiritual path in terms of eight steps. The final three steps (or inner limbs) are directly related to the theme of this chapter because they describe different levels and flavors of the concentrated states.

According to the Raja yoga system, the first step in the concentration continuum is *dharana,* which literally means "holding." In dharana, you take some object and attempt to concentrate your awareness on it. The object of focus could be anything: the breath, a sound, a visualization, a flower, a person. When your attention wanders, which inevitably it will, you gently bring it back to the object. When it wanders again, you gently bring it back again, over and over. This act of bringing the attention back each time it wanders is called dharana. We are making an effort to *hold on to* the focus object.

As I mentioned previously, we can compare the process of developing concentration strength to the process of exercising a muscle. When we exercise a muscle, we use that muscle to lift a weight over and over, and as a result, the muscle gets stronger. The stage of dharana is comparable to this, except that instead of working against the force of gravity, we're working against the force of distraction. Each return to the focus object is equivalent to a rep in weight lifting. It's hard work, but it's one of the main ways that the concentration "muscle" is built.

The second step in Raja yoga's concentration continuum is called *dhyana.* This word could cause some confusion, because the term is used in Buddhism in a similar but not identical way. Within the context of Raja yoga, dhyana is what comes after we have paid our dues, so to speak. We've brought our attention back over and over again to our object of focus, and finally, the attention doesn't wander, but stays put, gently resting on that object. That's dhyana. In the state of dhyana, our attention is like pouring a steady stream of oil upon an object, without any breaks or gaps in the stream. It's a smooth, continuous stream of contact with the focus object.

Once we are able to do this with a specific sound or a breath sensation, or other sensory category, we can generalize that ability to any other object. It's not like we have to learn the process entirely anew for each type of experience. Once we enter the dhyana phase, we find that when we're eating lunch, for example, our awareness flows unbroken onto the tastes and body sensations that constitute the enjoyment of the food. However, if while having lunch we start to engage in a conversation with someone, our awareness shifts immediately and flows totally onto just that person. When the person is talking, we're not caught up in our own thoughts and feelings; instead, there is a constant flow of presence and attention toward the person. When the person is done talking, we go right back to being completely absorbed into the tastes of the food we are eating as we take the next bite. The awareness moves easily from object to object, yet no matter what it rests upon, there is an unbroken flow of attention. This is dhyana according to Patanjali.

The third and final step in Raja yoga's concentration continuum is *samadhi,* which refers to unitive experience. Again, there is a possible confusion in terminology here, because in Buddhism samadhi often refers to *any* level of concentration, from the lightest to the deepest. In the state of samadhi as understood in Raja yoga, we not only have unbroken concentration, but we actually *become* the thing we are concentrating on. This is what is meant by the often-heard phrase "to become one with something." It sounds sort of mystical-shmystical, but it's an experience reported the world over by all who enter states of high concentration.

Let me explain in a simple way how this happens. If you carefully observe your day-to-day experience, you'll notice that whenever you see a flower or another person, or take a bite of food, or hear a sound, your awareness is usually divided. Part of your attention flows out into the objective experience and part of it flows back into your subjective thoughts and feelings. In that moment, those thoughts and feelings create the sense of an internal "I" who experiences the external "it." But imagine what would happen if, for a period of time, *all* the attention flowed into the "it," and none of the attention flowed back into your mental images, internal talk, and emotional body reactions. What would happen to the sense of "I" separate from "it"? The "I" would vanish, leaving only the "it" for a while. Initially, we can maintain such merging or oneness only for a few seconds, but in the case of veteran meditators, it can be maintained continuously for minutes, hours, even days.

The Raja yoga system actually distinguishes two kinds of merging: *sabija samadhi,* samadhi "with a seed," and *nirbija samadhi,* samadhi "without a seed." This terminology may sound a little strange to modern ears, but it refers to something very specific and well defined. In samadhi with a seed, all sense of self disappears, and only the object of concentration remains, shining in consciousness. This is what I described in the preceding paragraph. The object that remains is the "seed," which is still present even though the observer has vanished for a while.

Samadhi without a seed takes the concentration to an even more extreme level. In this state, awareness flows so completely onto the object of concentration that there is no time to fixate that object as something rigid, opaque, and extended in time and space. In other words, the object of concentration ceases to be an object, ceases to be a something. To draw a metaphor from modern physics, the object ceases to be a particle and becomes a wave. That waveform fills our consciousness, and we become that waveform, and we are that wave. As we merge with the wave, it links to all the other waves in the universe. Then the wave dies away into deeply fulfilling nothingness. Observer and observed both disappear. This is samadhi without a seed: a direct abiding at the Still Point of the turning world.

This level of merging is both incredibly rich and refreshingly empty. It contains the totality of the universe, and it contains nothing at all, no concrete object. Hence, it's referred to as samadhi without a seed or pure consciousness or true witness.

That's the growth of concentration as described in the *Yoga Sutras.* We progress from simple focus exercises (dharana), to states of continuous concentration (dhyana), and finally to oneness with the unborn Source (nirbija, or seedless, samadhi). If you can consciously taste moments of seedless samadhi in daily life, we'll say you attained the initial stage of enlightenment.

∽

Now let's look at Buddhism. Here we find descriptions of a process somewhat similar to what we find in the *Yoga Sutras,* although formulated from a very different philosophical position. Buddhists traditionally divide the levels of concentration into eight stages: four *dhyanas* (absorptions with form) and four *arupyas* (formless absorptions).

As you'll recall, Buddhists tend to use the word samadhi as a generic term referring to any state of concentration, from Patanjali's dharana to dhyana, up to and including the sabija and nirbija states. This difference in usage often leads to massive confusion and endless, pointless quibbling over whose path goes further. Fortunately, that need not concern us here. From now on throughout this work, I will use the term "samadhi" in its generic sense, as Buddhists do.

Note that many Buddhists regard concentration as good, but not sufficient for deep insight. They contrast concentration/calming practice with clarity/observing practice, seeing them as different things. We'll look much more closely at this distinction in chapter 4.

Shamanism

As I mentioned earlier, scholars of comparative religion use the expression "mystical experience" as a general term for what I've been describing thus far in this chapter. There are any number of books that attempt to compare mystical experience across traditions. One thing I find interesting is that some of the older, classic studies on comparative mysticism fail to mention the experiences of native peoples such as American Indians, Australian Aborigines, Africans, and Polynesians. This is a glaring oversight, considering that mystical experience was probably somewhat common within such preliterate cultures.

Consider the situation of our remote ancestors—humans living before the development of cities, literature, and technology. Viewed from the perspective of the modern world, how would we characterize their life? It seems to me that for most of human history, life was simple, uncomfortable, and full of things that people could not understand. One natural response to physical discomfort is to find ways to get comfortable. This eventually leads to the development of complex tools, building skills, and the rise of cities, writing systems, and technology. Analogously, one response to the mystery of things is to figure out how stuff works. This eventually leads to the development of science. Thanks to centuries of research and invention, we can be comfortable in our houses even in the dead of winter, and we don't get perplexed by phenomena such as eclipses or thunder or a woman's menstrual cycle.

However, there is another equally natural response to physical discomfort, and that is to simply *open up to the discomfort* rather than fight it. In the same way, instead of flailing to find answers, we can let go of the need to know and open to the mystery of things. This second response is the core of the religion of tribal peoples, usually referred to as shamanism. Shamanism is often described as an attempt to acquire power through contact with the spirit world. But what often goes unappreciated is that in most cultures the standard way to contact the spirit world is through physical ordeals, some of which can be quite severe. *Shamanic ceremonies, such as the sweat lodge or sun dance, build concentration power and force equanimity.* By equanimity, I mean a kind of detached, gentle matter-of-factness within which pleasure and pain are allowed to expand and contract without self-interference. The *combined* effect over a lifetime can bring enlightenment as a byproduct.

I imagine that the reason some of the earlier studies on comparative mysticism failed to mention native cultures is that in these cultures there is no technical vocabulary or intellectual model for enlightenment. People just experienced it. And they probably experienced it somewhat frequently, because everything about their ordinary life would have tended to push them in that direction. Because life was simple, it was relatively easy to enter states of mental quiet and high concentration. Whereas modern people struggle for years with the complexities of their wandering thoughts, native peoples could, by and large, become quite one-pointed after drumming or singing for just a few hours. So the simplicity of daily life would tend to make it easy for people to enter samadhi. Indeed, we could say that the formal meditation techniques used by people in postliterate civilizations are just a systematic way of doing what our remote ancestors did relatively naturally every day.

Thus, among our remote ancestors, one natural response to their situation would have been to live in states of high concentration, in equanimity with discomfort, and in acceptance of not knowing things. Another response would have been to figure out stuff and get comfortable, but that resulted in life getting so complex that samadhi seldom occurs spontaneously. Furthermore, as we become habituated to comfort, we lose the natural ability to cope with discomfort through equanimity. So our remote ancestors experienced two oppositely directed forces. Expansively, they were motivated to figure stuff out and get comfortable. The figuring out led to science, and the getting comfortable led to technology. Contractively, they would naturally enter states of surrendering to the Mystery by letting go of the need to know and surrendering to discomfort by dropping into equanimity. High states of concentration combined with detachment from the mind and body would naturally lead to a state of oneness with nature itself, a kind of contracting back to the simplicity of Father Sky and Mother Earth. Since both of these directions are natural, it seems to me that the ideal situation for humans would come about when both directions harmonize in a science of enlightenment. We'll explore that theme in detail in chapter 11.

So although native peoples may not have technical terms for various nuances of concentration, as are found in the other traditions, the fact is that the experience was there. Indeed, the absence of special vocabulary may indicate that samadhi wasn't a special state for them, but part of everyday life.

In Secular Contexts

One might think that samadhi only arises within a spiritual context, but that is not the case. People can also achieve secular samadhis, which don't occur within a spiritual paradigm, but are still potentially paths to enlightenment. There are individuals who, through performing arts—like playing the piano, or dancing, or martial arts—spontaneously enter states of very high concentration. Over months and years, that state of high concentration may deepen and go through all the standard stages described by the religious mystics of the world. It also broadens, and they find themselves going into these states even outside of their art. Maybe they first experienced it playing the piano, then noticed they would go into that state in other activities in daily life. Sports is another area where people sometimes fall into these states spontaneously. The locker-room term for samadhi is "to be in the zone." For example, Ted Williams, sometimes described as the greatest hitter who ever lived, reported that when he "entered the zone" his concentration was so great that he could see the individual stitches on the ball as it came at him at close to one hundred miles an hour.

Among people who develop a high concentration through a particular secular activity, some go beyond the state of high concentration. They don't just get completely focused when they dance, they tangibly taste a formless state of no self/big self as they dance. The dance, the dancer, and the audience all vanish into a pure doing of space. The dance continuously manifests from seedless samadhi—the Still Point of the turning world. The poet T. S. Eliot describes this beautifully: "Except for the point, the still point, / There would be no dance, and there is only the dance."

If a person enters samadhi without a seed while performing some art, they are, strictly speaking, no longer performing. The universe itself is manifesting through their art. If they're able to replicate that state in daily life, then their sport or art can be legitimately described as a path to enlightenment.

The most sophisticated premodern theory of performance can be found in the Noh theater of medieval Japan. There are several traditional forms of Japanese theater, but Noh is the most ancient form and goes back to the fourteenth century. Noh, not Kabuki, is the true classical theater of Japan, and in many ways is remarkably parallel to classical Greek drama. For example, there is a chorus and the actors wear masks. One of the main creators of Noh acting theory, Zeami Motokiyo, talked about what he called the "Flower." According to him, the Flower is the absolute epitome of art, and very few people ever reach it. The Flower is what happens when rigorous training, intrinsic talent, and deep no self come together. The art is no longer a creation, it's a manifestation.

Spontaneous Awakening

Enlightenment experiences can sometimes occur without any practice whatsoever, by accident as it were. Sometimes people just fall into a unitive or no-self state without any intentional seeking. Typically, this state wears off after a few minutes, hours, or weeks. This is because most people do not have the base level of concentration required to maintain the experience. Also, they may lack a conceptual framework with which to understand what is happening to them.

For example, I once heard of an older woman with little education who had a major enlightenment experience. As she put it, "One day, I just got big." She had had this major experience, but without any training or conceptual framework, all she could understand about it was that she had become "big." In her particular case, the experience was permanent, but typically, spontaneous no-self/big-self experiences do fade after some time.

An old friend of mine named Flora Courtois had an experience like this when she was in college. It did not fade for her, and she spent many years trying to find another human being who could understand what had happened to her. She went to her priest, who did not have a clue about what was going on, and she went to her school psychologist, who was similarly clueless. Years passed, and she thought she was the only person in the world who had ever changed in that way. Then she read some books on Zen, and she met some Zen masters and realized that she was not the only one. She discovered that there was a whole tradition of it all over the world, and a whole methodology for achieving it. You can read about her in a booklet she wrote called *An Experience of Enlightenment.*

At Home in Anybody's Church

Enlightened consciousness can be found inside the core of each spiritual tradition. But it can also arise in secular settings through concentrative activities, such as sports and the arts. And sometimes it arises without any particular cultivation; it just happens to certain people. My goal in this chapter has been simply to sensitize you to the rather extraordinary fact that individuals living in different times in different places, having totally different views of the world, all describe a basically similar sequence of stages of enlightenment. And most of these people didn't know about each other. Isaac Luria, the Jewish Kabbalist living in sixteenth-century Palestine, never heard of Saint Teresa of Avila, and Saint Teresa of Avila certainly never heard of the Buddha, and none of these people ever heard of Lao Tzu. Yet we can find a broad similarity in how they describe their experience. Surveying mystical experience across traditions and cultures, we are struck by two extraordinary facts. Fact 1: Despite enormous cultural and philosophical differences, mystics describe their experiences in rather similar ways. Fact 2: These descriptions sound counterintuitive and paradoxical to the average person.

I believe that those two facts imply that enlightenment is something distinct and universal for humans. The English writer Aldous Huxley referred to this universal phenomenon as the *perennial philoso-phy.* I like this phrase. *Perennial* means something that is constantly coming back, constantly popping up again, in different ages, within different traditions, and within different cultures.

It was one of the great mind-blowing experiences of my life to realize the essential unity of mystical experience around the world. For me, it was like discovering a kind of spiritual periodic table of the elements. Before that, like many people, I was confused by the differing claims and doctrines of the great religions. But now, I can see a unifying principle. Once you begin to have mystical experiences, you can feel right at home in *anybody's* church.

I owe a great debt of gratitude to Father Bill for providing the books that so vastly expanded my spiritual horizon at a pivotal juncture in my life.

To sum up, whenever we practice meditation, we are linked to a global phenomenon that has been a core human experience all over this planet for a long time. Whenever we practice meditation, we are sitting on the tip of a vast pyramid that extends out in space and back in time and directly links us to a global lineage involving thousands, perhaps millions, of extraordinary human beings, all the way back to our prehistoric ancestors. Knowing this moves me deeply.

CHAPTER FOUR

Calming and Clarifying

M any years ago, I received a telephone call from Bob Stiller, the founder of Green Mountain Coffee Roasters, a company well known in New England at the time and now as Keurig Green Mountain all over the world. I was delighted when he said that my work as a meditation teacher had come to his attention. He told me that he was interested in personal growth, and asked how I would feel about teaching mindfulness meditation to him, his family, his employees, and—as a public service of Green Mountain Coffee Roasters—the general public in northern Vermont.

I was very enthusiastic. The possibility that I could teach meditation in a medium-sized company, with the backing of the CEO and his whole senior management, was just too good to pass up.

Soon, I began working with the employees at Green Mountain once a week, guiding them in meditation. The same architect who built their roasting plant, which at the time processed twenty-one million pounds of coffee a year, interviewed me about how to build a meditation room. Two months later, he had constructed a beautiful little *zendo* (meditation hall) right in the middle of the company's human resources department. We began to offer free retreats to the general public.

That's when I started to notice something amusing. For me, coffee is a natural complement to meditation, because it helps to keep you alert. When I think of coffee, I think about how it makes my mind clear. This parallels tea, which was introduced into Japan by Zen monks to help them remain awake during long periods of meditation.

However, I've noticed that this is the exact opposite of what most people associate with coffee. The general public thought it humorous, even oxymoronic, that a coffee company provided free meditation for the public. Most people think that coffee makes you anxious and frenetic while meditation means to relax, calm down, and chill out. They seem like opposites.

While concentrating and calming down is certainly a part of meditation, it is only half of the story. The other half of the process is clarifying, that is, observing, analyzing, and deconstructing sensory experience. Clarifying leads to insight. This clarifying aspect of meditation is known technically as *vipassana*. One way to think about meditation is as a dialectical interplay between a calming-concentrating aspect (*samatha*) and a clarifying-dissecting aspect (*vipassana*). For simplicity, I'll just call these two sides of meditation the *calming part* and the *clarifying part*.

When I tell people that I teach meditation, their usual response is to tell me how much they need to calm down, relax, and let go of stress. Very seldom do they tell me how much they need to gain discrimination power or analyze the sensory components of their experience. Our cultural archetype of what meditation involves is skewed toward the calming side of the picture. The calming side makes sense to the average person. It's a little harder to understand how the clarifying aspect works and why it's also a good thing. So let's discuss the calming aspect a little more, then take a look at the clarifying aspect, and then see how the two might work together.

Concentration and Calm

To begin with, there is an intimate link between the experience of being highly concentrated and the experience of being calm and reposed. The two experiences go hand in hand. As you get ever more concentrated, your body gets physically relaxed, and your emotional turbulence calms down. Mental image activity lessens, and you become aware of a sort of uniform soothing darkness or a pleasant brightness in the mind's eye. Mental talk also dies down, and you begin to experience interludes of mental quiet in your head.

Thus, calming effects accompany the concentrated state, and this allows us to establish a kind of positive feedback loop between deepening calm and strengthening concentration. The more concentrated we become, the more we experience physical and mental calming. Then, the more we focus on those pleasant calming effects, the further concentrated we get. As we go deeper, the pleasure of the calming effects gets more intense, which motivates us to focus even more one-pointedly on that pleasure, which then produces even more calming pleasure, which then motivates us to focus even more intently on that pleasure.

It's a spiral that builds on itself, the pleasure of the calm and the one-pointed attention reinforcing each other in a positive feedback loop that takes us deeper and deeper. This feedback loop is the mechanism that facilitates the attainment of special deep states known technically as absorptions (*jhanas*).

The first time I ever went into a state of dramatically high concentration was during my first Zen retreat in Japan. The retreat was harsh and rigorous and lasted one week. The first sit of the first day was a half hour long, and at the end of it, I felt great. On the second sit, my legs started to cause me a little bit of discomfort, but I still felt great. During the third sit, my legs hurt from the beginning to the end of the sit.

By the fourth half-hour sit on the first day, I realized I was in big trouble because I was experiencing intense pain. It hurt so much my body was shaking, and I was sweating. And that was just on the first day! Because it was a Zen retreat, there was a zero-tolerance policy toward movement—you were not allowed to shift your posture at all during formal meditation periods.

By some miracle, I managed to make it through the retreat, and it was totally worth it. During the very last five minutes of the last half-hour sit on the final day, the physical discomfort had reached such intense levels that I thought I was going to pass out. My whole body was shaking, and I was on the verge of bursting into tears and sobbing. I didn't want to lose my composure in front of everybody, so I started to scream to myself in my head, "You're not a baby! Don't cry! You're not a baby! Don't cry!" Over and over and over again. It was awful.

And then something dramatic happened. I dropped into a stunningly altered state which I had never experienced before. I noticed that the pain was exactly the same, but it didn't bother me anymore. It just felt like flowing energy. The voice inside my head totally stopped for the first time in my whole life. I actually observed this shift taking place. First my mental voice was screaming at the top of its lungs, then it was just talking in a normal voice. Then it turned into a whisper, then it turned into a faint little hint. And then there was silence. I had never in my entire life had the experience of inner silence. It was absolutely worth every minute of the pain, because from that time on, I knew what it was like to hear the absence of chatter in my head.

Such was my first personal experience of one of the calming effects of concentration. In retrospect, I realized that the pain made me so focused that it put me into an altered state. There was no place else to go. I was focusing on the pain because I couldn't focus on anything else. But that focused one-pointedness produced a delicious restful condition in my verbal mind.

My whole body relaxed, even though I was in great pain. That was very interesting because it is the opposite of what I would usually do. Pain typically makes us tense up, but I think I relaxed because I was near the fainting point. When you are about to pass out, you get "faint"—your mind becomes light, tranquil, diaphanous, and your whole body relaxes. Even though my focus was on the pain itself, it was also able to produce pleasant calming effects on my mind and body.

This illustrates the intimate link between concentration strength and its pleasant calming impact on the mind and body. Because of that you can, in a sense, get something from nothing. Well maybe you can't really get something from nothing, but you can certainly get something very big from something very small.

Here's what I mean. There are subtle, fleeting, restful experiences available to anyone during the day: physical relaxation, an absence of body emotion, a brief pause in mental talk, and the darkness/brightness behind your closed eyes. These are visual, auditory, and somatic restful states that are available once you know what to look for. Most people aren't even aware that these states are happening. But if you use them as an object of concentration, then the small pleasure they produce becomes more pronounced, more pleasant. When you then concentrate even more, they become more pronounced, creating a feedback cycle. Through concentration, you magnify those tiny, subtle, pleasant experiences into something that is hugely enjoyable and available to you any time you want. It's not exactly getting something from nothing, but it's getting quite a lot from a very little. I call this approach Focus on Rest. You let your attention move between visual rest (darkness/brightness behind your closed eyes or defocused external gaze), auditory rest (mental quiet or physical silence), and somatic rest (physical relaxation and emotional tranquility).

Getting Caught in a Good Place

Because there is this intimate link between the pleasure of tranquility and the ability to concentrate, it's natural for people to look upon tranquility and concentration as an end in and of itself. The ultimate goal of such a path would be to have the deepest possible concentration and the greatest possible tranquility pleasure. This sort of ecstatic bliss-out is our cultural archetype of meditation.

There is a *potential* problem with that. It's a pitfall of the concentration path which doesn't happen to everyone but is nevertheless pretty common. I see it often in my role as a teacher. Let's say a person has been meditating for some time on a simple object of concentration, such as the breath. When they meditate, they get very relaxed and calm, time passes quickly, and they feel pretty good. Their meditation practice has given them a little edge on life, and that's great.

The problem is that, in some cases, year after year after year, there may not be dramatic growth beyond that point. Their meditation practice is pleasant and useful, but it's not delivering the life-changing results they should expect. This situation is a specific example of a general phenomenon I call "getting caught in a good place."

There are two main traps that prevent people from reaching their fullest potential on the meditative path. The first is mistaking the map for the journey. Thinking about and debating about the paths becomes a substitute for systematically practicing a path. The second common trap is getting caught in a good place: the path leads to something good, but growth slows after that. One of the main jobs of a teacher is to make sure that doesn't happen. Tranquility that fails to mature into insight is a classic example of getting caught in a good place.

The problem lies in an overemphasis on the calming aspect without enough of the clarifying aspect, leading to lopsided practice. The person is in a good holding pattern but doesn't make dramatic strides over the years. Their growth is linear, not exponential.

When I encounter this in a student, I tell them that there's good news and bad news. The good news is that they are going into deep states. The bad news is that they are not bringing enough sensory clarity into that experience to foster dramatic growth. When I show them how to do that, it changes everything. It kick-starts their personal growth again, and their meditation practice vastly deepens.

The Buddha's Discovery of Vipassana

The Buddha was not some sort of god or myth. He was an actual, historical person named Siddhartha Gautama. He was a prince, the son of the king of the Shakya nation, which was located in modern-day Nepal.

If we strip away the mythology around this person, we can get a pretty clear sense of what he was like as a flesh-and-blood human being. In my opinion, he was one of the most remarkable human beings of all time.

Even though Siddhartha Gautama lived about twenty-five hundred years ago, he was, essentially, a modern person in many ways. He was a rationalist, he downplayed the role of authority, and he was critical of the inequities of the caste system as it existed then. He was the only religious leader in the history of the world who asked people not to follow his teachings based on his authority. That's a quite modern, egalitarian, and refreshing point of view.

These things about the Buddha are quite impressive, but I think his most important contribution is that he was the first person in history to clearly articulate a new facet of meditation. Because there is this feedback link between calming and concentrating, people had had a tendency to look upon calm/concentration as the be-all and end-all.

They believed that the goal of the path was to get greater and greater concentration and go deeper and deeper into pleasant, absorbed states.

But according to the traditional accounts, the Buddha discovered *an entirely new attentional skill.* He found that you could use it to get deep insights into yourself, even the profoundest insights of enlightenment. He discovered how to develop a sort of internal microscope to carefully observe the nature of your own sensory experience. This discovery brought a whole new dimension to meditation: the dimension of clarifying and untangling. Clarifying and untangling fosters insight into fundamental issues—the nature of self, the nature of suffering, the nature of oneness, perhaps even the nature of nature.

Here is the traditional story of how he discovered this new way to focus.

Siddhartha Gautama was born into a royal family about five hundred years before the birth of Christ. A court astrologer said that Siddhartha would either be a world-conquering emperor or a world-changing guru. His father, being a king, did everything in his power to encourage Siddhartha to become an emperor, but the young prince saw how much suffering there was in the world. He also encountered *shramanas*—people who had shaved heads, wore special clothes, and did not engage in societal activities but rather pursued, among other things, concentration-style meditation and ascetic practices. He was very struck by the idea of becoming a shramana and overcoming suffering.

One night, he snuck out of his father's palace with the goal of seeking a meditation teacher. (As I've mentioned, concentration practices are found in all cultures, and there were such teachers available to young Siddhartha.) His first teacher, Aradakalama, taught him how to enter a very deep state of absorption and rapture. Siddhartha was something of a spiritual prodigy. He had an enormous natural aptitude for meditation. He was to meditation techniques what Mozart was to music, Bobby Fischer was to chess, or Muhammad Ali was to boxing. Techniques that ordinarily take years or decades to master, Siddhartha was able to perfect in a few months. After he mastered the deepest, most absorbed, blissful, and concentrated state that his teacher knew of, Aradakalama offered to make Siddhartha a co-teacher.

As I mentioned, part of the greatness of the Buddha was that he was very critically minded. He realized that, although there was no suffering in that deep absorbed state, it returned when he came out of that state. When he was walking around in ordinary life, he could discern that the seeds of suffering were still there. His deep concentration was ecstatic, but it hadn't yet engendered a fundamental shift in his being.

To his great credit, Siddhartha recognized this problem. He had achieved something amazing, something that felt incredibly good. His teacher even told him that he had, in effect, achieved all there was to achieve. But Siddhartha wouldn't let himself get caught in a good place, so he sought out another teacher, Uddaka Ramaputta, who knew about even deeper states of absorption.

Again, Siddhartha was able to master this new teacher's techniques very quickly. Uddaka Ramaputta declared that Siddhartha had achieved all there was to achieve, and offered him a co-teacher position. Even though the new state of absorption he had learned was even deeper than the first, Siddhartha realized that it still hadn't radically transformed his everyday self.

There were no other teachers available who could show him any deeper concentration state. So Siddhartha took up ascetic practices: doing extreme self-mortification, starving himself, and so forth. He did this for several years. Eventually, he had the courage to abandon that, too. It was destroying his physical body, ruining his health, and he still felt that he hadn't achieved a fundamental change in his relationship to suffering.

At this point, he felt that, although he had learned some important things, he had failed in his quest. So he sat down under a tree and vowed not to get up until he succeeded in finding what he was looking for.

And he found it.

What had he discovered? According to the traditional story, he discovered a completely new paradigm for the meditative endeavor. He realized that the cultivation of concentration and calm was not an end in and of itself. He discovered how to *microscopically investigate in real time the nature of sensory experience,* how to break the complex experience of self into manageable sensory elements. This led to an understanding that would permanently uproot the source of suffering, not merely suspend it due to an altered state. After that, people referred to him as a Buddha, which means an awakened person.

I call this microscopic investigation of sensory experience *sensory clarity*. It is the essence of mindfulness meditation, and an extremely powerful method of self-transformation.

Analyzing Sensory Experience

The clarification/insight side of meditation involves analyzing sensory experience into components and then tracking how those components interact. For example, if you are going through an emotional experience and want to practice meditation, you could decide to use a clarification meditation and, moment by moment, analyze your emotional experience in terms of basic sensory elements and their interactions.

Let me make that tangible. At any given instant, you may have emotional-type sensation in your body *or* you may not. By emotional-type body sensations, I mean things like teary-sadness in the eyes, tense-anger in the jaw, queasy-fear in the belly, pleasant-smile on the face, enthusiastic-interest over the whole body, and so forth. These kinds of body sensations are important components of any emotional experience.

Mental images are a second component. You mentally see the scene, the people, the situation. You get a mental picture of what your body looks like, and you get mental pictures of the scene around you. You relive the past or fantasize about the future. All involve mental images. So "image activity" is also an important component in an experience of an emotion.

And in your head, you hear yourself or perhaps others speak, you rehearse what you're going to say, or brood on what was said. You have judgments and rationalizations, and they come up in internal conversation. I call such thoughts "talk activity."

The three basic components of any emotional experience, then, are mental imagery, mental talk, and emotional-type body sensations. In order to have a quick way to describe things, I often refer to mental images as "See In," mental talk as "Hear In," and emotional-type body sensations as "Feel In."

So if you're going through an emotional experience, you could deconstruct it into three components: mental images, mental talk, and emotional body sensation. But what about when you're not going through anything specifically emotional? Do these three categories still arise? Absolutely. That's the beauty of the whole thing. *Any* perception of self involves one or a combination of those components. The ancient Greeks said "know thyself," but in fact, self-knowledge has many levels. You can know yourself in terms of your personal patterns. That's a good thing. But you can also know yourself as an inner sensory system. That's also good.

At any given instant, you either have mental images or you don't (two possibilities). At that same instant, for *each* of those two possibilities, you have two further possibilities: you either have mental talk or you don't. Do the math. We now have four (2 x 2 = 4) logical possibilities for any given instant. But at the same instant for *each* of those four possibilities, you either have body emotion or you don't, which multiplies the possibilities again by two, yielding a grand total of eight (4 x 2 = 8) basic states: three possible single occurrences (mental image, mental talk, body emotion), three possible paired occurrences (any two at the same time), and two possible extreme situations (all three inner components are active at the same time or all three inner components are inactive at the same time). Thus, we can analyze any subjective state into eight basic compositional patterns. This represents a somewhat oversimplified view, because each of the inner components can activate over a continuum that ranges from absolute rest to maximum possible intensity. But for simplicity's sake, we can represent them using a binary approximation involving "on" versus "off." Normally we're preoccupied with the *content* of our subjective experience, which, of course, can be enormously complex. But the basic *composition* is remarkably simple if we model it as three binary variables producing a total of eight (2^3) basic states. Let's list those eight possibilities.

Three single occurrences
1. mental image only
2. mental talk only
3. body emotion only

Three paired occurrences
4. mental image and mental talk
5. mental image and body emotion
6. mental talk and body emotion

Two extremes
7. all three active at the same time
8. all three restful at the same time

If you monitor your inner experience (memory, plan, fantasy, worry, will, desire, problem solving, judgment, conviction, confusion, and so on) in terms of the eight basic states, you'll notice something remarkable. When all three elements activate strongly, the perception "I am a separate thing" is very intense. But if only one or two activate mildly, the perception "I am a separate thing" becomes somewhat reduced. And most amazingly of all, every once in a while, the inner system spontaneously goes offline, causing your sense of a separate self to vanish. Something that fluctuates with time is a wave not a thing. And something that vanishes and reappears cannot be thought of as an abiding entity. If there's anything that abides, it is the Nothing from which sensory phenomena arise and to which they return. I will say more about this in chapter 9.

Initially, keeping track of those eight states may be fairly complicated. It may agitate you. It may not feel "deep" like meditation is supposed to feel. And it may take a lot of effort. So you might legitimately wonder "Why bother? Why not focus on pleasant restful states or something simple like the breath?"

Well, there is an important and powerful payoff to the clarification side of meditation. The payoff is that it leads to insights—"aha" experiences.

Some of these insights are trivial. For example, you might discover that every time you sneeze, you notice that a certain muscle in your back spasms. You didn't know that before, but you realized it because you were paying such close attention to sensory experience. Such an insight is extremely insignificant, but other insights can be quite profound, such as understanding the difference between pain and suffering, or realizing that you are not separate from the rest of the world, or that the thing you think of as "you" isn't what it appears to be. Such insights are staggeringly profound and permanently change your experience of your life.

A humble metaphor for how the clarifying aspect of meditation works comes from the realm of the office cubicle. Imagine you have a desk, and it is piled high with papers. Not only do you have a tremendous amount of work to do, but the system is also in total disorganization. It's just a blizzard of paperwork, and you don't know what goes with what.

A powerful way to deal with this situation is to make some categories for the papers. For example, you might sort them into incoming, outgoing, payables, and receivables. You would create a basket for each category and put the appropriate label on each container. Then you would sort the papers, one by one, putting each into its proper basket. You would have analyzed the pile of paper into its constituent components.

Not only is your desk now cleaned up and organized, you are now able to get some work done. You may even generate some insight through doing this analytical process. For example, if through the act of sorting you realize that the basket of payables is much fuller than the basket of receivables, you may have to look into your business model! You have gotten insight into your business's income stream.

The reason this metaphor seems so obvious is that we constantly do this kind of sorting or analysis in our external world. Categorizing and labeling are a mundane and extremely useful part of our everyday lives. Nothing could run without our doing so. However, practically no one makes use of this powerful technique for cleaning up their *inner* world.

I sometimes call this clarification aspect the "divide and conquer" strategy of vipassana. Ancient Romans used the phrase *divide et impera* to describe their strategy of breaking up a conglomeration of enemy forces into smaller units that could be defeated individually. If you will excuse my use of a martial metaphor in this context, I feel that this phrase neatly describes, in a nutshell, how vipassana works.

Breaking a complex experience down into its components makes it easier to understand, thus giving us insight. It also divides up a difficult experience into smaller, less individually challenging pieces. And this makes it easier to cope with. This ability to make life experience both insightful and manageable is the sort of "conquering" that vipassana affords us. What gets conquered is suffering and the distorted behavior that comes from suffering. If divide and conquer sounds too imperialistic and violent, an alternative description of the same thing is "untangle and be free." Personally, I like the phrase "divide and conquer" because scientists and computer programmers use it.

ळ

Although there is some disagreement among modern scholars regarding this point, according to the traditional narrative, the Buddha discovered a new way to meditate that involved clarifying and untangling sensory experience. States of calm and concentration were systematically cultivated in India before the Buddha's time. Also, asceticism was widely practiced prior to the Buddha's innovations. The original idea in asceticism was that the more you can be patient with pain, the deeper will be the purification of your soul. The Buddha tried such ascetical practices but eventually abandoned asceticism for a related but broader, deeper, and more refined paradigm: equanimity. The more equanimity you bring to pain (or pleasure!), the more it purifies consciousness. In this context, equanimity refers to a relationship to sensory experience—the letting go of craving and aversion around each experience, the ability to allow any and all experiences to expand and contract, without interfering. So in terms of meditation strategies, the Buddha made two huge original discoveries: the liberating power of sensory clarity and the purifying power of equanimity.

Samatha and Vipassana

As we have seen, the notions of concentration and calm have a natural relationship. It would be useful to have a single word that refers to calm and concentration as an integrated endeavor. In Buddhism, there is just such a word—*samatha* in Pali, or *shamatha* in Sanskrit. When we look at how the word is translated into Tibetan, it is very revealing. The Tibetan translation is *shi-gnas* (pronounced something like shee-nay). *Shi* means "calm," and *gnas* means "abiding." The gnas or abiding part could be interpreted as the ability to hold on to or to concentrate, and the calming or tranquilizing part is the shi. In Pali, *samatha* combines the notions of both high concentration and blissful calm in a single word.

By way of contrast, there is a word *vipassana* in Pali (*vipashyana* in Sanskrit) that refers to the clarifying side of meditation. Vipassana is a rich term, which combines three related notions in a single word. *Passana* literally means "to see." The prefix *vi* means two things: "apart" and "through." First, then, vipassana means to break things apart or separate them into their components (particles). This is the analytical, or "seeing apart," aspect. Second, vipassana means to soak your awareness into these components until you see their deepest nature, which is that they are nothing other than the vibrations of space (waves). This "seeing through" aspect is sometimes referred to by Burmese *Sayadaws* (vipassana masters) as "penetrating" each sensory event at the moment it arises. Third, vipassana results in "in-sight," the paradigm shift that occurs when you do enough seeing apart and seeing through.

So Buddhism traditionally characterizes meditation in terms of two contrasting but mutually complementary aspects: samatha versus vipassana. But I want to emphasize that this is one of many ways to analyze the endeavor of meditation. It's traditional and it's good to know about. A related alternative way to think about meditation is in terms of three components: concentration, sensory clarity, and equanimity. Yet another is to think of it as noticing a kind of primordial perfection that is always there so you don't need to meditate. (You still should though!) I'll be talking about those other formulations later on.

The Buddhist emphasis on cultivating systematic sensory clarity represents a unique innovation in the history of world spirituality. Because of this, there sometimes can be a prejudice in Buddhism against the calming and relaxing aspect of meditation, technically known as *absorptions*. Some teachers will dismiss such practices out of hand, saying that absorption practices "will never get you anywhere." But that's not really true. There is no real conflict between these two sides of practice, between samatha and vipassana. The two mutually aid and reinforce the other. Most people, however, start out with one side or the other.

You can work with the subtle, restful experience of mind-body self, which is a clever way to meditate. If you go into deep, pleasurable absorptions in meditation, this makes the senses seem porous, light, and open. Doing vipassana on such an attenuated experience leads to insight into impermanence, emptiness, and no self—and it's pleasant to boot!

On the other hand, you can work with the activated, solidified experience of mind-body self. It might seem obvious that you'd want to start out with the attenuated, calm, relaxed, samatha-influenced mind-body self, but that is not always true. For one, some people are not drawn to doing the pure samatha side of practice. Because of their personality, preferences, experiences, or some other reason, they simply like doing vipassana better. Furthermore, vipassana has the advantage that you can do it under any conditions. Samatha (at least early on) requires that you have a quiet room, time to really relax, aren't under a lot of pressure from life circumstances, and so forth. Vipassana, on the other hand, is rough and ready for anything. You can do vipassana perfectly well at a rock concert or on your drive to work. It doesn't have the hothouse-flower quality sometimes associated with the initial practice of samatha.

There are advantages to starting with either side of meditation. If you can't get to restful states for some reason, it doesn't matter, because you can sit down just as you are, with things very agitated and very solid, and begin to apply the vipassana side of the practice. Applying vipassana without a preceding attempt to develop samatha is some-times referred to as "dry" vipassana. It's not watered with the soft pleasure of calm, but it does get the job done.

Most people who are drawn to meditation are first drawn to the samatha side of things. That can be either good or bad depending on how they are taught. If they are taught skillfully, then the samatha practices can lead to great insight. If, however, they are taught unskill-fully, they can develop a kind of agenda or longing for certain desirable states. Then if they can't get to those desirable states, they are very frus-trated and they are constantly comparing. "Yesterday I was able to go deep, but today I couldn't get as deep," and so forth.

The medicine for that is to remember that the main goal in med-itation is not to get to certain good states, but rather to eliminate what gets in the way of those good states. If you do that, those good states will be available any time you wish. As the result of doing dry vipassana, you work through the craving, aversion, and unconscious-ness that prevents the blissful, restful states. As the result of having teased apart experience and clarified it over time, the blissful, rest-ful, absorbed states will arise automatically for you because you will have worked through the underlying blockages, or that which pre-vents those restful states from happening. I'll talk more about working through blockages in chapter 5.

So there is a complementarity between samatha and vipassana. If you do the samatha practice and experience wonderful, tranquil states, these represent a porous and attenuated self that can be relatively easily penetrated with vipassana. If you can't get to the restful states, that's okay. You do dry vipassana, and as a result, the blockages get decon-structed into their elements, and they lose their gripping force. After that, you automatically find yourself dropping into pleasant, absorbed samatha states simply because you've worked through the forces that would prevent those states from happening. It's a win-win situation. Samatha helps vipassana, and vipassana helps samatha.

If you really understand the complementary relationship between samatha practice and vipassana practice, you realize that, no matter what your situation, there is always something productive you can do.

CHAPTER FIVE

Insight and Purification

I sometimes have the honor of helping one of my meditation students go through the dying process. One of these was a colorful character named Gino, who kind of looked like Popeye the Sailor Man. Gino had been a sea captain, and had been torpedoed in World War II. In fact, his ship was blown out from under him twice, and he survived. He was a really tough character, the sort of guy that could get into a dock fight with four other guys and be the last man standing.

This extraordinary individual introduced himself to me by saying that he was getting kicked out of the nearby Zen center where he lived. He had gotten pissed off at the head monk and coldcocked him. Quite an introduction! He was wondering if he could come live at our meditation center. I don't know why we let him in, but we did. He turned out to be a very devoted practitioner who meditated with me for about five or six years and eventually became quite skillful.

Years later, he was diagnosed with terminal lung cancer. It was time to die, and he knew it, and he wanted to do it well. He had moved to Tulsa, Oklahoma, so I went out there for a while to help him through his dying process. However, it took longer than we had expected, and unfortunately, I couldn't stay on to guide him all the way to the end.

As I was leaving, he asked me for some final advice on how to optimize his experience of dying. I told him that, as far as I could see, he was facing five distinct types of challenging body sensations.

First, there was the pain of the tumor. Then there was the sensation of exhaustion because he couldn't sleep very well. Third, there was nausea, which is another distinct quality of sensation. Finally, on the emotional side, there was some irritability and also some fear present.

Gino agreed—these five body sensations were exactly what he was feeling. I told him that his job was straightforward: never lose track of these five qualities of sensation. Whichever one or combination of them was arising, be precise about where they are in the body. Note where the primary location is and whether it spreads out through the body. Keep infusing each one of these qualities with concentration, clarity, and equanimity. Allow them to get intense or mild, to shift and spread, to expand out and contract in, whatever way they wish. I told him this would reduce his perceived suffering and make dying a good process rather than a horrific one.

He had enough background in meditation to understand the instructions and to implement them, and indeed the dying process went well for him. His suffering was lessened because he was keeping track of what was going on in a state of concentration, sensory clarity, and equanimity—the essence of mindfulness. But more than that, he started to identify each of the different flavors of sensation with the *purification* of the psychological and spiritual blockages acquired from his previously badass lifestyle. He felt that the various intense sensations were cleaning out specific negative things he had done and the bad ways he had treated other people.

For example, when I was talking to him on the phone once, he excused himself saying he'd be right back. In the distance, I could hear him vomiting into the toilet. Then he came back and described how, during that vomiting jag, he just worked through a big piece of karma relating to his son.

As he infused those five types of body sensation with concentration, clarity, and equanimity, he could actually feel them reaching down into the memory bank where the guilt and regret were stored and cleaning them out. For him, each sensation was correlated with a specific thing it was purifying. The exhaustion cleaned him out in one way, and the fear cleaned him out in another. As this was happening, he was gaining insights into the meaning of his life, including the nature of various intense conflicts he had had with people. Because of this practice, his dying process became a process of insight and purification, wisdom and catharsis.

During the time I was staying with Gino, guiding him through his transition, I got a call from a former student, Ben. Before taking early retirement, Ben had been in the entertainment industry as a producer, writer, and comedy performer. His unexpected call led to one of the most moving scenes I had ever witnessed.

Ben was totally freaking out. Earlier that morning doctors had discovered an enormous tumor in his abdomen, and there was a very real possibility that it might take his life. Ben was relatively young, and this turn of events was totally unexpected. In panic and desperation, he was calling me for support. I reviewed for him the principles and practices I had taught him, reminded him of how to deconstruct fear by breaking it into mental image, mental talk, and body emotion. I also reminded him that a final diagnosis had not been made yet. But my attempts at comforting him were not very successful. I sensed he was on the verge of losing it.

Then it hit me. Why not have Ben talk to Gino? Gino, who at that moment was going through the process that Ben might be facing in six months or so. I went to Gino's room and explained the situation, then handed him the phone. In the intervals between coughing, vomiting, and convulsing, Gino gently assured Ben that there was nothing to fear in the dying process—it's just a return to a simpler, more primordial mode of being. And he described how the sensations he was currently experiencing had become for him a process of spiritual cleansing and empowerment. The power of Gino's words was palpable. This was not a theoretical discussion. He was speaking about dying from the place of dying.

It was an incredibly moving scene: the former badass sea captain, from his bed of agony, comforting the freaked out Hollywood actor. The interaction helped Ben calm down enough to start untangling the fear with a focusing technique. Although waiting for the biopsy was still tough for Ben, it was less hellish than it would have been otherwise. Contrary to expectations, Ben's tumor turned out to be benign. Often meditation works this way: we measure its value in terms of the suffering that would have happened but didn't—thanks to the fact that we have a practice.

As you can see from this story, when we apply concentration, clarity, and equanimity to sensory experience, moment by moment, we generate a process of insight and purification. Over time, this improves our lives, the lives of those around us, and the world in general. It can make dying bearable, even meaningful.

Breaking Things Down

A common strategy in the sciences is to take a complex phenomenon and break it down into its natural components. Analysis of these components allows us to understand the complex phenomenon at a deeper level, to have some control over it, and to predict things about it.

The field of chemistry gives us a good example of this. The set of known substances in the world is enormous and their structures often quite complex. There's everything from monosodium glutamate to clouds to gasoline to sugar crystals to biological macromolecules. But scientists are able to explain this vast diversity in terms of roughly a hundred basic elements. That's because they came up with an elegant classification—the periodic table of chemical elements. This allowed them to distinguish the basic building blocks. This in turn revealed that a relatively small set of elements can explain the enormously diverse range of substances and chemical properties. This basic strategy of analyzing complex phenomena into simpler elements is part of the "secret sauce" that makes science so powerful.

One very complex phenomenon that is of central importance for all human beings is our sensory experience. Human experience is quite complex; just think of everything that has ever happened to you since the day you were born. Fortunately, there is a natural way to break down any experience into much simpler components. When we look at an experience in terms of these simpler components, it's much easier to understand, to manage, and to gain insight. This sort of analysis is the secret sauce of mindfulness meditation.

When you think about it, all of human experience can be understood as *sensory* experience. That is, we only know about self and world through our senses. Recall that thought is *sensory* (mental image and mental talk) and emotions are *sensory* (mental image, mental talk, plus emotional body sensations). So following the example of chemistry, let's create a periodic table of sensory elements, a way to classify sensory events in terms of basic elements.

In the West, we tend to think that there are five senses, but in Buddhist theory, there are six. The six senses in Buddhist theory are hearing, seeing, smelling, tasting, the feeling body, and the thinking mind.

Personally, I like to slice up the pie of sensory experience slightly differently. I separate body experience into physical-type body sensations and emotional-type body sensations. For simplicity, I include the chemical senses, smell and taste, into the category of physical-type body sensations. I separate mental experience into a visual component (mental images) and an auditory component (mental talk). This creates a nice symmetrical system: the core subjective self—thoughts, emotions, will, conviction, confusion, judgment, reaction, memory, problem solving, fantasy—all arise through the "inner activity" of mental images, mental talk, and emotional body sensations. The perception that there's a physical world around us arises through "outer activity"—physical sights, physical sounds, and physical body sensations. Let's look briefly at the nuts and bolts of this formulation.

Thinking Mind

The thinking mind is quite a complex phenomenon. Human thoughts created relativity theory, Gödel's incompleteness theorems, Shakespeare's plays, Hegel's philosophy, and Hitler's ideology. What system of analysis will allow us to break down something as complicated as all thinking into relatively simple constituents?

If you look very carefully, you will see that most of the thoughts that we are consciously aware of come either as internal conversations (mental talk) or internal imagery (mental images), or a combination of the two. In terms of mental talk, we find that we think in words, phrases, sentences, and narratives. If you're multilingual, your mental talk will be in more than one language, but it is still grammatical human speech. Sometimes we hear our own voice, and sometimes other people's voices. Sometimes it's a dialogue; sometimes it's a monologue. What I call mental talk can also take the form of nonverbal tunes or music or internal onomatopoeia.

The other mode of the thinking process is imaging. We see things in the mind's eye, such as vague forms, scenes, faces, situations, or spatial relationships. Mental images are like the things that we see in the external world, but usually are not vivid or stable like physical objects or photographs. For most people, mental images are nebulous, semitransparent, half-formed, and fleeting. However, for a minority of people, mental images *are* vivid and stable. Such people are said to possess eidetic imagery. Artists often possess eidetic imagery.

Some people think mainly in the internal auditory mode, some think more in the internal visual mode, and for most of us both are present. This is how thought appears to us generally: in inner words and mental pictures. Thus, we can easily deconstruct the thinking process. The myriad of complex meanings is simplified into a tetrad of basic states: mental image without any accompanying mental talk, mental talk without any accompanying mental image, image and talk at the same time, or absence of both image and talk (a moment of total mental tranquility). This tetrad represents a great reduction in complexity and gives us a powerful handle on thought because it allows us to keep track of what's going on in the mind in real time and in a tangible way.

But isn't there more to thought than surface images and mental words? What about subconscious thought? It turns out that the visual versus auditory analysis works out beautifully well for that too. Visual thought takes place in certain locations. For many people, images associated with memory, planning, and fantasy tend to occur in front of/behind the eyes. Self-images tend to occur where the body is, and when your eyes are closed, the images you get of your surroundings tend to be arrayed out and around you. Also for most people, mental talk tends to occur in the head or at the ears. The locations where images might occur could be referred to as "image space," and the locations where talk might occur could be referred to as "talk space." "Mind space" would then be the union of those two spaces.

Notice that this formulation not only makes mental experience qualitatively tangible (visual experience versus auditory experience), but it also makes it spatially tangible (mental images and mental talk occur in specific locations and have width, depth, and height). We can think of image activity and talk activity as the independent components of a "thought vector." Thought now becomes a tangible, time-varying vector field. The magnitude of that vector represents the overall intensity of thought, and its direction represents the relative contributions of visual versus auditory qualities. For most people, image space tends to center in front of/behind their eyes—an area sometimes referred to as one's mental screen. Talk space tends to be somewhat posterior, in the head and/or at the ears. Viewed this way, your mind sort of has a front side and a back side, just like your body does.

The clarity aspect of mindfulness practice has several facets. One facet of clarity is discrimination skill, the ability to separate. Another aspect of clarity is detection skill, the ability to pick up on what's subtle. A natural place to begin observing the mind is by discriminating image versus talk. At some point, surface pictures and explicit words tend to die away. At that point, you begin to detect a subtle undercurrent, a sort of subterranean stirring in image space and talk space. That's your subconscious mind! You don't see explicit images or hear explicit words, but you know which part is visual and which part is auditory by its location. Unblocking the natural flow of this subtle mental activity nurtures intuition, wisdom, and creativity. But you can't unblock it until you can detect it. Parsing thought into image and talk opens the door for that possibility.

The ability to keep track of the distinct components of our experience is incredibly useful. First, you learn to separate experience into a few basic components. This sets the stage for detecting and untangling the subcomponents of those components, and then the sub-subcomponents, until we can get down into the ultimate building blocks or substance that underlies all experience. This makes experience trackable. The basic mantra of mindfulness is simple: trackable implies tractable.

The Feeling Body

Turning from the mind to the body, we see a similar potential. Embodied experience is a very complex phenomenon, but we can break it down into two main constituents: physical-type body sensation and emotional-type body sensation.

Physical-type body sensation requires no special explanation. A pain in your knee, the feeling of your muscles working, the sensation of cold, and an itch on your scalp are all physical-type body sensations.

The notion of emotional-type body sensation is, at first, an unusual concept for some people. As a culture, we don't often talk about emotions as something that occurs in the body. We tend to think of them as mental, cognitive events. However, if we have a very strong emotion, it's quite easy to contact the body sensations associated with it. Those body sensations are the primitive "juice" of the emotion.

So these are the two basic qualitative categories of body sensations: physical and emotional. These two big components of body sensation can be broken down much further into sub-subdimensions.

For both physical-type body sensations and emotional-type body sensations, we can distinguish subqualities of the feeling: hot feels different from cold, pressure feels different from an itch, embarrassment feels different from anger, anger feels different from fear, fear feels different from sadness, sadness feels different from a burn, a burn feels different from a cut, and they all feel different from the touch of your clothes, or the sensation of the blood circulating, or the feeling of the breathing process, or tiredness, or being very alert and energetic. Tiredness has a quality of body sensation associated with it, as do sleepiness, boredom, and impatience. Doubt, indecision, and confusion are things that occur in the mind, but they often also have associated body sensations.

There are many flavors or qualities of body sensation; however, these flavors are not infinite. I suppose perceptual psychologists could get into long discussions about exactly how many fundamental sensation types there are, but I would say, based on my own experience, that there can't be more than a couple of dozen really distinct ones. If we limit our consideration to just emotional-type body sensations, the most common flavors are anger, fear, sadness, embarrassment, impatience, disgust, interest, joy, love, gratitude, humor, and smile.

If you want to be happy independent of conditions, you'll need to learn how to have a complete experience of each basic type of body sensation. On the spiritual path, we have to learn how to have a complete experience of anger, so that anger does not cause suffering which then distorts our behavior. For the same reason, we have to learn how to have a complete experience of fear, sadness, and so on. We even have to learn to have a complete experience of physical pain, as well as other unpleasant feelings in the body such as fatigue and nausea. When I say, "Have a complete experience of x," it's just a quick way of saying, "Experience x with so much concentration, clarity, and equanimity that there's no time to coagulate x—or yourself—into a thing." You and x become an integrated flow of energy and spaciousness.

Learning how to have a complete experience of discomfort sets us free. Learning how to have a complete experience of pleasure deeply fulfills.

For example, erotic/sexual sensation is a major pleasant quality. In India, Tibet, and China, there's a whole tradition of transmuting sexual experience into spiritual energy. In the West, this endeavor is sometimes referred to as Tantric practice, but scholars are quick to point out that using the Sanskrit word *tantra* as a synonym for "sexual" is historically misleading and inaccurate. Putting aside the controversy over the name (and ignoring New Age hype), the spiritualizing of your amatory life is really quite simple and straightforward. The body sensations of making love are spiritual to the extent that they are complete, that is, experienced in a state of concentration, sensory clarity, and equanimity. To know what true love is, we need to experience it as it truly is. In Tibet, that's called the oneness of bliss and void.

In addition to quality of the body sensations (the basic types), there's the issue of intensity. Intensity represents a dimension of body experience that's independent from quality/type. Anything from a mild irritation to a homicidal rage is really part of one family: the anger family. Both have the same basic quality or flavor, but present at a different intensity level: rage is just a higher intensity version of irritation. Likewise, anything from slightly uncomfortable anticipation to paralytic terror is an example of the fear flavor. Intensity, then, is another way that we can categorize or track our body sensations while meditating.

Clarity gives us the ability to detect sensory events that are subtle, or not very intense. This combined with equanimity allows us to have a high degree of fulfillment on demand during the day. So subtle pleasures can be very significant. On the other hand, subtle discomforts can also be very significant. If the spread of a subtle discomfort is not detected and "equanimized," it might coagulate into enormous perceived suffering. Thus, the combination of clarity and equanimity applied to subtle experiences is helpful both for elevating fulfillment and reducing suffering.

A third dimension of body feeling is its *spatial distribution,* meaning location and shape of body sensations. Once we understand that body feelings are tangible, then we can start to talk about the location of a feeling, the geometric shape of a feeling, and so forth. We can talk about how a feeling may have its primary location in one part of the body and spread more subtle influences throughout the rest of the body. The way I like to define it, mindful awareness is "concentration, clarity, and equanimity working together." Clarity helps us to detect and discriminate qualities, intensities, and spatial patterns in what we see, hear, and feel. It gives us the ability to analyze our sensorium in terms of:

- how much,
- of what,
- where,
- when,
- interacting in what ways, and
- changing at what rate.

Interestingly, this set of categories corresponds to the most common variables that scientists use for quantifying the natural world. The last variable, changing at what rate, corresponds to what modern scientists call the "time derivative" of a function. It's one of the main things that you learn about if you take calculus.

Many people contributed to the historical development of calculus, but the name most commonly associated with its invention is that of Sir Isaac Newton. Newton, however, used a different word for what we now call the time derivative. He called it the *fluxion,* which is Latin for "mode of flow." Tracking rates of change in sensory experience leads to insight into impermanence—a huge theme in the Buddhist tradition. This makes a nice parallel with science. Buddhist meditators learn to "take the derivative" of what they see, hear, and feel.

How Thoughts and Feelings Intertwine

When we become skilled at tracking the subtleties of our internal sensory landscape, we can encounter our experience in a clearer way. Take for example the experience of anger. When you have an experience of anger, you have talk in your head: "He said such and such." "How dare he do such and such." "The next time he does such and such, I am going to do such and such." "But what I would really like to do is such and such." We hear words like these in our mental "talk space."

Meanwhile on the internal screen (the mind's eye), there are pictures that go with these words. We might picture ourselves striking back or stalking off. Taken together, these internal words and pictures constitute the thought component of the anger experience.

While these are going on, a tight quality is happening in the gut, a shaky quality is arising in the legs and spreading through the rest of the body, a hot quality is moving over the face and also spreading subtly over the rest of the body, and a pressured quality is arising in the chest. These feelings are the emotional-type body-sensation component of the anger experience.

These three components of anger—mental image, mental talk, and emotional body sensations—often occur simultaneously. Without clarity, they become a tangled skein. Without equanimity, that tangled skein coagulates into a solid mass of congealed suffering. And what's true of anger is true of *all* mind-body experience. If we develop an ability to discern the components of the experience, we can begin to keep track of what part is thought and what part is feeling. But if you don't have the skill of keeping track of the components, then you get this mixture, this tangling together of the feeling body and the thinking mind. And the result of the tangling together can bring about two undesirable consequences: the first quantitative, the second qualitative.

The first undesirable consequence of tangling is an illusory intensification of the experience. This is a *quantitative* effect. It makes the suffering associated with an uncomfortable experience seem much worse than it actually is. Without sensory clarity, the different components of the experience don't just add together, they crisscross and mutually multiply. For example, if we have ten units of discomfort in the body and ten units of negativity in the mind, what we actually have is twenty (10 + 10 = 20) units of undesirable experience. That is what you will experience if you have sensory clarity—just what it is. However, if you don't keep track of what is going on, each of the ten units of discomfort in the body will interact with each of the ten units of negativity in the mind, cross-multiplying to produce the illusion of one hundred (10 x 10 = 100) units of undesirable experience. If I have to be uncomfortable, I'd much prefer twenty units to one hundred. Sensory clarity skills give me that choice.

Imagine adding a few more units of undesirable experience, and it's easy to see why we can become so suddenly overwhelmed. For example, if we double the amount of each component, there will be twenty units of discomfort in the body and twenty units of negativity in the mind. Assuming you maintain sensory clarity, the effect is marginal; the distress only rises a little (20 + 20 = 40).

However, if we allow the thoughts and feelings to tangle together, they multiply, and we now have the experience of four hundred (20 x 20 = 400) units of distress, even though in reality we only have forty (20 + 20 = 40). This explains why things can get out of hand so quickly. Such exacerbated suffering will often distort our response to a situation, leading to even more suffering. This is the essence of the vicious cycle that Buddhists refer to as *samsara*.

The second undesirable consequence of tangling is a *qualitative* effect, and it's a bit conceptually subtle. But it's also very useful to know about. The tangling of three sensory strands—mental image, mental talk, and body sensations—imparts an illusory quality of "thingness" to the experience of self. If you are able to fully untangle those strands, the illusory quality of thingness goes away.

I'll be discussing this in more detail in chapter 8.

The Basic Model

The basic model for the mindfulness-based spiritual path is to take some type of experience and infuse it with a high degree of concentration, sensory clarity, and equanimity. Concentration means to focus attention on just what you deem relevant. Sensory clarity involves discerning the components that constitute an experience and detecting their subtle essence. Equanimity means that we give permission for these components to expand, to contract, or to be still—to do whatever they naturally would do. Equanimity is a radical noninterference with the natural flow of our senses. In other words, we can take any type of experience and attempt to be focused, precise, and allowing with it.

Greeting experiences this way—both in formal practice and as we are doing things in day-to-day life—catalyzes a process of insight and purification. In a chemical reaction, the role of the catalyst is to speed up a process that would occur naturally but perhaps very slowly. The catalyst interacts with the reactants in a way that can dramatically speed things up. Similarly, concentration, sensory clarity, and equanimity interact with the experiences of life to speed up a natural process of psychospiritual evolution.

Whether they know it or not, all human beings are involved in the path to enlightenment by virtue of living daily life. Nature (or grace, or spirit, if you're comfortable with such words) is constantly pulling us toward the enlightened state. The main difference between a practitioner and any other person is the speed at which they are intentionally moving along this path.

To sum up, infusing concentration, clarity, and equanimity into an experience functions like a catalyst facilitating a natural process of insight and purification that is just waiting to happen. Thus, the Fundamental Theorem of Mindfulness is:

Concentration + Sensory clarity + Equanimity + Time =
Insight + Purification

Insight

Spiritual insight (prajna) is like a many-faceted jewel. We have already talked about some sides of insight: the insight that physical and emotional pain don't have to turn into suffering, the insight that pleasure will yield deeper satisfaction if we don't tighten around it, the insight into how the sense of a particulate self arises through a tangling together of thought and feeling, and insight into the mechanism of how we can experience merging or uniting with another.

The basic premise of mindfulness meditation is that consistently infusing the qualities of concentration, clarity, and equanimity into ordinary experience over time causes a fundamental shift in our paradigm. It is for this reason that mindfulness is sometimes called insight meditation.

Purification

Most growth modalities—from nineteenth-century psychoanalysis to twentieth-century Scientology, and just about everything in between—share a common paradigm. It goes something like this: we store influences from the past in the subconscious, those influences inappropriately affect our behavior and perception in the present, and our job is to somehow remove those distorting influences. There are many different names for those influences, such as imprints, engrams, complexes, residues, and fixations. In India, and cultures influenced by India, they are referred to as *samskaras,* which means something like grooves or impressions. *Samskara* is a Sanskrit word. Yet another Sanskrit word for the same thing is *vasana,* which means something like habit influence. The notion that we carry subconscious, limiting forces from the past was discovered in India centuries, nay, millennia before Freud and Jung.

The samskaras are located in the deep subconscious. We are not aware of them on the surface. But we notice that despite our best intentions to be different, year after year we seem to be pulled into the same coagulated patterns of perception and action. And despite the fact that we may believe that there is a spiritual reality constantly present, our daily experience is one of separateness, materiality, discomforts, and banality. We don't seem to have a beatific vision every time we turn our head. We don't typically feel each body event as the touch of Spirit.

So if, as many believe, we really are imbedded in spiritual reality, why don't we see it? Why isn't every vision beatific? It's because of these fixating forces deep down in the subconscious. And our job, according to a plethora of self-help paradigms, is to become free from those forces.

In the Buddhist, Hindu, and Abrahamic contemplative traditions, the process of becoming free of those limiting forces is sometimes referred to as purification (*vishuddhi* in Sanskrit; *catharsis* in Greek). Purification could be described as the process that breaks this material up, digests it, metabolizes it, and (pardon the metaphor) excretes it. Purification is what it "tastes like" as we are getting free from those limiting grooves. It's a sort of immediate reward. *You sense that the limitations of the past are being metabolized and a brighter future is being created because of the way you're experiencing a certain something in the present.* Once you learn to taste purification, your growth goes exponential. The ability to taste purification is the sign of a mature spiritual palate. It's what allowed Gino to die well.

Just as there are many facets to the insight process (prajna), there are many different ways in which we can talk about the purification process (vishuddhi). If you want to use a theological paradigm, you would say that purification is the working through of our sinfulness, gradually burning away what's lodged between the surface self and the spiritual Source of self. For example, a form of meditation is practiced in the Eastern Orthodox Church that is in some ways remarkably similar to mindfulness. It's called *nepsis* (sober observation). It expresses the idea of purification using the Greek word *catharsis,* which means "cleansing." It is a doctrine of the Eastern Orthodox Church that we can cleanse away enough sinfulness to experience *theosis,* which means literally "becoming like God." According to the Orthodox Church, theosis is the goal of human life. The Christian notion of theosis is clearly distinguished from the pagan notion of *apotheosis,* which refers to a human being claiming that they are a god.

In Christianity, sin is original, but purification is possible through a combination of effort and grace. In Buddhism, purity—sometimes called the Buddha-nature—is original, meaning that consciousness is by nature pure. But we are subject to three fundamental impurities (*kleshas* in Sanskrit). The three impurities are craving, aversion, and unconsciousness (*raga, dvesha, moha* in Sanskrit). So our pure consciousness gets mucked up, and that leads to suffering. Buddhism sees the samskaras as impurities, not in the sense of uncleanliness or sin, but impurity in the sense of admixture. It's a metallurgical metaphor. Consciousness is by nature like gold, but these three impurities are mixed in the ore. In this paradigm, purification means the removing of that which is foreign to the gold, leaving just the pure gold. Through meditation, we smelt away the kleshas. We refine the ore, and we are left with what always was—the pure gold of pure consciousness.

The modern psychoanalytic paradigm of purification says that there are various unpleasant memories, incomplete experiences, and holdings stored in the deep mind—the repressed pool of poison and pain of the Freudian subconscious. From a Buddhist perspective, that old material gets worked through by pouring clarity and equanimity into the experience of the moment. That clarity and equanimity percolate down into the subconscious and give the subconscious what it needs to resolve/dissolve its issues. Moreover, unlike many psychological models, in the Buddhist formulation it is not *always* necessary to remember specific events or the content of past experiences. The Buddhist paradigm holds that most of the purification comes about because clarity and equanimity seep down into the subconscious, where the subconscious uses them to untie its own knots.

Often when we meditate, we are not consciously aware of much happening. It just seems like we are sitting there. Much of the time, our mind may be wandering, and when our mind is not wandering, it goes to sleep. After a while, we become aware that we are physically uncomfortable, and then we come back to our object of meditation for a couple of seconds. Sometimes meditation practice goes on and on like this, and it doesn't seem as if anything of real value is taking place. When we tell our friends what we experienced at a meditation retreat—mostly pain, sleepiness, and confusion—they may well say, "You paid good money for that?"

But all the while, clarity and equanimity are slowly but surely trickling down into the subconscious. They rewire us at the most fundamental levels without us *necessarily* knowing it at the time. How do we know that it's happening? We notice that things are changing in daily life. Our behavior and perception seem to be improving spontaneously. It is almost as though somebody is performing plastic surgery on your soul; you have been under anesthesia, and when you wake up, you look different, and you are not quite sure what happened in between. In meditation, a lot of the learning that takes place is of this type. Meditation can clean out stored materials without necessarily requiring that you recall specific memories, traumas, and such.

We might refer to this paradigm as the "trickle down" model for reaching the subconscious. This contrasts with the "dredge up" model used in much of psychotherapy. In the dredge up model, we reach down and explore a specific complex. This leads to a specific personal insight that then improves our quality of life. Dredge up and trickle down could be looked upon as mutually complementary processes. For some meditators, trickle down purification may be sufficient. But when that's not the case, they can utilize the services of dredge up experts, that is, competent mental health professionals. It's important to appreciate the awesome power of meditation practice, but it's also important to realize its limitations. Sometimes other elements are required—therapy, 12-step programs, openness to social feedback, having a list of explicitly stated ethical guidelines, and so forth.

Another possible description of the purification process is a somewhat mechanistic paradigm that I am fond of. In this paradigm, the six senses (what I like to call inner and outer see-hear-feel) have a kind of viscosity to them, like molasses. We have all heard the expression, "flowing like molasses on a cold winter's day," meaning something that flows very slowly. If however, we warm the molasses up, it becomes incomparably more fluid, and flows quickly.

Pervading our inner and outer see-hear-feel experience is a kind of subtle internal friction or viscosity that keeps our senses from flowing freely. This microscopic coagulation in the natural flow of the senses creates a kind of internal friction. It causes our visual field to congeal, giving us the impression that space is rigid. It causes our internal conversations to congeal, giving us the impression that thoughts are real. It causes our body sensation to congeal, giving us the impression that the body is material. This microscopic second-by-second self-interference in the sensory circuits is analogous to microscopic muscle tension. There are dozens of tiny microtensions subliminally present within each inner or outer experience. It is the sensory system working against itself, a sort of micro self-conflict.

In the mechanistic model of purification, the idea is to remove the microscopic, subliminal self-interference within the sensory circuits. This view is congruent with the paradigm of psychotherapy, which also seeks to reduce self-conflict. The difference, however, is that therapy talks about getting rid of *macroscopic* self-conflicts. Psychological-type purification is very important, but in meditation the emphasis is on dealing with the *microscopic* self-conflicts. As we infuse clarity and equanimity into our sensory circuits, their internal friction lessens. Inner and outer sense experience goes from jagged ice to flowing water, and from flowing water to vaporous steam. Chemically, ice, liquid water, and steam are the same, but their physical characteristics are quite different. Analogously, frozen see-hear-feel and fluid see-hear-feel are sensorily the same, but their spiritual characteristics are quite different.

I call this the "rheological" paradigm of purification. Rheology is a branch of engineering that describes nonlinear flow in nature. In the rheological paradigm of purification, the goal is to remove this microscopic, ubiquitous, and invisible coagulation from the substance of consciousness itself.

[∞]

Let's review. We have considered four paradigms for purification: Christian, Buddhist, psychological, and rheological. In the Christian paradigm, the blockage that separates self from Source is called sin.

Its radical removal is viewed largely as a matter of grace, but personal effort also plays a role. In Buddhism, the impurities are seen as secondary. Their radical removal is viewed as feasible with effort. But it is also true that certain Buddhist traditions emphasize letting go of effort and letting the nature of consciousness itself do the work. This trust in the nature of consciousness is the Buddhist analog of Christian faith and grace.

The Buddhist view contrasts with the psychological view in certain ways. Western psychology is often interested in dredging up specific biographical material to aid in repairing specific aspects of personality. In Buddhist practice, clarity and equanimity are poured into the sensory circuits, causing a global transformation throughout the whole of the subconscious. The practitioner may not even be consciously aware of any specific biographical content. One just notices that life is getting easier, behaviors are improving, and the only explanation is that the subconscious must be reorganizing itself due to the infusion of clarity and equanimity. Don't get me wrong; I'm not implying that the Buddhist view is better or that meditators might not need therapy. I'm just pointing out a contrast.

The rheological paradigm views purification as the sensory circuits learning how not to interfere with themselves. The theme of reducing self-conflict, inappropriate holding, and fixation sounds similar to a lot of what's talked about in psychotherapy, but there's a fundamental difference between the psychotherapeutic paradigm and the rheological paradigm. In the psychological model, the self-conflict, inappropriate holding, and fixation that are addressed belong to a large temporal scale—patterns that have persisted in a person's life for a week, months, years, or decades. The rheological paradigm addresses self-interference at a microscopic scale—holdings and fixations that go on continuously below the threshold of awareness at the timescale of a few seconds or even a few hundred milliseconds.

Personally, I think each of these paradigms of purification can be useful. Psychotherapy repairs areas that Buddhist meditation may not get to. Materialistic rheology and religious theology are not necessarily pointing to incompatible realities.

The Amphibious Human

Any experience—simple or complex, pleasant or unpleasant, internal or external, bizarre or banal—can be greeted with concentration, clarity, and equanimity (or not). It would be convenient to have a word that indicates the degree to which a given sensory event is being experienced mindfully. The word I use for that is "completeness." When we greet a sensory event with little mindfulness, our experience of that sensory event will not be very complete. If we experience a sensory event with a medium level of mindfulness, that experience gets closer to being complete. If we greet an experience with the fullest possible mindfulness, that experience becomes as complete as can be. Regardless of how ordinary a sensory event may be, when it is experienced with radical completeness, it becomes utterly extraordinary—indeed, paradoxical.

There is a deep complementarity between having complete experiences and purifying consciousness. By trying to experience each event in life as completely as possible, we purify consciousness, but the more consciousness gets purified, the easier it is to have complete experiences. When there is maximal concentration, clarity, and equanimity, an experience becomes maximally complete, and any maximally complete experience is much like any other complete experience. They all have "one taste"—the taste of rich vacuity combined with dynamic tranquility. Which is totally paradoxical. Complete pain causes rather little suffering and doesn't turn into aversion. Complete pleasure brings lasting satisfaction and doesn't turn into neediness. A complete experience of confusion creates a basis for spiritual intuition. A complete experience of desire is desireless. A complete experience of boredom is endlessly fascinating. A sensory experience is just some tiny part of the universe—the wind touching your face, an act of making love, tying your shoes, being angry with a student—yet when we experience any of these completely, it links us to the fullness of Creation and the vacuity of the Creator.

I like to think of humanity as destined to be amphibious, moving back and forth between two worlds like a frog. I imagine that a frog is happy because it's a creature of two worlds. When it is appropriate to be on dry land, it is comfortable there. When it is appropriate to be in the water, it is comfortable there. A frog can go back and forth between water and land any time it wants, as frequently as it wants. If it gets tired of the water, it can go to dry land, and if it gets tired of dry land, it can go to the water. It enjoys unimpeded freedom of movement between these two realms.

We human beings were also meant to traverse two realms. We were meant to submerge beneath the water of oneness into the world of completeness, fluidity, connectivity, and vacuity, and then to come out into the solidity, separateness, and somethingness of dry land for certain kinds of functions. The problem is we have forgotten how to get back into the water, and now we are stuck in the arid zone. Most humans have no way to refresh in the cooling waters of the Source.

∽

Here's the top-page summary:

> Ordinary experience, when greeted with concentration,
> clarity, and equanimity catalyzes a process of insight
> and purification which culminates in the ability to have
> complete experiences whenever you want.

This theory is quite elegant. It has all the marks of good science. A good scientific theory has simplicity, generality, and power. Simplicity means that it is not overly complicated. Generality means that it applies to a wide range of circumstances. And power means it gives you a good handle on what is going on.

The theory of meditation has all these marks. It well deserves the name "science of enlightenment."

CHAPTER SIX

The Many Faces
of Impermanence

S piritual wisdom is like a many-faceted diamond. Different teachers emphasize different sides of this precious gem. For example, the Buddha put a great emphasis on how enlighten-ment delivers freedom from suffering. Some Zen masters, no doubt influenced by Taoism, describe it primarily in terms of becoming one with everything. The facet of wisdom that has been personally most enriching for me is impermanence.

You might be wondering how impermanence could be enriching for a person. At first sight, impermanence seems at best trivial and at worst pessimistic. Trivial: everyone knows that things come and go, so what's the big deal? Pessimistic: if everything eventually passes, why bother doing anything at all?

In this chapter, I will show that the notion of impermanence is neither a banality nor a bummer, but in fact the very antithesis of these—something both profound and empowering.

"Impermanence" is the standard English translation of the Pali word *anicca* (pronounced *uh*-nee-*tchuh*). *Nicca* means "permanent," and *a* means "not," so anicca literally means "not permanent." The English word "impermanence," however, does not come close to conveying the richness of that notion within the Buddhist tradition. I would say that the concept of impermanence in Buddhism is as deep and mani-fold as the concept of energy is in physics. If you are familiar with the history of science, you know that the concept of energy has deepened and evolved over several centuries. The same is true for the concept of impermanence in Buddhism. Just as wisdom is a jewel with many facets, the particular facet of wisdom called "insight into impermanence" has itself many subfacets, many nuances and levels.

In early Buddhism, impermanence was closely linked with another concept, dukkha, which is usually translated as "suffering." The Buddha said that human suffering is caused by grasping. One way grasping can cause us to suffer is when we pin our happiness on things that cannot and will not last. Most people depend *solely* on things like health, wealth, reputation, relationships, appearance, family, or children for happiness. The problem is that these things are not eternal. People change; our health eventually deteriorates; wealth comes and goes; war may follow peace. All sources of conditional happiness are impermanent. In the words of Ecclesiastes, "All things must pass." If we make these impermanent things the cornerstone of our happiness, then we set ourselves up for inevitable suffering, or dukkha. So in early Buddhism, impermanence had a negative connotation. We suffer because we count on impermanent things for our happiness. We pin *all* hope of happiness on things that will not last.

But is there an alternative? Yes. Go ahead and pin *some,* even most, of your happiness on things that won't last. But be sure to allocate at least some time and energy for exploring the dimension of happiness that does last. Ironically, the dimension of happiness that does last is itself a facet of impermanence. It's the positive face of impermanence—the flow of *Creator Spiritus* that is always present, surrounding each moment of conditional happiness, embracing it from within and from without.

In everyday life, we tend to perceive ourselves as objects, as things. Human languages both reflect and reinforce this perception. But in point of fact, self is not just a thing; viewed deeply, it's also a doing, a wave. A wave is anything that goes through fluctuations, gets stronger and weaker, has peaks and troughs, spreads and subsides. Our sense of self certainly goes through such fluctuations. When you are alone at night, safe under the covers, your sense of self is somewhat diminished. On the other hand, if you walk into a room full of judgmental strangers, and everybody stops to stare at you, your sense of self grows larger.

It wells up as a wave, a billowing of self-referential mental talk, mental images, and emotional body sensation. Later, as you grow comfortable with the people in the room, the amplitude of that self-wave subsides a bit.

When we look carefully, we discover that the sense of self is not a particle that never changes, but rather a flow, a wave of thought and feeling that can increase and decrease and is therefore not permanent. Because it is a fluctuating wave, not a solid particle, the Buddha described it as *anatta*. *An* means "not," and *atta* means "self as thing." It's not so much that we don't have a self, rather it's that the self we do have is not a thing. It is an impermanent, fluctuating activity, a *process* not a particle, a *verb* not a noun.

The Stone Buddha Dances

I sometimes ask people an intentionally weird, multiple-choice question: Are the mountains dancing? The possible answers I offer are yes, no, and it depends. The answer I like is: it depends. Depends on what? Two things: how minutely we investigate the mountains and how patiently we investigate the mountains.

In many languages, the word "mountain" is a metaphor for that which is permanent and unchanging. However, if we were to look at the mountain not at the macroscopic level of the rocks, but at the microscopic level of the molecules, we would be struck by the enormous amount of gyration, movement, and vibration. To borrow a phrase from the 1950s rock-and-roll star Jerry Lee Lewis, "There's a whole lotta shakin' goin' on." Below the molecular level is the atomic level, below that is the level of protons and neutrons, and below that, quarks, and below quarks, perhaps superstrings. At each progressively subtler level, the vibrations are higher frequency and more dramatic. At the quantum level of physical reality, we find the ultimate frequency of vibration known as the Planck frequency, which is roughly a million trillion trillion trillion cycles per second. In other words, beyond a certain spatial scale of fineness, the mountain is essentially *nothing but* movement. Viewed with very minute, microscopic awareness, the mountain would appear to be a literal dance of energy. That's the spatial perspective.

Now let's talk about the temporal perspective. If we look at a mountain for ten years, it doesn't seem to change very much. However, if we took a time-lapse video, a shot each century for millions of years, then played the film back at regular speed, what would the mountain look like? It would look like streaming protoplasm, undulating with a graceful fluid motion, expanding here, contracting there. In other words, if we look in slow motion, we see all sorts of movement that we would not see otherwise. How is this relevant to ordinary sensory experience? Is there something we can do that is analogous to seeing in slow motion? Yes, if we look patiently enough, if we have great *equanimity,* we will be thrust into an altered state, where time dramatically slows down. You might have experienced something like this in your own life—perhaps associated with a dramatically life-threatening situation or a dramatically life-affirming situation. Everything seemed to run in slow motion, and you were looking as from a distance, unafraid, knowing exactly what to do and having seemingly an eternity to do it. In the language of mindfulness, you spontaneously dropped into a state of profound equanimity. Within that state, it is possible to experience self and world, ordinarily so solid, as a kind of effortless flow.

Viewed with the patience of centuries (from deep equanimity), or with the precision of the microscopic (with great sensory clarity), seemingly solid experiences are in fact a dance of energy. This holds true for all our experiences, from the most ordinary to the most outré. We may say that a certain sensation seems very solid, a certain thought seems very gripping. We look at the wall, and it seems unchanging and rigid. However, if we can look patiently enough and precisely enough—if we have sufficient clarity and equanimity—then our moment-by-moment sensory experience is an effortless flow of impermanence.

There is an ancient Zen book that gives a criterion whereby you can know if you are enlightened or not. The criterion goes like this: if you visit a temple, and the stone Buddha on the altar dances for you, then you are enlightened. Now is this just some sort of zany Zen metaphor, intentionally designed to blow your mind? Not at all. They mean it quite literally. The question is: How can a stone Buddha dance?

Let's say that you are in a Chinese temple, looking at a giant stone Buddha. You look to the right, look to the left, then you look at his belly, look at his leg, then look over the entire sculpture at once. Your vision flows over the stone Buddha, and each time there is an eye shift, a completely new visual impression of the stone Buddha arises. Most people are not explicitly aware of this constant visual shifting in day-to-day life. During a typical day, how many times does your head turn, how many times do your eyes move from one side to another, how many saccades—small shifts in your visual axis—occur? Neuro-scientists estimate that it's about a hundred thousand! And with *each* shift, a new world arises, and an old world dies. Typically, we don't consciously notice such transitions; they are all part of the automatic processing of the brain. However, if we trained ourselves to be mind-ful in visual space, we would be aware that moment by moment, at all sorts of spatial and temporal scales, the center of our visual awareness is constantly shifting within the so-called material world. We would also notice that at each one of those shifts, something wells up, but something also subsides. At first, it might be something like snapshots taken at different angles. But as your visual mindfulness deepens, you would begin to see a smooth and continuous flow of visual welling-up and subsiding. It is very much like the graceful movements of a jel-lyfish, or seaweed in a tide pool, or like the movements of the earth if seen in time-lapse photography. The world becomes soft, pliant, and elastic. It's like a fluid version of one of those Picasso paintings where you see a face from many angles. Picasso was trying to portray what our visual field actually does—to paint this dynamic 3D process on a static 2D surface.

The stone Buddha comes to life through the dance of your eyes.

Masks of Impermanence

When we really attend to what is, we become aware that *impermanence is characteristic of all our experiences,* even the experiences that seem very permanent. If we look carefully enough and patiently enough, any experience will show us its impermanence. That is important and useful, because impermanence can turbocharge our spiritual growth. In order for that to happen, we have to be able to detect the impermanence. So I would like to describe some of the guises in which it presents itself.

Frequently students tell me that they haven't experienced impermanence yet, or that they would like to experience it, or that they don't understand what I mean by it. This indicates to me that they are thinking that impermanence is something special. It's not. It's something ordinary that will become extraordinary if you consistently pay enough attention to it for a long enough time. If you have ever had a pain that got stronger and then got weaker, you have experienced impermanence. If you have ever heard a sound get louder and then fade, you have experienced impermanence. If you have ever watched your mind get agitated and then calm down, you have experienced impermanence. Seen this way, no human being can claim they have not experienced impermanence. When people say things like "I have not experienced impermanence yet," what they mean is they have not reached the point where impermanence informs and empowers them in a significant way. So how does one come to an extraordinary experience of impermanence—an experience of impermanence that alters one's world view and liberates one's mind and body? This comes about by *carefully* paying attention to "ordinary" impermanence *consistently, for a long period* of time.

Impermanence is simply the changing-ness of experience, and everybody has contact with the changing-ness of experience. However, most people have not developed an *intimacy* with the changing-ness of experience. They may not have the sensitive radar to detect its various guises. They may not have cultivated a palate that appreciates all its subtle flavors. They may not have realized its earthshaking potential. They may not appreciate its ubiquity. But no one can say that they have not *experienced* impermanence.

When Buddhists talk about having insight into impermanence, they just mean appreciating the normal changing-ness of experience at deeper levels of poignancy. One way to think about this is in terms of three aspects: the trivial aspect of impermanence, the harsh aspect of impermanence, and the blissful aspect of impermanence. Let's look at each of these a little more closely.

At first impermanence may present itself in a kind of *trivial* way. For example, you are meditating, and you start feeling an itch. You get preoccupied with it for a while. Then something distracts you, and when you come back, the itch is gone. You didn't actually feel it go, you are just aware that something previously present is now absent. Your attention was broken, but you still noticed that something changed. This level of understanding impermanence is based on a lack of continuous concentration. A deeper appreciation of impermanence comes about through continuous concentration.

As your concentration skills grow, and you are able to focus on things more continuously without being distracted, you begin to appreciate how things *continuously* change. But continuous change does not necessarily imply smooth change. At this stage, your experience of change may be abrupt, jagged, perhaps even harsh. For example, you are watching a pain in your leg, and you notice that it is pounding, twisting, stabbing, shooting, crushing, or exploding. Now these are very abrupt and uncomfortable modes of movement, but they are movement nonetheless. They are ways in which the pain sensation is changing. It seems like somebody has stuck a knife in your leg and is twisting it to the right, to the left, jabbing it in, pulling it out. It is harsh, it is abrupt, it is jagged, but it represents a continuous contact with changing-ness.

This doesn't happen only with painful experiences. The same can happen with intense pleasure. For example, during lovemaking you may have continuous contact with strong pleasure sensations. But because of craving, these sensations impact the body in a harsh and jagged way. There's intensity, yes, but it's coagulated and driven. It fails to deliver the smooth, easy waves of timeless fulfillment that love was meant to be.

Eventually, your concentration and equanimity skills mature to the point where your experience of change is not only continuous, but smooth as well. A softening takes place. The impermanence becomes fluid, soothing, bubbly, more like an effortless breathing in and out. This is because your focus is like a high-resolution monitor or a high-definition TV screen, and you are able to perceive subtler movements with clarity. To make a techie metaphor, it's as if you have increased the sampling rate or bandwidth of your change detector. You can't force this to happen, but as you are paying attention and developing an acceptance of the harsher kinds of impermanence, they break up into gentler kinds of impermanence—stately undulations, effervescence, effortless spread, and collapse. When this happens, the impermanence starts to comfort you, it becomes like a massage.

In point of fact, even when it was pounding, cutting, crushing, and exploding, it really was massaging you, but that's a kind of rub-down that you don't quite recognize as a rubdown, because it was just a little bit too harsh. It's like the difference between light Swedish massage and intense deep-tissue massage. Unfortunately, nature often starts out with the intense, deep massage mode, and we do not realize that we are being massaged. We may think we are being tortured. But we have to be willing to go with it. If it wants to pound, let it pound; if it wants to twist, let it twist; if it wants to crush, let it crush. Through that, some of the gross resistance to the flow of imperma-nence gets broken down, although it may not seem like it at first. At some point, you will experience the gentler aspects of impermanence, the soft-massage style. I describe this third stage of impermanence as a pleasant flow of energy—a smooth, effortless effervescence that's nurturing and enlivening.

At this point, we are on the edge of an important transition, because now we can yield to the flow and let it "meditate us." The perception "I am meditating" fades into the background and is replaced by the perception that "impermanence is meditating me." You can think of impermanence in this guise as your helper in meditation.

The great Burmese master U Ba Khin had an interesting and useful way of talking about impermanence, which I am sure was never used in earlier Buddhism. He spoke of "activating" impermanence. At some point, you may experience impermanence as a kind of energy that has been activated within you and helps you along with the meditation. It is a kind of impermanence you can ride and surf. In Hindu meditation, this is sometimes called *kundalini* or *shakti*.

Here is where we start to perceive an aspect of impermanence that is more positive than the earlier association of impermanence with suffering. Instead of only representing a pessimistic philosophy, we are now talking about a helper along the path. As far as I know, the Buddha never explicitly talked about impermanence in such terms. I think we should have a name for the positive side to impermanence, so in my system, I call it "Flow." I find having a word that emphasizes the positive side of impermanence very useful in teaching anicca to the modern world.

Flow itself comes in many different flavors. The main forms of Flow I like to distinguish are *undulatory* Flow, *vibratory* Flow, and *expansion-contraction* Flow. Undulatory Flow is continuous, wavy movement, like a jellyfish, an amoeba, or a lava lamp. Most people initially experience this flavor of Flow over their whole body. The whole body feels like seaweed in a tide pool.

Vibratory Flow is like champagne bubbles or sparks of electricity. If you have ever experienced the "high" that runners enjoy or the "pump" that weightlifters speak of, you have contacted this flavor of Flow. A similar feeling is the vibratory sensation you get after taking an invigorating shower, or the glow feeling you have after making love, or the endorphin rush some people seek. If you have enough microscopic clarity, you'll discover these pleasure types are really Flow in the form of scintillating mist or effervescent champagne bubbles throughout your body.

Taking a run or an invigorating shower or making love—what do each of these experiences have in common? Each one of them represents an intense experience of body. In the relaxed period that follows, if you observe microscopically, you will discover a fine vibratory phenomenon. This is in fact the nature of all body experience, but it is easier to detect at such times because of the intense involvement with the body that preceded.

Expansion-contraction Flow involves inward and outward movements, stretching and squeezing forces, effortless puffing out and equally effortless collapsing in. It's not uncommon in meditation for people to get a sense of vastness that encompasses everything and a sense of lightness that pervades everything. But look carefully. That immense vastness is not static; it's a dynamic force that spreads outward. And that pervasive lightness is not static; it propagates a flavor of contractive thinness, constantly calling consciousness back to the dimensionless point whence it arises. Expansion-contraction Flow is fundamental in that it underlies all other flavors of Flow. All three—undulation, vibration, and expansion-contraction—are often present at the same time.

For many people, their first experience of Flow is in the body. Later they will begin to notice various flavors of Flow in the other senses, including the thinking process itself. Of course, not everybody experiences impermanence in the ways I have described, and you certainly should not struggle trying to get experiences of undulations, vibrations, or expansion-contraction. However, if you do experience Flow, either as a result of formal meditation or spontaneously as the result of everyday living, it is useful to understand what it signifies and how to work with it.

Before we go further, I need to make one minor point regarding terminology. Technical terms mean different things in different contexts. In the field of positive psychology, "flow" refers to the intrinsic reward associated with a highly concentrated state, a topic we discussed earlier in this book. It has come into popular use in that sense. It's not unusual to hear people say things like "I entered a flow state," by which they mean they entered a state of enjoyable concentration. It's wonderful that we now have a commonly known English word for that phenomenon. So we should thank positive psychologists like Mihaly Csikszentmihalyi for that. However, notice that within my formulation, Flow refers to dynamic qualities that may be present within sensory experience—change, energy, force, movement, and such. In terms of science, detecting Flow corresponds to taking the "time derivative" of sensory experience. Obviously, flow as spoken of in positive psychology and Flow as spoken of within my system have a natural relationship: the former facilitates the latter.

Flow as Purifier

When a body worker massages you, that person's fingers move through the substance of your muscles and transfer energy into them. This works out the kinks and lumps in the substance of the muscles. This is a good analogy for the Flow of impermanence. When you let impermanence work on you, the energy in its waves and vibrations softens the substance of consciousness, works out knots in your soul. It breaks up the coagulated places in all your senses: visual, auditory, and somatic. This is impermanence as a purifier, something that breaks up blockages, cleans out impurities, refines the ore of who you are. As this is happening, it may seem as though consciousness is becoming porous. Within that porosity, you can feel anicca's waves and vibrations churning up gunk from the depths of your soul. They push gunk up, digest it, then excrete it from your being. You can feel your senses being scoured by the Flow of impermanence. The cleansing of the doors of perception is not a poetic metaphor, it's a palpable reality.

Impermanence is related to central ideas found in various spiritual traditions. The words used may not initially look anything like "impermanence." If you just looked at their literal meaning, you would never in your wildest dreams imagine that they had anything to do with what Buddhists call impermanence.

For example, Chinese culture recognizes something called *qi,* which is described as a kind of energy that flows in channels through a person's body. The East Asian medical/martial notion of qi is closely related to the Buddhist experience of impermanence. If you receive an acupuncture treatment and really tune in to what is happening with the needles, you will detect what in Chinese is called *deqi* ("getting qi"). You feel expanding, contracting, vibrating waves going out from that needle, doing stuff that seems to be good for your body. You might not think that would be related to a philosophical concept like impermanence, but it is.

As you'll remember, in Buddhist practice we get insight into impermanence by being very precise and very open to things. When the acupuncturist puts a needle in your skin, the pinprick produces a sensation of pain. It is not a big sensation, nothing more than a mosquito bite, so it is fairly easy to be completely open to that sensation, especially if you believe that the needle is going to help you. When you are needled in acupuncture, it is easy to have equanimity with these little pin pricks. It is also easy to be very precise about them, very mindful about exactly where they are located. In English, we even have a verb, "to pinpoint," meaning to be spatially precise about something. Receiving acupuncture automatically gives you an experience of precise and accepting awareness of the body.

But this is exactly what we do in mindfulness practice! When we develop body mindfulness, we attempt to be very precise about the locations of sensations, and we try to have equanimity with them to the best of our ability. In essence, we take the ordinary aches and pains we experience while sitting, and convert them into a kind of acupuncture stimulus. As a result of pinpointing them and opening to them, they start to flow and vibrate, creating an experience analogous to the deqi of acupuncture.

I'd like to clarify something about the relationship between the Taoist notion of qi and the Buddhist teachings on impermanence. People familiar with the Buddhist tradition tend to associate the concept of impermanence with two things: the nature of objective reality and the ubiquity of suffering. Everything that is compounded eventually passes away. So if we pin all of our happiness on people, objects, and situations, we set ourselves up for inevitable and perhaps horrific suffering. This aspect of impermanence is an important and useful *philosophical* statement. But there's also an *experiential* side to impermanence. As we carefully observe our senses, we become poignantly aware of their vibrant, vibratory, and dynamically spacious nature.

Qi is usually conceived of as an objectively existing entity that can be controlled and manipulated. But what's the historical origin of this concept? I suspect that it originally arose as the result of people detecting energy flows in their body and noticing how those flows tend to move in certain patterns. Whether qi objectively exists as a physical force is contentious, but as a sensory experience, its significance is undeniable. Therein lies the link between Buddhist impermanence and Taoist energy. As intellectual concepts, they seem quite different, but as sensory experiences, they're closely related.

Impermanence is also related to what is called the Holy Spirit in the Abrahamic religions: Christianity, Judaism, and Islam. The phrase "Holy Spirit" may sound sort of mystical-shmystical, maybe even annoying, or intimidating, or off-putting. But the English words "Holy Spirit" come from the Latin *spiritus sanctus,* which in turn is just a translation of the Greek *hagia pneuma,* which itself is a translation of the Hebrew *ruach ha-kodesh.* In Hebrew, *ruach* means "the wind," something that has power but is insubstantial and constantly moving. The Holy Spirit is a kind of wind that blows through us and comforts us. It is the Paraclete, the comforter that purifies us and links us to our Source. (See chapter 10 for a Christian take on how the Holy Spirit dissolves the somethingness of self.) So activating impermanence, receiving the Holy Spirit, and getting qi are very different phrases based on very different paradigms, but as *experiences,* they can be closely related.

On the spiritual path, one has to develop a sensitivity to vocabulary. Two teachers may use very similar vocabulary and yet be referring to rather different things. On the other hand, two teachers may use words that do not seem similar at all but that actually refer to related phenomena. Developing discernment, a sensitivity to how words are used in different contexts, is a benchmark of spiritual maturity.

Forty-five years ago, I was studying languages and philosophy in graduate school, and I had never done any meditation practice. If somebody had said to me, "Several decades from now, you will be stating in print that the Judeo-Christian concept of the Holy Spirit, the martial arts concept of qi, and the Buddhist concept of anicca are related," I probably would have said, "Please shoot me now." As a scholar, I thought these concepts had absolutely nothing to do with each other—that they possessed no connection historically, linguistically, or conceptually. But that was before I had experience. Experience transformed me from a dignified academician into someone spouting seeming non sequiturs. That's impermanence!

This idea that impermanence can be a positive, purifying force is revolutionary. At first, the notion of impermanence may scare us a little bit because it seems to remove all sense of security. If everything in the universe changes and vanishes, then there would seem to be nothing upon which we can rely. The only thing that doesn't change and vanish is the changing and vanishing itself. But as we have seen, that changing and vanishing can become a powerful source of comfort and security. There is a sort of "taste" we get when we become aware that the Flow of impermanence is purifying and cleansing us. For lack of a better term, I call it the "taste of purification." The ability to taste purification is the sign of a mature spiritual palate, so to speak.

Children usually cannot understand how an adult could possibly like a bitter taste such as coffee or a burning taste such as hot chili. But as we grow older, we come to appreciate and seek flavors that children don't. We call this the maturing of the palate. The same thing can happen with our spiritual palate. As our spiritual taste buds mature, we begin to savor certain qualities that we couldn't detect or appreciate previously.

The taste of purification is very hard to describe, but in essence, it is a kind of joy. You may be in great pain, but there is a deep joy because you feel blockages being worked out each time you greet the pain with equanimity. You can feel how the energy in the pain is wearing away the separation between you and your spiritual Source. You sense that holdings from the past are being ground up, digested, and metabolized by the peristaltic and vibratory movements of impermanence. The grinding and digesting is both painful and liberating at the same time. This is the taste of purification. Once you are able to detect and appreciate this taste, you become capable of doing practices that were unthinkable when you began your meditation career.

To develop this taste, you have to start somewhere. You can begin with experiences that are relatively easy and not too overwhelming. For example, you can sit and watch itches or little aches and pains come and go in your body. When we meditate, often we will simply observe an itch without necessarily scratching it, or we will sit with a straight back even though the muscles may be a bit tired. These are little things that anybody can do. If we do this enough, we start to get a sense of what that taste of purification is like. Then we are not afraid to do the same with sensations that are a little more intense, or perhaps a *lot* more intense.

We do not have to actively seek out uncomfortable situations in order to purify our consciousness. We can just wait for life to give them to us, which it always does sooner or later. If we understand the taste of purification, we will not be frightened by the prospect of the unpleasant things that will happen in this life. Eventually, we will encounter intense discomforts, things that we wish were not happening. But if we understand about the taste of purification, all the discomforts that we will have to face are guaranteed to have a silver lining. It is good to practice with small things so that you will have a momentum going for you when things get heavy.

Some people are drawn to actively seeking intensely challenging situations, not just little things like itches and aches. Why would someone do that? In order to put themselves in a situation where they will literally be driven into a state of equanimity and Flow by the sheer intensity of the ordeal. Those of us who have lived in Asia and participated in traditional monastic training love to tell what I call "Buddhist war stories." These are stories about the really intense stuff that we did or saw in Asia. There is a danger in telling these stories, however, because when people hear them, they may well say to themselves, "If that is what I have to do to get enlightenment, I think I will try it in another lifetime."

But it is certainly not the case that heavy-duty practice is absolutely required for enlightenment. The issue is to experience things *fully*, be it an itch, an ache, or for that matter a pleasant sensation like smiling. You could travel the entire path to enlightenment if you had a radically complete experience of your smile every time you smiled. If every single time you smiled for the rest of your life, you infused it with total concentration, clarity, and equanimity, you would discover in the midst of the smile that the facial muscles contract and the smile sensation expands simultaneously—both sides of impermanence are there working together to manifest the self of the moment as a smile. Indeed, you would eventually experience all the expansion and contraction, all the yang and yin of the universe inside your day-to-day smile. So something as mild and ordinary as a smile has the potential to bring the same level of enlightenment as the intense and strange ordeal that I am about to describe.

When I lived in Asian monasteries, I observed mind-boggling intensities of practice. But what struck me was that these austerities were by and large not done with white-knuckled endurance. Rather, they were done with a smile on the face and a lightness in the body because monks did not undertake these practices until they were ready. By that, I mean that they had developed a momentum of the purifying force of impermanence. For such people, when things become intense, the taste of purification will immediately arise. The reward is instant, so the ordeal does not degenerate into a grim endurance contest.

There is a tradition of going to special places in order to do intense practice. For example, early Christians went into the desert, Tibetans go into caves, and Theravada monks go into forests. In Greece, the most famous center of Christian contemplation is on Mount Athos. Japan has two equivalents to Mount Athos: Mount Koya, where I was ordained in 1970 as a Shingon monk, and Mount Hiei. The English language guidebooks always compare Mount Koya to Mount Athos. They are both mountains in remote areas with a harsh physical environment. Originally, there was nothing but monasteries on Mount Koya, and no women were allowed. The no-women rule was abandoned on Mount Koya quite a while ago, although I think it's still observed on Mount Athos.

You may recall that my initial training in Shingon meditation occurred during one hundred days of continuous practice in isolation, in the dead of winter, and in total silence. I went in one person—a scattered, wimpy, would-be scholar—and came out quite a different person. Not enlightened, but incomparably more focused and courageous. As far as I'm aware, I was the first Westerner to ever complete the Shingon basic training. By the end of that, I thought I was pretty hot stuff. My best friend at the time was a monk of the Tendai school who had studied on Mount Hiei, near Kyoto, the old capital of Japan. When I completed my one-hundred-day training, he suggested that I go meet his teacher on Mount Hiei. It turned out that his teacher was one of a small group of extraordinary ascetics sometimes referred to as the "marathon monks" of Mount Hiei.

Recall that I thought I was pretty tough because I had done one hundred days in isolation. By way of contrast, marathon monks commit to *twelve years* in isolation! During those twelve years, they must undertake several seemingly impossible ordeals. For example, they have to walk down the mountain, go into the city of Kyoto, visit every major shrine and temple in the city, chant the appropriate mantra in front of it, and then climb back up the mountain. This cycle takes over twenty hours, and they must do it for one hundred days in succession, once each year for twelve years. That leaves a few hours to sleep, and the rest of the time, they are hiking and chanting mantras for over three months.

It is almost an inconceivable ordeal, but I've seen it done with a smile on the face. Why? Because in each moment, they are tangibly aware that this austerity is doing something for them; they can actually feel the purification happening despite the intensity. Eventually, this taste of purification gets so strong and delicious that it eclipses the pain.

Twice during this twelve-year period, they have to do a special ceremony in which they essentially sit for nine days without eating, sleeping, or taking liquids! You might think this is a legend, or perhaps even a pious fraud, but it is a public event. In fact, it is sometimes televised live on Japanese network TV. The master I talked to said that the first two days of the nine-day sit were pretty rough, but after that, it wasn't so bad. The momentum of impermanence and purification just took over, and the time went fairly quickly. He told me, however, that afterward it took him a full month to recover his normal sleeping cycle.

You might think that this is pretty interesting, but what after all is the point of such austerity? Did all that intensity do any good? After completing his twelve years, what was this man like in terms of his day-to-day functioning? From what I observed, my friend's teacher spent his days serving people. They would come to visit him with their problems. They might need some counseling or encouragement or advice or inspiration. Certainly, meeting with someone like him would provide living proof that no matter what you are going through in your life, you can get through it, and perhaps be empowered by it, just as he had been. He became an inspiring figure for masses of ordinary people who would come just to talk and sit with him.

Now all of this may seem rather foreign, exotic, and remote from your reality. You may well be wondering what it has to do with you. But it is totally relevant to the lives of ordinary modern people. There is every probability that a person who lives a comfortable life in, say, North America will still have to go through experiences comparable in intensity to those of the marathon monks. Because something will happen to them directly or to someone they care about deeply.

For example, when my father died of lung cancer, I watched him go a week without sleeping, hyperventilating twenty-four hours a day, slowly suffocating to death. This is certainly as physically intense as anything undertaken by monks at Mount Hiei. He had all the best care that Western medicine could provide and all the amenities of middle-class North American life, yet he still had to face that reality. I don't know to what extent he was subjectively aware of it, but as an outside observer, I could certainly see all the types of impermanence working within him, grinding away his somethingness. I think he was probably aware of this at some level, despite the fact that he couldn't speak to say so. Even though he had never meditated, and he had no explicit spiritual path, he had lived as a really good person, and everybody liked him. That good karma was there, and even though he had no background in concepts like the purifying action of impermanence, his basic goodness must have helped him. So the kinds of austerities and intensities that people put themselves through in traditional training may at some point become reality for you, even if you do your best to avoid discomfort.

Impermanence as a purifier can in some ways be compared to the process of digestion. During digestion, the peristalsis, or undulation of the stomach and the intestines, helps break the food down into its components. Then what is useful among its components is absorbed and becomes part of our mass and energy, and what is not useful is excreted by further peristalsis. I have talked about the notion that we all have a sort of pool of poison and pain within us, deep down in the subconscious, that consists of holdings from the past—what might be described as a layer of residue. When impermanence is experienced in its purificatory guise, we can literally feel its peristaltic movements reaching down into this "pain body" and breaking it up into a kind of energy. The impermanence absorbs what is nutritive from the past to enhance the content of our being. We can also feel it sort of excreting what is not nutritive, a kind of releasing process wherein spiritually toxic aspects of this residue are expelled. I realize that this may sound a bit weird and maybe even gross. However, the experience itself is quite natural and very beautiful.

Fuel for the Spiritual Reactor

When we speak of the Flow of impermanence, it is very important to realize that it is not something separate from ordinary experience. There is not some special world of flowing energy from which we must eventually be pulled away, back into the clunky and lumpy ordinary world. On the contrary, the energy flow *is* the ordinary world; it's what happens to the ordinary world when that world is experienced with extraordinary attentiveness. In the science of enlightenment, complete experience is the name of the game. Some people who encounter Flow don't realize this, and so they fall into the belief that the world is one thing, and spirit quite another. This creates a conceptual dichotomy between spirit and matter, between God and the world. This is a very common misconception, and in a way, it is easy to see how people could fall into it. But Flow, spirit, qi are just what happens to the ordinary senses when they are experienced with extraordinary concentration, clarity, and equanimity. God is what the world looks like when experienced with radical fullness. Spirit is what matter tastes like when it's tasted to the core.

When people experience Flow in any of its pleasant flavors—expansion, contraction, undulation, vibration, bubbles, electricity, kundalini—there is a tendency to want to focus only on that, to see that as the good stuff, the goal of meditation. But the goal of meditation is something deeper and more subtle. The goal of meditation is to gain insight, to know that spirit energy is simply what happens to ordinary experience when it is greeted with extraordinary attention. Conversely, the materiality of objects, the somethingness of the self, the rigidity of space, and the linearity of time are simply what happens to Spirit when it encounters the nebulosity and viscosity of the untrained human nervous system. This reminds me of Einstein's famous statement that matter is frozen energy.

Strictly speaking, my comment about the "untrained nervous system" is not quite accurate. The actual situation is more complex. *During the first few hundred milliseconds of preconscious processing, every experience is a flow of pure spirit. Nebulosity and viscosity enter in a bit later as we become conscious of the experience.* So there are two sides to spiritual training. One side involves developing clarity and equanimity. Clarity reduces nebulosity and equanimity reduces viscosity. The other side of training involves detecting the momentary primordial perfection that's always there for everyone. Success with that second side of training brings you to the realization that you never needed to do any training! I'll talk more about this in chapter 10.

In order for insight into impermanence to occur, we have to make the following correlation over and over again: An ordinary, solid, sensory event arises. We greet it with concentration, clarity, and equanimity. As a result, it eventually breaks up into Flow. In order to go through this three-step process enough times, we have to be willing to look at the parts of our experience that are still solid and separate. That means that we have to be willing, and indeed enthusiastic, about the prospect of focusing on what is solid and opaque, and not want to focus *only* on what is fluid and transparent.

When you start to experience Flow and energy, if you only want to experience that, and are not equally interested in watching ordinary solidified, objectified sensory events, then your spiritual path will be self-limiting. You will dissolve to a certain degree, but be unable to go any deeper, because your spiritual reactor has run out of fuel. $E = mc^2$. The source of further energy (E) lies in your remnant mass (m), the ordinary, coagulated, opaque sensory arisings. There's a natural alternating process, like the cycle of the seasons. We freeze, we melt, we freeze, we melt, but with each repetition, the freezing becomes more subtle, which allows for the subsequent melting to be even deeper.

Understanding the nonduality of spirit energy and ordinary experience is very important. We must watch how ordinary experience becomes waves of impermanence over and over—a hundred times, a thousand times, a hundred thousand times—before we really believe that *all* ordinary experience is impermanent. Eventually it sinks in: every statue dances.

When Flow is unimpeded, we say that we are living in the world of oneness and spirit. When Flow stiffens up, we say that we are in the world of separateness and materiality. There is absolutely nothing wrong with the world of separateness and materiality, as long as it is not the *only* world in which we are constrained to live. Unfortunately, this is exactly the case for the great majority of human beings. They are constrained to live in rigid space and linear time.

> Ridiculous the waste sad time
> Stretching before and after.
> T. S. ELIOT, "BURNT NORTON"

Flow as Guide

When Christians speak of the Holy Spirit, they describe it not only as that which comforts and purifies, but also that which *guides*. And indeed, another of the many masks of impermanence is that of a guide. For one thing, impermanence can function as a kind of feedback loop, because it tells us when we are approaching complete experience. As concentration, clarity, and equanimity deepen, the experience presents itself more as wave, less as particle.

But impermanence is also a guide in another sense. When people talk about having an inner guide, they usually mean an archetypical figure that communicates to them through internal talk and mental images. Yes, you can call this an inner guide if you want, but it is not the *innermost* guide. The innermost guide does not teach through words or archetypal visions but rather by example. That no doubt sounds somewhat enigmatic; let me try to explain.

The Flow of impermanence functions without any will or desire. It's a kind of effortless effervescence. As we encounter this effervescence, it begins to inform our entire being, and we begin to take on some of its qualities. At the microscopic, preconscious level, every human being functions as an effortless flow of nature. But at the macroscopic, conscious level, there are all sorts of push and pull, driven-ness, rigidity, and solidity. When we encounter the effortlessness of Flow at the microscopic level of our being, some of that effortlessness begins to inform the macroscopic level of our being and teaches us by example.

The metaphor I use is an extremely undignified one given the nobility of the experience; nevertheless, I can't resist using it. Consider an Alka-Seltzer tablet. It is quite solid, however it does have a certain potential inside it, and that potential becomes activated when we drop the tablet into water. Lo and behold, out of that solidity a great deal of fizz arises. The more fizz there is, the more quickly the solidity of the tablet disappears, until it literally dissolves itself.

In the same way, we have a very solid sense of self, a very solid sense of body, a very rigid sense of space, and a very congealed sense of matter. If we drop those solid tablets into the waters of concentration, clarity, and equanimity, lo and behold, something gets activated. All we have to do is keep that bubbly part next to the solid part, and the bubbly part starts to influence the solid part. It presents a model; it teaches the solid part. Eventually the big, gross, congealed part simply gives itself back to the bubbles, and becomes nothing but bubbles. In other words, the parts of us that *are* in Flow show the parts that are not in Flow how to be in Flow. Flow sets up a positive feedback loop. The more we attend to some part that's in Flow, the more that Flow informs all our parts.

Flow as Unifier

Another facet of Flow is as an *integrator* or *unifier*. At the beginning of mindfulness practice, our job is to make distinctions. We have to make a clear distinction between mental experience and somatic experience so that when these two arise together, they don't tangle and cross-multiply. We discover that when we are able to keep these two domains of experience distinct, they merely add together and are manageable, but when they become conflated, they multiply with each other into overwhelm.

Going further, we learn to break mental experience into visual thinking (mental image) and verbal thinking (mental talk). And we learn to break somatic experience into emotional flavors and physical flavors. All these are *empowering distinctions.* Being able to track our thinking process in terms of visual and auditory components allows us to experience thought as a tangible sensory event. Being able to detect the often-subtle emotional flavors that arise in the body prevents them from distorting our perception and behavior. We learn to distinguish outer stimuli (physical sights, physical sounds, physical body sensations) from inner reactions to them (mental image, mental talk, emotional body sensation).

The English word "mindfulness" is roughly equivalent to the Pali word *vipassana.* The prefix *vi* in Pali implies separation, and *passana* means "to see." But as this process of seeing-as-separate reaches finer and finer levels, we start to experience a commonality. When you study anatomy, at first you learn to distinguish the various organs and their parts. But when you get to the cellular level, you realize that there is a unifying principle underlying the separate components of the body. Furthermore, at the level of that unifying principle, the human body, the body of a worm, and even the body of a tree are composed of essentially the same building blocks—cells. In the same way, at a microscopic level of observation, the mental images, internal talk, and emotional feelings that constitute the "I" can all be experienced as being made of the same stuff, the vibrating Flow of impermanence.

This realization integrates your personality at a profound level. Your personality becomes a single flow, a pure doing, an integrated activity. This is what is behind the apparent paradox that those who vehemently claim that there is "no such thing as a self" usually have powerful, impactful personalities.

Moreover, the same Flow of impermanence that makes up the inner world of thought and emotion also makes up the outer world of physical sight, physical sound, and physical body sensations. In other words, both the "I" and the "it" are made of the same stuff: Flow. *This realization breaks down the fundamental barrier between inside and out-side, unifying the subjective and the objective into a single, I-Thou doing.* When we tune in to the impermanence deeply enough, there is no fundamental distinction between mind and body, or between inside and outside. A single arabesque of energy cuts across everything.

Imagine a valley containing several kinds of vegetation that are quite distinct. Imagine also that wind is continuously blowing through that valley. If you focus on the different kinds of vegetation themselves, you get a sense of separateness. If you focus on how the wind moves through them, you get a sense of unity. In the same way, as you attend to the inner sensory activity as a wave and the outer sensory activity as a wave, the two waves flow together into a single integrated self-world wave.

This could be described as an experience of merging, a passing away of the separation between inside and outside. By having experiences like this many, many times, two deep sources of suffering begin to disappear: our fundamental alienation and our deep-seated fear.

When all that we see, hear, or feel begins to flow, then it all becomes like one taste: the impermanence taste, the Flow taste. Flow is the Great Leveler. It breaks down distinctions in an empowering way. A person on a mature spiritual path becomes familiar with both empowering distinctions and empowering unifications. The unifications break down the distinctions, paving the way for detecting even finer distinctions, which are then broken down to create an even deeper unification.

Imagine that you hear a sound in the outside world, for exam-ple the sound of a bird singing. When this sound is experienced as Flow, you have the sense of sound as a rising and falling waveform. At the same time, in your mind's eye, you might see a bird, but that too is a wave, an image wave, a wave of internal light that rises onto your mental screen for a while, and then ebbs away. At the same time still, you might have a feeling reaction to the birdsong, one of joy, for example. This joy is also experienced as a rising then subsiding wave of pleasure in the body. Rather than three discrete objects of sense expe-rience—birdsong, bird image, and bird joy—you experience three interpenetrating bubbly waves that integrate into one bubbly wave. You experience it as an unbroken flow of sensory motion, rather than separate chunks of sensory impressions. Oneness is no longer a philo-sophical abstraction, it is now a daily sensory reality.

Sasaki Roshi had a very eccentric way of talking. For example, sometimes instead of calling a pine tree by its usual Japanese name, *matsunoki,* he would say *matsunoki toyu hataraki,* which means "the activity called pine tree." He also used phrases like *ningen toyu hataraki,* "the activity called human being," and *kami toyu hataraki,* "the activity called God." This is a very idiosyncratic use of the Japanese language. He talked this way to remind people that all the objects in the world can be experienced as waves of impermanence, not just as concrete, separate things.

So impermanence is a unifier, in that it gives an underlying char-acteristic that unifies mind and body, inside and outside. We come to experience things in terms of their activity. Every individual thing in the universe has its wave nature, and therefore, the universe itself can be thought of as an integrated world-wave. When we experience a grain of sand, its grain wave is united with the universe wave. This sounds nice, but what does it actually mean? Well, to see a grain of sand means some-thing is arising in external sight space. In order to know that it is a grain of sand, visual associations must arise in your image space. Those visual associations are usually below the threshold of awareness. Furthermore, each visual association triggers a cascade of subtler visual associations, and each of those subtle visual associations triggers yet another cascade of even subtler visual associations. The wave of visual association spreads wider and wider, but as it spreads, its components get finer and finer. To borrow a notion from calculus, that association wave points to the whole universe "in the limit." If equanimity is not deep, the intense See Out (physical sight) and the subtle See In (mental image) are both coagulated, and you have the ordinary experience of an *I* looking at an *it.* But if the See Out of the sand and the See In of visual association are not fixated, they become a single wave. The entire universe points to the grain of sand as its child, and the grain of sand points to the entire universe as its parent.

Admittedly, that sounds a little mystical-shmystical. Here's what I mean: In the objective world, there's a pyramid of physical causality

The luminous net

that lies behind the grain. The base of that pyramid spreads out to encompass the entire universe, because any one thing comes from a relational net that is ultimately connected to everything. On the other hand, there's a visual association wave triggered in you by the sight of the grain of sand. Although that association wave may not literally include everything in your subconscious, it implicitly points to your whole inner *imago mundi*. The grain of sand triggers subliminal mental images. That's what allows you to understand the grain of sand in context. However, each of those associated images requires its own wave of association, and each of *those* associated images sets off an even finer wave of associations. Of course, this does not actually go on forever, but it does potentially point to everything you've ever seen or could even imagine seeing. It's a little bit like how light propagates. Each point on the spreading spherical wave front becomes a new source for another spherical wave front.

All this happens below the threshold of awareness. An experienced meditator can detect these spreading waves of association constantly happening in image space. Because the content is below the threshold of awareness, the wave is in a sense empty, but because it points to everything that you know or can imagine, it's also huge. Taken together, the combined experience is a simultaneous sense of vastness, thinness, and all-encompassing connectivity.

In the objective world, the grain of sand arises through a converging net of physical connections. And in the observer's consciousness, the grain of sand is understood through a diverging net of mental associations. A relational net converges from the whole world creating a product: grain of sand. An associational net diverges to your whole mind creating a concept: grain of sand. Matter and mind are dual in the mathematical sense of that word. They are partial mirror images of each other, inverse lattices so to speak. As William Blake wrote, you really do:

> See a World in a grain of sand,
> And a Heaven in a wild flower,
> Hold Infinity in the palm of your hand,
> And Eternity in an hour.

Flow as the Spiritual Source

We have talked about many facets, many modes, many functions of impermanence. We have talked about impermanence as sort of a pessimistic worldview, we have talked about impermanence as a characteristic of experience, and we have talked about impermanence as something that helps us along in our meditation. We have also talked about impermanence as an integrator that frees us from our fundamental alienation and connects us to the All. There is, however, one more facet to impermanence, and it is this facet that I personally find most fascinating. However, until you have experienced some of the other aspects of impermanence, this final aspect may seem enigmatic, esoteric, and irrelevant. If what I am about to say strikes you as nonsense, I hope that you will just read the words and have equanimity with any confusion and annoyance that may arise. Sometimes we have to be satisfied with wisdom at the level of just remembering someone's words.

At the deepest level, impermanence is none other than the activity of our spiritual Source. Flow is the peristalsis of a formless womb. That formless womb gestates time, space, self, and world into existence moment by moment. Now I am quite aware that this may seem like a very strange point of view to most people. Isn't the world always there? Isn't the self a thing? Aren't time and space a rigid, always-existing stage? And if for an enlightened person time, space, self, and world wink in and out of existence moment by moment, then how in God's name would such a person be able to function in the material world?

There was a time when many people believed that lunar eclipses meant that a monster was eating the moon. If you didn't know any better, that might appear to be the case. As the eclipse progresses, you can imagine the outline of the monster's jaw biting deeper and deeper, until the moon is swallowed. Almost no modern person would look at things that way. A shift in paradigm has occurred. The phenomenon of a lunar eclipse is now interpreted as the earth's shadow moving across the moon. Eclipses still happen, just as they always have, and just as frequently as ever, yet they are not *interpreted* as before.

For human beings, world and self seem to be solid objects, time and space seem to be a rigid always-existing platform. This occurs for enlightened people and for unenlightened people. However in the case of the enlightened person, a paradigm shift, a shift in interpretation has occurred. Before enlightenment, when self and world arose as solid objects, that person believed they really were solid. After enlightenment, self and world still arise as solid objects a lot of the time, but the enlightened person now knows that they *appear to be solid only because he or she is not paying close attention right now.*

Even for a deeply enlightened person, the experience of contact with Flow and emptiness does not necessarily go on uninterrupted. It may happen frequently during the day, but not necessarily continuously. Even a very liberated person still spends a lot of time experiencing the world in the ordinary way. What then is the difference between an ordinary person and a liberated person? The difference is a matter of freedom. An enlightened person has the ability to experience self and world as a Source wave. And when they are not experiencing things that way, they understand why that is the case. It is just because they are not paying close attention!

Freedom lies in being able to live in both of these worlds—the normal paradigm and the enlightened paradigm—and to know when to go to which, and to be able to do so anytime. This is why enlightenment is sometimes referred to as *liberation.* Liberated people live a lot of the time in their body-mind just like anybody else, but they are not *confined* to it. When a liberated person drives their car to the local store, they go in and out of the two paradigms hundreds of times during that trip. Self-as-separate and scene-as-solid arise just in time to make the right turn, to beep the horn, or to signal, then they dissolve back into direct contact with the Source wave. Then an instant later, it all congeals just in time to take the next action. Then they go back to the formless again. So even experiences as seemingly unspiritual as driving during rush hour on a smoggy Los Angeles freeway can be celestial—as pleasant and peaceful as sitting in a mountain hermitage.

There is a story about this that I love to tell. You may have heard some quaint Zen stories from Asia, but this is a Zen story from the United States, one that happened in Los Angeles. Years ago, it was a fad for people to spend time in sensory-deprivation tanks—tubs filled with high-saline water, so that you float like a cork, which more or less removes the sense of gravity. The water is body temperature, so you don't feel hot or cold, and the tank is light-proof and acoustically baffled, so no light or sound gets in. In such a simplified sensory environment, people tend to get very relaxed, and they also tend to go into interesting altered states.

Some friends of mine owned a place where you could rent time in these contraptions, and they told me this story. They had overheard a conversation between two Buddhist nuns from the Zen Center of Los Angeles. One was a senior practitioner, and the other was a relative neophyte. After they were finished with their sessions in the sensory-deprivation tanks, the young nun said, "Wow, that was far out!" To which the more senior nun replied, "Yeah, you're right. Really far out. It was exactly what I experience when I drive on the freeway!"

CHAPTER SEVEN

The Realm of Power

One way to view the path to enlightenment is as a journey—a journey from the surface of consciousness to the Source of consciousness. A reasonable question to ask when undertaking a physical journey is, "What general direction are we going? East? Southeast? West?" In the same way, we might also ask what general direction we are traveling in when we make the *spiritual* journey. People often think of spirituality as a kind of turning away from the world. Geometrically speaking, that would represent a turn of 180 degrees to face in a direction that is the opposite of the world. In that way of thinking, the spiritual journey is away *from* the world. But the way I like to describe the spiritual journey is not as a 180-degree turn, but as a 90-degree turn. Here's what I mean.

We can look upon consciousness as having layers to it, like a many-layered cake or the geological strata of the earth. Our ordinary experience of self and world arises on the topmost layer. Our spiritual Source is the deepest layer. In between surface and Source, there is a thick slab that must be traversed. Therefore, a turn in the direction of our spiritual Source would be a turn of 90 degrees. Instead of just moving along the surface of experience, we begin to *burrow down* into experience toward its Source.

While moving through the intermediate level between surface and Source, some people encounter unusual phenomena which may be either frightening, empowering, or both. In this chapter, I would like to talk about those phenomena and how to work with them. But first let's look a little more closely at this tri-level model.

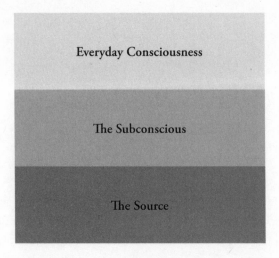

Figure 2: A Three-Level Model of the Spiritual Journey

As I mentioned, the surface level (everyday consciousness) represents the world of ordinary experience. What characterizes ordinary experience? We have the sense that there is a thing inside us called a self; the self is surrounded by other selves that are also things; material objects are solid; and these are all fundamentally separate. Moreover, events in the objective world and subjective states of thought and emotion arise and pass along a continuum of time that seems to extend in a linear way endlessly forward and backward. Finally, ourselves, the other selves, and material things seem to be embedded in a rigid framework of always-existing space. So at the surface of consciousness, self is a thing, objects are solid, space is rigid, and time is a two-way, endless line. This is the ordinary view of things; it's the perspective that is natural at the surface of consciousness.

There is nothing intrinsically problematic about this ordinary perspective. The problem comes when it is the *only* perspective available to a person, which unfortunately is the usual case. Enlightenment, or freedom, comes when we also have a complementary perspective that we can access at any time. To have this complementary perspective, we must come into direct contact with the third level of consciousness, the Source. When we are in direct contact with the Source, self is not perceived as a separate particle, objects are not perceived as solid, and space becomes elastic and can collapse to a dimensionless point, taking everything with it to the Unborn. And time is cyclic—self and scene arise from and return to that unborn Source over and over. We can call this perspective many things, such as God, Brahman, the Tao, the Unborn, the Undying, the nature of Nature, Zero, Emptiness, Completeness. The words don't really matter. What matters is direct contact.

In some descriptions, the Source is referred to as our "ground of being." This is a phrase used by Meister Eckhart, one of the greatest of the Christian mystics. Born in 1260, he was the bishop of Cologne, a Dominican friar, a famous academic, and also a great meditation master. Contemporary influential Protestant theologians like Paul Tillich still use Meister Eckhart's metaphor of God as the ground of being.

If we want to think of that third layer as the ground of being, that is okay. The only difficulty with that terminology is that when we say the word "ground," we tend to think of something that is extended in space and somehow solid. The ground of our being is the source of the experience of space: it generates the experience of space, it's not inside of space. And it is anything but solid! However if we think of the word "ground" as referring to that from which things arise and to which they return, then ground is a good word for God. If you want to think of God as your ground, then you can call that experience God. On the other hand, if you're a skeptical materialist, you probably don't like words like ground or Source or God. No problem. Call it something else. Call it a state of maximal conscious rest, or the sensory analog of a physical system being at its ground state, or call it "regression in service of the ego." You can call it whatever you want, as long as you actually *experience* it. Anyone who has had the experience is allowed to describe it any way they want. (For the record, I think of myself as a skeptical rationalist. It's just that I happen to be quite comfortable with the G-word. And I'm also a materialist, but for me, matter tastes like Spirit.) The pre-Socratic Greek philosopher Heraclitus put it nicely when he said, "It is both willing and unwilling to be called by the name Zeus."

Moving from ancient philosophy to modern science, consider the word "ground", as it's used in physics. The "ground state" of a system means the state of greatest stability, deepest repose. Certainly, this would be a good description of what the human mind/body system experiences when we have direct encounter with the Source of consciousness.

One of the fundamental themes in physical science is that things tend toward their ground state. In a similar way, we human beings are constantly pulled toward the Source. It's like a gravitational force, but we may not be aware of it, and a lot of times, we scramble in the opposite direction. But given half a chance, we will sink down into our ground state. By "half a chance," I mean the systematic cultivation of concentration, clarity, and equanimity. In other words, meditation is what gives us the chance to feel the tug of the ground state, of God. The ground state is formless—it is in fact a doing, an activity, not a thing—and that's why to describe it as a layer or level of consciousness is useful but also misleading.

So one way to describe the spiritual path is as a journey from ordinary surface experience to the ground state, the Source of all states, both ordinary and altered. The vehicle we ride, that carries us from the surface down through intermediate layers of consciousness to Source, is that of concentration, clarity, and equanimity. Now let's talk about some experiences that may occur along the way.

The Subconscious: The Intermediate Layer

When I speak of the intermediate realm of consciousness, it may sound abstract and esoteric, but what I am calling the intermediate layer is none other than what is commonly referred to in the West as the subconscious.

It's very revealing to look at how the subconscious is described by various schools of psychology. The notion of the subconscious came into the Western world through the works of Freud and Jung, but these two men had radically different points of view. Freud described it metaphorically as a dark cellar filled with ghosts, demons, cobwebs, snakes, and centipedes. It is where the repressed poison and pain of our life, the trauma of unresolved past experiences, fixations, and conflicts are stored.

From the perspective of Buddhism, there is a certain truth to this model because the aspect of the subconscious that Freud was interested in corresponds to what in Buddhism is called the *samskaraskandha*—the "aggregate of (limiting) conditionings." According to Buddhism, it is conditionings that prevent our ordinary consciousness from directly contacting *nirvana*, that is, the Source. If you have something between your two hands, like a ball, it will impede your hands from touching each other. The impurities and blockages in the intermediate realm are like that ball, separating the everyday mind from the enlightened mind. If we were to pop the ball, then the two hands could automatically come together and stay together.

From this perspective, the path is really not so much a journey from surface to Source as a clearing away of what lies between surface and Source. As a result of this clearing, surface and Source fall together, and we find ourselves constantly touching transcendence in each moment of ordinary experience.

So one view of the intermediate realm is that it is where the blockages lie, and when we direct the light of sensory clarity and pour the water of equanimity into any experience, the brightness and softening percolate down into those areas to clarify and dissolve the blockages. The surface gets closer and closer to the Source until, finally, the two touch in the experience of enlightenment. From that time on, the ordinary experience of day-to-day life rests in contact with the ground of all experience.

Freud's student Carl Jung took a somewhat different direction in his understanding of the subconscious. For Jung, the subconscious is the world of archetypes, the world wherein angels, ancestors, entities, and spirit beings are real and relevant. From the Buddhist perspective, this point of view also has truth to it because the subconscious can be looked upon as the *sambhogakaya*—"the realm of archetypal bodies." When journeying from surface to Source, some people encounter celestial and empowering experiences in the sambhogakaya. It may seem to them as though they are meeting spirit beings or angels, visiting the worlds of the gods, or achieving psychic and healing powers. It may seem to them that they can remember former lives, or that they can travel outside of the body.

Whether such powers actually exist in the objective world, I don't know, although in general I tend to be rather skeptical. But one thing is certain. In this intermediate realm, some people do get very vivid subjective experiences of these phenomena. Likewise, I don't pretend to know the ontological status of spirits and entities. They can certainly seem real—if by real we mean a sensory experience that can be extremely vivid and tangible. But sensory vividness is not the same thing as objective existence. For me, the really important question is how to harness these phenomena toward optimal growth. To do that, we need to become somewhat indifferent to what they mean but utterly fascinated with how they move.

Considering what we've said so far, the intermediate layer could paradoxically be described as either the realm of power or the realm of blockage.

It is of the utmost importance to remember that not everyone encounters unusual experiences or special powers when they traverse this intermediate realm. Neither does everyone meet the archetypal monsters of their impurities there. Many people travel the whole way from surface to Source and are never aware of anything other than very ordinary experiences, like the touch of their clothes, the aches in their body, or the sensation of their breath. That's all that ever happens to them, and yet they are able to traverse the whole territory.

I frequently hear people say things like, "I've been meditating for a number of years, but I've never had any unusual experiences or strong emotions. What am I doing wrong?" I ask them if they are consistently bringing concentration, clarity, and equanimity to ordinary experiences, and if they notice whether their day-to-day life has been improving. If they answer yes to both questions, I tell them that they are doing fine. Extraordinary phenomena are not required for extraordinary growth.

When people *do* have unusual experiences in the intermediate realm, those experiences may manifest in a variety of ways. People may see weird images, monsters, or skeletons. They may get very hot or cold, shake, move in strange ways, or become hypersensitive and emotional for no apparent reason. These represent samskaras or blockages percolating up from the subconscious and becoming tangible. If you happen to have such experiences, the trick is just to observe them with concentration, clarity, and equanimity so that the purification process continues. No matter how intense, bizarre, or powerful an experience may be, it can only come up as some combination of physical sensation in the body, emotional sensation in the body, mental image activity, and internal talk—our old friends.

Just as some people have very ordinary experiences for the whole path, and some people encounter weird and disturbing content, so others have heavenly, entertaining, empowering visions. And some people get a mixture of both hellish and celestial experiences. There are many possibilities, and we should never think that, just because we haven't encountered an archetype or left our body, we are not making progress. Neither should we think that we must eventually uncover hidden monsters or have unusual sensations in order to make progress.

Whatever the experiences may be, it's how we relate to them that really matters. Indeed, it could be said that one litmus test for spiritual maturity is how a person relates to the experiences of the intermediate realm. The spiritually mature person treats all events encountered on the path from surface to Source in exactly the same way: greeting them with concentration, clarity, and equanimity. The spiritually *immature* person develops cravings and aversions with respect to these phenomena. They fear certain types of experiences and desire other types of experiences. Or they worry they won't have any special experiences at all.

There was once a Zen monk who started to get very successful in his meditation. He could sit for hour after hour and day after day without moving. He got so deep in meditation that even the gods started to admire him. They would show up every day and shower flowers on his head, give him offerings, and worship him. This went on for a while. Finally he yelled, "Beat it, guys, you're boring me!" and whacked them away with his stick.

This story is told to Zen monks as a caveat: do not develop a craving for even the most celestial content that may come your way during meditation.

Want not, fear not

Eruptions in the Everyday

For the first five or six years of my practice, I never had any unusual experiences. My main focus was just trying to deal with the pain in my legs and the wandering in my mind. But then I started having intense visionary experiences. Visionary material is very interesting; once it gets going, it's not necessarily limited to when you're sitting in formal practice. The images can erupt during your waking hours and may continue while you're just walking around.

In my case, these image eruptions consisted of huge and very realistic-looking insects. They weren't like static photographs, they moved with the distinctive articulate quality that you would find in a living arthropod. They were extremely vivid and lifelike, and worse still, gigantic! They seemed to be five or six feet long, actually.

These visions continued for a year while I was in graduate school. I'd be walking to classes, and there would be these monstrous vermin greeting me along the path.

It was not a problem though. In fact, I functioned quite well. It wasn't like a psychotic or schizophrenic state, it was just a phenomenon of the intermediate realm. I interpreted it to mean that I had dropped into that realm and some material was presenting itself. I just treated it like any other mental image activity—it was just a form of visual thinking. I tracked how my awareness moved over the surface of the images (whether it was drawn to the right, left, top, or bottom). I attempted to look at the images with equanimity. If the images created emotional reactions in my body, I would try to bring concentration, clarity, and equanimity to those sensations, noticing the flavor—fear, sadness, interest, for example—the location, the felt size, shape, and whether the impact was local in my body, global over my whole body, or both.

Because these arthropods moved in realistic ways, I would also focus on their movement qualities as a flow of expansion and contraction. I paid close attention to how parts of the images would fade in and fade out. I was very cognizant of the Flow of impermanence in the images. In other words, I simply applied the standard mindfulness procedures to these weird hallucinations. I didn't try to ignore them. I didn't try to suppress them. I did not take messages from them. I just recycled them as objects of the meditation practice, no matter how bizarre they got.

As this went on, I discovered something rather extraordinary. You might assume that when you bring mindfulness to this kind of material, it would automatically get weaker and start to dissolve. And in fact, that's what often happens. But the opposite can also occur. Sometimes the more matter-of-fact you become, the more *realistic* the hallucinations become. And that's what started happening for me. I thought through the logical consequences of this. If I continued to bring concentration, clarity, and equanimity to this phenomenon, just give it total permission to do its thing, then it might become so vivid that it would be as tangible as the so-called real world itself. I decided to let that happen, and this led to a great insight.

Impermanence is not merely a characteristic of sensory experience. Impermanence is also the creative flow of nature that ferments sensory experience into existence moment by moment. The more concentration, clarity, and equanimity I brought to this visionary material, the more I was able to literally see how the Flow of impermanence was molding these visions into realness. When I completely surrendered to the Flow of expansion and contraction, it began to manifest that parallel reality the same way it manifests ordinary reality.

That's why those images were becoming so realistic: I was able to detect the creative Flow of impermanence animating them from within, like the hand of some invisible puppeteer, expanding and contracting to bring life to an empty puppet. The more I let that Flow move without blocking it, the more it functioned creatively as it does in nature, and therefore the more realistically it manifested visual material. It occurred to me that if I were to completely unblock the Flow, the manifestations could become as vivid and tangible as the real world.

You might think this would make a person freak out. In fact, quite the opposite should occur: it gives you liberating insight. You see how impermanence creates something that is obviously not there. A sort of figure-ground reversal takes place. It's not that you become convinced that the hallucinations are real, rather you understand how conventional reality is in some ways a hallucination.

Relating to the Realm of Power

As I mentioned, an important gauge of a person's spiritual maturity lies in how they relate to the phenomena of the intermediate layer, the realm of power. Indeed, we can classify an individual's spiritual journey based on how they react to this realm. First let's examine three extreme cases: Freak-Out, Diversion, and Plumb Line. After that, we'll look at another possibility: a compromise scenario.

Freak-Out

In the case of freak-out, you start out living on the surface of consciousness, just like everyone else. Then for some reason—a cultivated path, some special condition like an illness, trauma, sleep deprivation, drugs, fasting, or maybe just due to random chance—you turn 90 degrees from the surface and start to go down into the intermediate layer. There you encounter some unusual phenomena and get frightened. Like somebody whose head is held under water, you flail around to get back to the surface of consciousness, to ordinary reality, gasping to catch your breath. The experience is so uncomfortable that you decide to never risk repeating it. You stay on dry land for the rest of your life. You are too scared to go back down, so you never bore through the intermediate realm to what is beyond. This represents an extreme relationship: you turn 90 degrees (downward), start to move toward the Source, get freaked out, and turn around 180 degrees (upward) in order to get back to normalcy.

Diversion

In the case of diversion, as you start to move toward the Source, you encounter phenomena of the intermediate realm, and you like them. They're interesting; they're empowering; they're enticing. So you move out into that realm and begin to explore.

But here's the problem. Remember that in order to move toward the Source, you turned 90 degrees from the surface. If you get preoccupied with the phenomena of the intermediate realm, you have turned 90 degrees again, and are now traveling *horizontally* out into that realm, rather than *vertically* down to the Source. It's like you were driving from San Francisco to Los Angeles for an important meeting. But along the way, you turned here and there to entertain yourself with the scenery. Somewhere along the line, *without realizing it,* you're no longer moving north to south. Instead, you're now headed east toward Denver!

Once you go out horizontally into the intermediate realm, there is no end to the new and interesting stuff you can experience: encounters with angels or entities, psychic abilities, out-of-body experiences, bright lights or colors, past lives, weird internal sounds. The scenery is really cool, but you're never going to make that important meeting. You just keep moving out further and further, parallel with the surface, having new and fascinating experiences but not getting any closer to the Source.

This is the territory of the New Age. Of course "New Age" is just a twentieth-century term for a phenomenon that liberation teachers have been warning people about for millennia. But let's be clear about one thing. These phenomena themselves are not a problem. The problem comes when you start putting all of your spiritual energy into them. When that happens, you believe you are making spiritual progress, but in fact you are not, and worse still, you don't realize it. The vocabulary used by those who travel around in the realm of power is sometimes quite close to the vocabulary used by those who plummet straight to the Source.

In previous epochs, for every person who was interested in traversing the vertical path to the Source, there were many more people who were interested in the ego ornaments of the realm of power. This makes perfect sense. The realm of power runs parallel to ordinary surface experience, so it is easier for people to relate to. In the world of surface, conventional reality, people are preoccupied with status. The realm of power can feed that preoccupation, just as "mating and rating" do on the surface. That's why getting caught in the realm of power is referred to as spiritual materialism. I sometimes joke that I would like to have a T-shirt that says: "My entity is older than your entity." Of course, this is just a joke, but that is exactly what the status trip of the realm of power sounds like. I've heard that some people have even claimed proprietary rights and tried to service mark the entities that they purport to channel!

Don't get me wrong. As I mentioned, the powers themselves are not a problem. In fact, *they're a good thing.* They're a good sign on your journey because they are a way to contact deep levels of the mind. If you're seeing the forms of specific spirits, it means that you're getting close to the formless Great Spirit. Moreover, you can use the powers from this realm to help other people, but that's best done *after* you've plummeted through this realm to the Source rather than before.

Wuguang, my teacher at the Buddhist temple in Taiwan, was a Tantric wizard. His primary interest was in acquiring psychic powers, but that interest had developed *after* his enlightenment. He cultivated these powers because that was his way of helping people. It was the normal thing to do given his cultural background. He cured illnesses, located runaway children, and exorcised people who were demonically possessed. It wasn't because he was particularly interested in this *mishegas* for himself. He was already liberated; he lived in the Source. If you're interested in this stuff, it's okay to put a lot of time and energy into it *after* you have contacted the Source. Because only then do you see the powers for what they truly are. You realize where they ultimately come from and what they're really made of.

Zen masters often refer to the intermediate realm as *makyo. Ma* is an abbreviation for *mara,* sometimes translated as "devil." But in this context, mara just refers to blockages or impediments, things that can "bedevil" one's progress. The Zen masters don't want students to get tripped out on the content of the intermediate realm, thereby missing their golden opportunity to get an insight into the nature of nature. It's very affirming to have angels shower you with flowers, but that is a trivial experience relative to the affirmation that comes when you directly contact the Source of all things—the formless womb whose peristalsis forms angels, demons, flowers, and garbage cans.

Plumb Line

In this reaction to the realm of power, no matter what arises, you greet it with concentration, clarity, and equanimity. If nothing special happens, you pay attention to the nothing special with concentration, clarity, and equanimity. If something special happens, and it is frightening and painful, you greet it with concentration, clarity, and equanimity. If something special happens, and it is blissful and affirming, you greet it with concentration, clarity, and equanimity. You make no distinctions. You just auger down, deeper and deeper, until you touch the Formless—the place from which both conventional reality and altered reality arise.

A good historical example of Plumb line is Saint John of the Cross, a Christian mystic poet who lived in sixteenth-century Spain and belonged to the Carmelites—one of the main meditative orders in the Roman Catholic Church. Saint John described the journey to the Source as a going up rather than a going down, but the idea is the same. He metaphorically described the path in his *Ascent of Mount Carmel.* In it, he drew a picture of Mount Carmel and the different stages of the ascent from the base to God at the peak. Each stage on the way he labeled *nada* (nothing) and at the very top he wrote *y en monte nada* ("and at the peak, nothing"). Of course, the nada of that peak is a very, very special nothing; it is the divine Nothing, which is sometimes called emptiness in Buddhism. It is a nada that is simultaneously a *todo* (everything).

Saint John wrote that if you want to climb Mount Carmel, you cannot let yourself be frightened by the beasts you may encounter along the way, neither can you stop to pick any flowers. This description beautifully captures the essence of spiritual maturity. You are not freaked out by the weirdness, and you're not decorating yourself with cool stuff either.

The Compromise Scenario

Between the extreme of going horizontal, which we might call the path of sorcery, and the extreme of going straight down, which we might call the path of liberation, there lies a continuum of in-between angles—oblique paths, so to speak. An oblique path has two components of motion. There is some horizontal movement into exploring the phenomena of the intermediate realm, but at the same time, there is some vertical movement toward the spiritual Source. An oblique path could be 45 degrees, where you move into the realm of power and toward the Source simultaneously and at the same speed. Or you could be angled a little bit more toward sorcery (more horizontal, going broader out into phenomena) or angled a little bit more toward liberation (more vertical, going deeper, approaching the Source). Many people follow one of these oblique angles; they are not on a spiritual materialism trip, nor are they just purely plummeting to the Source. So we can measure a continuum of spiritual orientations, depending on how close your vector is to vertical. As a general rule, the more vertical, the more mature. *This range of oblique angles between pure power tripping and pure purification represents the spectrum of classical shamanism.*

I like to refer to shamanism as the *really* old-time religion of this planet. Even relatively old religions like Hinduism and Judaism have only been in existence for a few millennia. Shamanism, the natural religion of tribal humanity, is at least twenty thousand years old, probably much older—no one knows for sure. In the big picture, the natural religion of our species has been shamanism, and compared to it, all the other religions of the world are new kids on the block.

Within shamanic cultures, there is often a distinction between the path that is oriented toward the special powers and the path that is oriented toward ego transcendence. The path of the powers brings knowledge of the spirits. But ego transcendence brings knowledge of the Great Spirit.

The only shamanic practice that I have had any direct contact with is one from North America, specifically that of the Lakota, or Western Sioux. In their language, they have two words: *pejuta-wichasha* and *wichasha-wakan. Pejuta* means an "herb" or a "medicine" or a "power," and *wichasha* means a "person," so pejuta-wichasha is literally a medicine person or person with power. *Wakan,* on the other hand, means the Great Mystery or the Great Spirit, so a wichasha-wakan is a spiritual leader, a person whose shamanic ordeals have taken them beyond the ego.

In Carlos Castaneda's early books, his teacher, Don Juan, lays it on the line in a way that couldn't be clearer. He uses exactly the same language that my teacher Wuguang used. Don Juan says that there are some people who have power, but they can't see. There are some people who can see, but they don't have power. And there are some people who can both see and have power. What Don Juan means by "seeing" is of course insight—understanding how consciousness works at the deepest level.

The Buddha said essentially the same thing. He had a student who was an *arhat,* which means a fully enlightened, fully liberated person, like himself. But the populace doubted that this person was an arhat because he didn't have any special powers. The people came to the Buddha and said, "What's the deal here? He can't levitate; he can't tell us the future; he can't heal people." The Buddha responded by saying that they didn't understand the nature of the path. Liberation is dimensionally independent from these powers. The Buddha confirmed that the arhat was liberated, but his path had not involved any unusual experiences.

By way of contrast, the Buddha had another student who was a master of the psychic powers, but had very little actual liberation. He wasn't enlightened, but he thought he was hot stuff. So the Buddha used a clever strategy to demonstrate this confusion to him at a gut level. The story goes that this particular student's psychic powers were so great that when he visualized phenomena, other people around saw them too. The Buddha said, "I have a request. Use your psychic powers to manifest a tiger." The student readily complied, magically evoking a ferocious tiger from the ethers. It was so real that he became terrified of his own creation. Then the Buddha said, "You see, you are not what you thought you were. You are not liberated. You are not yet free from fear."

Upaya: Using the Powers for Liberation

It might sound like I'm warning against the phenomena of the realm of power, speaking of them as a bad thing. But actually, it's quite the opposite: contacting such unusual experiences can potentially be a good thing from the viewpoint of our ultimate goal. This is because if you happen to experience any of these phenomena, it's a sign that you have gone deep into consciousness, and therefore, if you bring the qualities of concentration, clarity, and equanimity to that experience, you will be able to purify yourself at a very deep level.

In other words, I am suggesting a sort of reverse way of looking at the power phenomena. The usual way that people view these phenomena is to see them as a conduit that carries messages from the deep mind to the surface. I suggest that the reverse way of looking is more productive. Power phenomena represent a conduit that can carry clarity and equanimity from the surface down into the deep mind—giving it what it needs to untie its own knots, to self-purify. The most important thing in working with unusual phenomena or altered states is to see them as a convenient venue for reaching and liberating the depths of your consciousness. Viewed this way, they become what in Buddhism is called upaya. This word is usually translated as "skillful means," but a more contemporary and idiomatic translation might be "working smart."

There are several ways to work smart with the realm of power. Let's consider some specific cases. Suppose that you're meditating, and you experience dramatic heat, or nectar-like energy circulating through your whole body. From the perspective of mindfulness practice, we would view this as a manifestation of anicca, or impermanence. Instead of getting tripped out on the sensation itself, the intrinsic *content* of the experience, become fascinated with the changing *contour* of the experience. You track the undulation or vibratory movement moment by moment. You see the experience as a verb, not a noun, a doing, not a thing. This will bring insight into impermanence down to a "cellular level" of your being, and move you in the direction of that formless doing that is the Source.

Or suppose that you get the impression that you have left your body. There is something significant about this experience, and there is something not so significant. Unfortunately, people often focus on the insignificant part and fail to utilize the significant part. The insignificant part is the impression that you can move around outside your body. The significant part is that you have entered a state of radical equanimity, a deeply detached witness-state from which you can observe your thoughts and body sensations with great matter-of-factness. Almost everyone who has out-of-body experiences gets tripped out on the entertaining impression that they can move around outside their body. Almost no one thinks of it as a platform from which to do systematic deconstructive observation, and that's sad, because they miss a golden opportunity. By focusing on the transient impression that you have become free of your body, you miss your chance to get the transformative insight that *you were never trapped there to begin with!*

How about the experience of reading people's minds or remembering former lives? When people have experiences like this, they are touching the part of the deep mind that is a sort of universal mind. There is a window of opportunity here as well, a chance to experience oneness with all minds, all lives—past, present, and future, mystic as well as real. In this case, the oneness is an expansion of consciousness to encompass all possible experience, without getting fixated in any one particular experience. By getting overly involved in the impression of being able to read specific minds or remember specific incarnations, you lose the opportunity to have the experience of embracing all minds and incarnations. If you do get the sense that you know what other people are thinking or can remember other lives, notice how spacious your consciousness is getting, and give it permission to get even bigger—so big that it literally becomes space itself, viewing everything, gazing at no particular thing. Then you will experience what in traditional Buddhism is referred to as the formless absorption state (jhana) called boundless consciousness.

Some people have experiences of intense pleasure or ecstatic bliss during practice. Some even say that the goal of meditation is to experience such pleasure. However, the goal of meditation is subtly but significantly different: it is to transform your relationship to pleasure, so that any kind of pleasure brings profound fulfillment. Bringing concentration, clarity, and equanimity to pleasure vastly elevates the fulfillment that pleasure delivers. If what you are focusing on happens to be the intense pleasure of meditative bliss, then this will retrain your "fulfillment circuits" at a cellular level. In fact, when you read the original sermons of the Buddha that appear in the early portion of the Pali Canon, there is much talk about how nirvana is experienced when you break through the highest meditative bliss.

Bliss during meditation is a great thing. Experience it tangibly as a body sensation and track your level of equanimity with it. Notice how every once in a while, you will greet a wavelet of bliss without any tightening around its arising, or any grasping around its passing. When that happens, notice how much more deeply fulfilling that detached pleasure is. In this way, the bliss of meditation becomes more a source of insight and purification and less a source of entertainment and craving.

Bliss is sometimes paired with the phenomenon of light. The light which may sometimes appear in the intermediate realm can be very intense. Perhaps you have experienced something like this. Have you ever half woken up from sleep and become aware of bright light that is not external? That's what I'm talking about. In the Christian tradition, the experience of bright light during meditation was referred to as "the uncreated light of Mount Tabor." Christian contemplatives believe that this light is what Jesus experienced during the Transfiguration that took place on Mount Tabor, a hill located in Israel near the Sea of Galilee. So they look upon that light as a special grace. But they also say that for true union with God, you must go beyond the light and into the darkness.

That is true. If you happen to experience luminosity in your meditation, look at it very, very carefully. You'll see that it arises due to incredibly subtle and rapid vibrations. In other words, within it can be found an almost inconceivably fine-grained vibratory flavor of impermanence. As you focus more and more on its subtle impermanence, the light breaks up, and you go beyond the light to the Source that is beyond dark or bright.

Finally, what if you see angels, allies, ancestors, entities, or avatars? It's fine to sometimes use these archetypes as a conduit to get information *from* the depths, but I recommend that you mostly use them as a conduit to bring clarity and equanimity *to* the depths. Become fascinated with how they move, and less tripped out with what they mean. Then you will be able to see the hands of the formless puppeteer, literally animating the images from within—the doingness that is the Great Spirit that lies behind the somethingness of any specific spirit.

This is how to work smart in the realm of power: use the phenomena as platforms to reach and unlock the flow of Source.

∽

Meditation teachers tend to fall into three categories vis-à-vis how they deal with the intermediate realm. Zen or vipassana teachers tend to caution people about it. Hindu or Tibetan teachers tend to be positive about it. Personally, I like to take the middle ground. It's good that you are experiencing the realm of power. For one thing, it is a sign that you are dropping deep, and for another, it's a platform from which you can do some very profound insight and purification work. But in order to do that, you have to be able to treat it like any other phenomenon. Break it up into body sensation, mental image, and internal talk, then break those up into waves of impermanence, and then watch where the waves go to when they cease. When you are directing attention to the place where things go when they cease, you are directing attention toward the Source where things come from when they arise.

Now you have a three-layered model of consciousness that can be used as a map of the spiritual path. In traditional Buddhism, these three layers are referred to as the *trikaya,* which in Sanskrit means three bodies: *nirmanakaya, sambhogakaya,* and *dharmakaya.* Nirmanakaya: the phenomena of the surface, which we are all aware of. Sambhogakaya: the phenomena of the intermediate realm, which I've described here in some detail. Dharmakaya: the Source itself, the formless womb whose peristalsis gestates time, space, self, and world into existence. It expands and contracts and gives birth to gods, ghosts, angels, avatars, saints, sinners, garlands, and garbage cans.

CHAPTER EIGHT

The Real No Self

One of the most perplexing and potentially off-putting teachings of the Buddha is the teaching of anatta, often translated as "no self." In the Pali language *an* means "without," and *atta* means "self" in the sense of thing, essence, or separate particle. The Buddha taught there is no thing inside us called a self.

This concept is totally counterintuitive. It goes against our ordinary ways of thinking; it goes against our normal perception. At best, it would seem to be a rather unsatisfying way to look at things. At worst, it comes off as downright ridiculous. I can still remember the first time I encountered this Buddhist notion. It was in my early teens. Walking through a bookstore somewhere in L.A., I picked up a book on Buddhism, randomly opened it to a page, and read a line. It said something like "All of your problems go back to your belief that you have a self. There is no thing called a self." "Bullshit!" I screamed mentally as I slammed the book closed in irritation. Now, sixty years later, I find myself making the same claim I read in the book. Have I drunk the Buddhist Kool-Aid? Well, maybe a little. But it's mostly because I spent some time carefully observing how the perception "I am" arises.

Of course every adult human has a *sensory experience* of self. If we ask "Through which of the sense gates does this perception of self arise?" we will see that it arises from a mixture of thought and feeling. Certain kinds of body sensations are more self-referential than others. The touch of our clothes is somewhat related to ourselves, but the body sensations we experience when somebody criticizes or praises us are much more related to the sense of self. They are both body sensations: the touch of our clothes and the feeling that we experience in our body when we are embarrassed in public or when we are praised in public. However, the latter feeling is qualitatively more associated with our sense of individual existence or self. In addition to the body component, there is self-referential thought: internal conversations and mental pictures that are associated with who you are, what you look like, and so forth.

Actually, there are several scales we might use to analyze the experience of our finite I-am-ness. At the broadest scale, we tend to identify with any and all mind-body experience: I am my mental image, mental talk, and body sensation. At the narrowest scale, we tend to identify particularly strongly with *self-referential* mental image, mental talk, and body sensation. Self-referential mental images are mental images of your own appearance. Self-referential mental talk is your judgment about how cool or uncool you are. Self-referential body sensations are the emotional sensations associated with being praised or blamed. Between the broadest sensory scale of self ("I am any and all mind-body states") and the narrowest sensory scale of self ("I am self-referential mind-body states") there is a midrange scale: I am thought plus body emotion. That's the system of mental image, mental talk, and emotional body sensation that I described in chapter 4. That's the system that my students mostly work with for gaining insight into no self. Of course, any of the three scales can be interesting and productive to work with, and each is, in its own way, natural. Defining the sensory self broadly as any and all mind-body experience is intuitive; even a child can understand it. On the other hand, working with the self-referential thought and emotion can be both enormously challenging and enormously freeing.

There's a reason that I mostly have people work at the middle scale. The reason is that mental image + mental talk + body emotion represents a natural system—a system that can be reactive, proactive, interactive, and occasionally inactive. Here's what I mean. When you have the perception of seeing the external world, hearing the external world, and being touched by the external world, the sense of an "I" that sees externally, hears externally, and feels externally arises because the inner system reacts to those outer stimuli. When the inner system is not reacting to outer stimuli, it may begin to proactively spin memories, plans, and fantasies. Also, it has an interactive mode. A mental image may trigger mental talk or body emotion. Mental talk may trigger a mental image or body emotion. Body emotion can build up until it drives us to form mental images and mental talk. So the system interacts with itself. Is there anything else this system does besides reactivity, proactivity, and interactivity? Yes, it sometimes goes inactive, creating *one kind* of no-self experience.

Something that reacts to its environment, pro-acts to change its internal state, and interacts with itself constitutes a natural system. It would be convenient to have a name for that system. Let's call it "inner activity." Consider for a moment the awesome range of phenomena covered by the rather bland-sounding term "inner activity": memory, plan, fantasy, problem solving, will, desire, doubt, indecision, confusion, conviction, unpleasant emotion, pleasant emotion, intuition, insight, enlightenment. . . . Enlightenment? Yes! Enlightenment is the ability to form a clear see-hear-feel representation of that which precedes each arising of see-hear-feel.

Is that all there is to I-am-ness? Well, yes and no. That's all there is to *finite* I-am-ness. But if you look carefully, you'll be able to find what might be referred to as transfinite I-am-ness—an I-am-ness that is simultaneously boundlessly large and boundlessly small. Where do you look for *that*? Well, one way to find that would be to continuously eyeball the I-am-ness that's behind your I-am-ness that's behind your I-am-ness that's behind . . . until you come to an I-am-ness that's not limited to mind-body. This is the method called "self-enquiry."

An alternative approach is to carefully observe the body-mind experience, breaking it into its components, subcomponents, and sub-subcomponents until you come to the realization that mind-body experience is literally made out of expanding-contracting space. This latter approach is the classical observing practice of Southeast Asia—vipassana.

Although the self-enquiry approach and the analytic observation approach are in some ways different, both of them require and develop concentration power, sensory clarity, and equanimity, and both of them result in an experience of transfinite self. People in the self-enquiry community tend to refer to that experience as the true self, whereas people in the Buddhist community tend to refer to it as no self. But, hey, a rose by any other name . . .

When we are unable to keep track of mental image, mental talk, and body emotion as components, they tangle together. Then we get a perception of self as a separate, vulnerable particle, rather than as an interactive, uninhibited wave of personality. The self-as-particle is a kind of illusion. When thought and feeling become *untangled* through sensory clarity and decongealed through equanimity, then we get a very different perception of what self is.

The somethingness of self and the duality of subject versus object is built into the structure of every human language I'm familiar with. I can't talk about the topic of no self without saying the word "I." And every time I say I, I'm using a pronoun, and when I do that, I reinforce the sense that there is a thing called "I."

It is very confusing because when people ask questions, the questions are always put into grammatical form, and the answers must also be put into grammatical form. People ask questions like "Who gets enlightenment? Who meditates? Who is talking to me now?" But the interrogative pronoun "who" grammatically requires a substantive, a noun, to answer it. To construct a proper response, you have to use "this" or "it" or "he" or "she." There is no other way in any human speech to respond grammatically to that question, so the answer always reinforces the illusion. I guess that is why some meditation teachers completely refuse to answer such questions. They just remain silent or they let out a yell or utter a seeming non sequitur. For example, the student asks, "Master, what is the self?" and the master replies, "Three pounds of flax."

Getting Rid of Something That Was Never There

The sense of self as a separate, vulnerable particle is a kind of illusion that arises when we lose track of inner see-hear-feel activity. There is a good metaphor in the physical world for this type of illusion. If I have two kinds of thread, one white and one red, and I tangle them together and hold them at a distance from you, you get a very clear impression that there is a unified pink mass. If you get closer and view it more carefully, however, what happens to the pink? It seems to disappear. When you clearly see what is actually there, you see the individual red and white threads, and no pinkness whatsoever. In the case of self, the analog of pinkness, the property that goes away is "thingness." *reify*

But we can go further still. In the next step, we penetrate the inner see-hear-feel components themselves, and then we penetrate their sub-components and their sub-subcomponents. When we scour down into the infrastructure of the thinking mind and the feeling body in this way, we discover their atoms. But their atoms are not things either. Their atoms are a sort of effervescent "quantum foam."

That opens the door to an understanding of the fundamental substance from which the thought and feeling are constituted, and a new sense of self arises. It is not a self in the ordinary sense of the word. Self in the ordinary sense of the word is an illusion; it is that pink, and the illusion of pink has gone away. The new self is not a noun, it is a *verb*. It is the activity of personality that arises effortlessly from the Nothingness moment by moment. And we might refer to that as a fluid self or our true self or big self. But in the Buddhist tradition, we usually choose to call this experience *insight into no self*. I know this terminology is confusing. The trouble starts when we talk about the pink going away, because that is not exactly correct. The pink was never there to begin with!

It's often said that if we practice meditation, we lose our ego, or we get rid of the ego. That is not quite accurate because we can't get rid of something that was never there. Instead, we simply see the sensory situation as it is.

Just because the sense of self as a thing goes away does not for a moment imply that the activity of personality goes away. The enlightened people who constantly talk about no self often have strong, charismatic personalities. You might think that's paradoxical, but it is a logical consequence of the experience of no self. It happens because the sense of self as something material has gone away, and all the energy that was bound up in that is now freed up for a fluid expression of personality.

We can draw a metaphor from physics. When expressed in conventional units the equation $E = mc^2$ implies that a little bit of matter is equivalent to a great deal of energy (because c^2 is very large). When someone has seen beyond the illusion of the limited self, a huge amount of energy is freed up for the expression of the personality. That's why people who are deeply enlightened often have expressive personalities.

When we talk about the experience of self-consciousness, it usually implies something uncomfortable. When you think about it, that is very strange. Why should self-consciousness be uncomfortable? Look carefully at the experience. What causes the discomfort is holding on to or interfering with the natural flow of self-referential thoughts and feelings—a kind of viscosity within inner see-hear-feel activity. The self-as-wave cannot flow smoothly.

Once we can experience self in terms of its sensory components, we can then allow those components to arise uninhibited moment by moment. When we do so, our subjective experience of who we are becomes wave-like. Experiencing our inner see-hear-feel self as an effortless activity is extremely fulfilling, but it is also empty and vacuous because it doesn't congeal into a thing.

So enlightened people often have expressive, engaging, and charismatic personalities. That's because their internal fluidity manifests as external spontaneity. They possess the doingness of self as opposed to being possessed by the somethingness of self.

Encouraged to Let Go

For many people, the thought of experiencing themselves as "not a thing" seems like it would be a negative experience. It's just not an attractive idea. It sounds like we are making ourselves and the world into something dead or bleak. At first, I had exactly the same reaction to this concept, but a Japanese Zen master helped me to overcome this fear.

Before I tell you how this happened, let me address the importance of having a teacher. There are a couple of reasons why it is difficult to make progress in meditation without a teacher. Usually we need somebody to inspire us, to answer our questions, and to encourage us. It's not necessary to surrender at the lotus feet of some putative "perfect master." I don't go for that approach myself. But I have noticed that most people make better progress if they have at least one competent coach. We need somebody to encourage us, somebody to work with us who knows the territory, someone who can speak with experiential confidence, someone we can interact with when we have questions and confusions.

Personally, I find the notion of surrendering to a teacher to be off-putting. Moreover, although in some ways it can be a comforting belief, it's been my experience that the notion of a perfect master is a myth—indeed, a potentially pernicious myth. On the other hand, many questions and confusions regarding practice are best addressed through interaction with a competent guide. A competent guide understands how each dimension of human happiness can be addressed through the practice. A competent guide will eventually encourage you to apply your practice to each of those dimensions. By dimensions of happiness, I mean five things: reducing suffering, elevating fulfillment, understanding yourself at all levels, positive behavior change, and manifesting a spirit of love and service. Moreover, a competent guide knows the potential limitations of meditation and will encourage you to supplement your practice with other modalities, if needed. Other modalities would include things such as counseling therapy or 12-step programs, for example.

In addition to these obvious things, another function that a teacher performs is to exemplify the practice and help us get over certain fears that we might have about where the practice might lead.

In my very first interview with Sasaki Roshi over thirty years ago, he blew my mind. He said, "Shinzen, you have been a monk in Japan. You know what this path is about. *I expect you to come to the place where you no longer need to make an object of the self or the world ever again!*" He said this very emphatically, very forcefully. Then he rang his little bell to signal the end of the interview.

He had chosen these words carefully. He didn't say, "Come to the place where you no longer *make* an object out of the self or the world again." He said, "Come to the place where you no longer *need* to make an object out of the self or world again." He didn't say that I should become *incapable* of making self or world into an object, he just said that I had to come to the place where I was no longer *driven* to make an object of self or world.

I understood what those carefully considered words were meant to convey; nonetheless, they really scared the bejesus out of me. I was afraid of the consequences because it sounded to me more or less like being dead. In essence, he was challenging me: "Here is the edge of the Grand Canyon. Jump off!"

This is one of those situations where having a role model can be really useful. Over the decades, I have had the chance to observe senior Asian masters very carefully. I may not be able to do what they do, but I understand what they are doing. A tennis pro may not be able to do what a world master does, but they can clearly *see* what a master does.

When you watch deeply attained masters, you can tell by the way they move their heads, by the way they carry their bodies, by the way they focus their eyes that they have no expectation that a world will be there. When they look within, they have no expectation that a mind will be there. Deeply enlightened masters have the body language of Ray Charles—someone totally comfortable with the fact that the world no longer exists as an object. Despite that—indeed, because of that—they are incredibly happy, incredibly self-expressive, and incredibly efficacious in influencing the world around them.

Contrary to my fear, I had these examples that nothing bad happens if you jump off the edge of the Grand Canyon.

Don't Fight It

While it's common to find the idea of no self to be off-putting at first, it's also common to become sort of attached to no-self experiences once they start occurring in meditation. When I first became interested in Buddhism, I studied it intellectually at a university. I read a lot about no self. When I began to actually meditate, I had this idea that I would only be making progress if I were somehow getting rid of the self. On the other hand, if I was aware of having a self, then I thought my meditation was a failure.

Without realizing it, I developed an aversion to the natural arising of self. If I was chanting and would lose myself in the chant, I felt that that was good. If I felt my self arising during the chanting, that was bad. This belief tormented me for a long time.

Many years ago, I lived at a residence community called the International Buddhist Meditation Center in downtown Los Angeles. Despite the name, it was not required that you meditate in order to be a resident there. Some of its residents were into the practice and others were not.

Brian Victoria, a good friend of mine who also has a lot of experience in Japanese Buddhist monasteries, lived there also. The two of us were really into meditation, and we would lead a sit each morning, and afterward we would chant. Everyone from the house was invited, but relatively few people ever showed up.

By the end of these sits, I would often be in a nice focused place—my samadhi was good. Then we would briefly chant, and that state would get even deeper. I would dissolve into the chanting. I thought that was really great. No self, no problem! At the end of the chant, we would strike a final bell and then briefly savor the morning silence for a magical moment.

But inevitably, one of the non-meditators would choose exactly that moment to flush a toilet or slam a door or start a conversation in the stairwell. Immediately, my state of no self would evaporate. In its place arose a spasm of inner reactivity, a storm of inner see-hear-feel. "I was *there*, goddammit, why did they have to flush a toilet? Now I am not in the no self anymore." I really begrudged the arising of this inner activation. I would be mad at myself because I could not stay in no self. I felt that I had failed, and I was grumpy at whoever had made the noise.

I don't know if I would have ever understood how to overcome this aversion, had it not been for my contact with Sasaki Roshi. I started interpreting for him. He would always say there are two things you must learn. You must learn how to let go of self, and you must learn how to manifest self. I heard that over and over again.

He also sometimes said, "You want to know what a Zen master is? I'll tell you what a Zen master is. A Zen master is a travel agent. I provide reusable round-trip tickets that allow you to travel effortlessly between heaven and hell."

During one of my *sanzens* (a personal interview with a Zen master), as usual, I gave a totally incorrect answer to my koan. In response, he said something that did not seem related to anything at all. He said, "Jesus Christ died and went to heaven, but I prefer to go to hell." And then he rang his bell to signal the end of the interview. *Ring-ring-ring.* And I left.

I had no idea what he was talking about. I just remembered what he said, and trusted that eventually it would sink in and make sense. It took years for the metaphoric lightbulb to go on, but I eventually understood what he meant. He was showing me where I was stuck in my practice.

Let's translate the poetry of his Zen into the prose of vipassana practice. He was saying something like this: "Shinzen, I know you have meditated for a lot of years, and when you sit in the zendo, you go into some pretty deep states. You really enjoy it when there is an absence of self, which is sort of heavenly for you. But when you grow up, like me, you will relish the *opposite* of that experience even more."

The opposite of the no-self experience is a congealed spasm of inner activity, a subjective charley horse, an inner see-hear-feel storm. Because he was a master, he could discern that I was still resisting, still not 100 percent accepting the arising of the self. He was telling me that, when I finally grew up, I would actually come to prefer the arising of the self to the experience of its nonarising.

Eventually I got it: don't fight this arising of the self overtly, and don't fight it subtly. When it arises, let it arise. Don't resist it. But do try to bring clarity and equanimity to it, because you are going to learn as much from the eruption of self as you learn from the cessation of self. In other words, the quicker and louder you can say "Yes" to each new arising of self, the deeper and clearer will be the "No"—the no-self state that inevitably follows.

If you find yourself in a really nice deep state and then, suddenly, you are not in that deep state, it can be upsetting. You may feel like you got tossed out of Eden, and an angel with the fiery sword is preventing you from getting back into paradise. You begrudge the fact that you've been expelled from heaven, and flail to get back—but to no avail.

But there is something you can do in that place of frustration and agitation. Get on board with nature's program! Totally let the see-hear-feel self arise unimpeded. Don't try to beat it down or regret the fact that it is erupting. Be willing to go back to square one, because it is not really square one. Allow yourself to love and relish the inner see-hear-feel storm. Your job is to clarify it, in both senses of the English word "clarify." Something is clear when we know its components, and something is clear when it becomes transparent. There is an intimate link between these two sorts of clarity. Seeing *separately* and seeing *through* reinforce each other. Just let the self spasm and give it permission to do so for as long or as short as it wants. And be grateful, not begrudging. You may no longer be in heaven, but you're not in hell either. You're in purgatory. Not necessarily a fun place, but definitely a productive one.

No Self: The Industrial Strength Version

For me, the most powerful version of no self comes about when you are able to experience your selfhood being loved into and out of existence moment by moment as you go about the activities of your day. I call that the *real* no self. That may seem like a tall order. Let's take it step-by-step.

It starts by tracking the experience of self in terms of mental image, mental talk, and emotional body sensations. This involves the dimension of clarity that I call resolution, the ability to separate the components and subcomponents of a sensory event. Clarity allows you to track your I-am-ness in terms of the same variables that characterize quantified science: how much, of what, when and where, interacting in what ways, and changing at what rate.

In addition to resolution, clarity also involves sensitivity, that is, detection skill. Detection skill is the ability to pick up on subtle sensory events. Just before each conscious mental image arises, there's a spread of subtle subliminal visual thought. Just before each conscious mental sentence arises, there's an analogous spread of subtle auditory thought. Moreover, a local body sensation will often produce a global spread of subtle activation.

The ability to detect subtle events is closely related to the ability to detect the instant when something arises, an ability that we might call temporal sensitivity. With time, your ability to detect the *absolute* beginnings of things will improve. Hopefully, at some point you'll notice that each moment of self is born as a wave of pure space simultaneously spreading and collapsing.

William James famously described the situation of an infant's first sensory experience as a "blooming, buzzing confusion." Indeed, it blooms and buzzes but it's not confusing, it's soothing. The buzz is a kind of creamy effervescence; the blooming is the budding and fading of space itself. This blooming and buzzing is not just the original situation of a newborn child, it's also constantly present in adult life. It's the situation that precedes each conscious moment of selfhood that we experience during the day. But if we are born many times during the course of a typical day, does that mean that we also die many times? Most assuredly! That may sound discouraging, but it's not—not at all. In fact, it's deeply empowering. I call it the "power of Gone."

CHAPTER NINE

The Power of Gone

And until you know of this:
How to grow through death
You're just another grumpy guest,
On the gloomy earth.

GOETHE, "HOLY LONGING" (SHINZEN YOUNG, TRANSLATOR)

Students sometimes ask me whether there is a quickest path to enlightenment. My standard answer is that there may be, but I don't think that humanity knows it yet. In our current stage of the science of enlightenment, different approaches seem to work for different people. That's why I like to give a wide range of contrasting techniques for students to choose from. However, just as a thought experiment, I have sometimes asked myself what I would say if I were allowed to teach only one focus technique and no other. Which technique would I pick as the quickest path to enlightenment? It's a difficult choice, but I think it would be the technique I call Just Note Gone.

Most people are aware of the moment when a sensory event starts, but are seldom aware of the moment when it *vanishes*. We are instantly drawn to a new sound, or new sight, or a new body sensation, but rarely notice when the previous sound, sight, or body sensation disappears. This is natural because each new arising of sensory experience represents what we need to deal with in the next moment. But to always be aware of sensory arisings and hardly ever be aware of sensory passings creates an unbalanced view of the nature of sensory experience. It also causes us to miss one of the more interesting ways to contact the Source.

Practicing Just Note Gone is pretty straightforward. Whenever a sensory experience suddenly disappears, make a note of that fact: clearly acknowledge when you detect the transition point between all of it being present and at least some of it no longer being present. You can use the mental label "Gone" to help you note the end of the experience. If nothing vanishes for a while, that's fine. Just hang out until something does. If you start worrying about the fact that nothing is ending, note each time that thought ends. There is only a finite amount of real estate available in consciousness at any given instant. Each arising somewhere causes a passing somewhere else.

There is a lot to be said about the passing of sensory experiences. When you first begin, it may be difficult to keep track of what's going on. But with time, you start to clearly track inner and outer sensory activity. At some point, you become very aware that these sensory events not only well up, but that they also subside. And then at a further point, you become more and more *interested* in how they subside; your attention is directed toward the passing of things. This classic progression from simply noticing events, to riding on a rhythmic pattern of arising-passing, to fascination with continuous passing is described in the *Visuddhimagga* (*The Path of Purification*), the classical Southeast Asian manual for vipassana practice.

I define the moment of vanishing to be when all or part of a sensory experience disappears. It might not be that the whole sensory event goes away, but at least some *portion* of it abruptly subsides. A gradual fading is not a Gone, but will continue to fade and fade, and then at some point, there will be a transition from a subtle level of existence to actual nonexistence. That moment when it winks out is a Gone.

My simple one word label for detected endings is "Gone." But as with many of the labels I use, we have to be careful, because the meaning is not identical to the meaning in colloquial English. When we say "gone" in everyday English, it typically implies gone for good; it's gone, and it ain't coming back. But Gone as a label in my system of mindfulness merely denotes the situation of detecting an abrupt diminishing.

It doesn't mean that what ended won't come back; in fact, it may come back instantly.

Also, Gone does not imply that every part of a sensory experience has vanished. Let's say that you are observing a mental image of a person—there's a head, trunk, arms, legs, and so forth. At some point, maybe the left arm abruptly evaporates, but the rest of the person's image is still there. That is a partial vanishing; part of what you were observing disappeared. That counts as a Gone.

So Gone does not imply gone for good. Gone doesn't mean that every single part of what you were observing disappears. It means that all or part of something suddenly subsides. And it doesn't even have to subside all the way. It might just abruptly diminish to a lower level or a smaller size.

As I like to define things, Flow is any change. Something may change by increasing in some way; something may change by decreasing in some way. Gone is the label for any *abrupt* decrease. Put another way, Gone is a special case of abrupt Flow.

The way I define Gone in this chapter may seem rather complex and subtle. What's the point? Recall that in chapter 1, I described how basic scientific definitions are sometimes honed over a long period of time. A modern high school student, if they're willing to be patient with their textbook, can have an understanding of calculus that is deeper than that of its genius creators—Newton and Leibnitz. It took me twenty years to hone my current definition of Gone. With it, a beginning meditator can sometimes get a taste of the stage that, according to the *Visuddhimagga,* immediately precedes enlightenment.

One might say that the moment of arising represents nature affirming a sensory event—metaphorically saying "Yes" to it. Paralleling this, one might say that the moment of passing is nature negating—metaphorically saying "No" to that sensory event. To be able to *clearly* detect Gone could be thought of as the ability to experience nature saying "No." The ability to appreciate Gone goodies, like relief, tranquility, and such, could be thought of as the ability to *deeply* experience nature's "No."

There are four factors that facilitate having a clear and deep experience of Gone: the totality of your momentary focus, the totality of your momentary equanimity, the quickness of your momentary focus, and the quickness of your momentary equanimity. Here's what I mean. The totality of your focus refers to pouring the whole bucket of your awareness on each new arising. The totality of your equanimity refers to how deeply you open to each new arising. To pour the whole bucket of your awareness on each arising while simultaneously opening to it could be described as affirming that arising—saying "Yes" loudly in response to nature's "Yes." The ability to do those two things at the very instant when something arises could be described as saying "Yes" quickly. This brings us to the basic axiom of noting vanishing. The more quickly and completely you affirm each arising, the deeper and clearer will be your experience of its passing.

I've noticed that there's a tendency to assume that Gone is a very esoteric category. Often, people think that if they dedicate themselves to meditating on it for twenty years, they may someday become worthy to note a Gone. Please disabuse yourself of that notion. Every in-breath comes to an end. Every out-breath comes to an end. Those are physical-type body sensations, and they come to an end. Don't ever say that you can't detect any vanishings. You can find two Gones in every breath you take.

You might think that such Gones are trivial, but they are not. All Gones are created equal. Or, as I sometimes like to say, all Gones are *uncreated* equal. I say it as a joke. It might seem like an enigmatic and strange way to talk, some kind of gimmick to get your attention or to make it sound like I know something you don't. But all Gones are uncreated equal. The thing that vanishes might be quite ordinary and banal, but its moment of vanishing points to something extraordinary and deep—the Uncreated, the Source of consciousness.

You hear a cat meow, and that sound comes to an end: Gone. You turn on a light in a room, and the darkness comes to an end: Gone. A verbal thought goes through your head, you note it, and it vanishes: Gone. You may think that these are too quotidian, too banal to have any significance, but these are all covered by the definition of Gone.

As you pay attention to these everyday Gones, you are gradually, gradually developing a sensitivity—the ability to detect the unborn Source of consciousness. Each one of those Gones represents a teeny tiny learning that in and of itself would seem rather trivial. But once you begin to sum that learning over many instances—over weeks, months, perhaps years of practice—you start to notice that those moments of Gone momentarily direct your attention toward something that's actually not a thing, and therefore can't really be experienced in the senses but can be *contacted*. That not-thing that you are contacting is the Source.

The Source can be indirectly *contacted* through the vanishing moment of the senses, even though it, itself, is not strictly speaking an experience. Put another way, the aftereffect of each vanishing becomes more and more sensorially well defined.

Regarding Gone, there are some things that are intuitively obvious, and some things that are actually quite counterintuitive. It's intuitively obvious that if you're having an unpleasant experience in your body and/or mind and you're able to pay attention to the moments when parts of it vanish, you'll get a sense of relief. Noting Gone allows you to experience that this too *is* passing, which will give you a lot more comfort than just trying to remind yourself, this too *shall* pass. It also makes sense that noting Gone could create stillness and tranquility within you. Relief and tranquility are a natural consequence of the nature of vanishing. They intuitively make sense.

But some effects of Gone are not intuitively obvious. It's not intuitively obvious that noting the vanishing of a neutral or pleasant experience can result in something delicious, but it can. Indeed when any sensory experience—whether it's pleasant, painful, or neutral—vanishes, it can potentially leave a sense of satisfaction in its wake. This is hard to explain logically but can be experienced personally. In India, there is a word that means both "cessation" and "satisfaction" as a single linked concept. The word is nirvana. It means "to blow out," like a candle flame. It also means to quench your thirst in the sense of being completely and totally fulfilled.

Where things go to is where things come from. Each time you note Gone, for a brief instant your attention is pointed directly toward the richness of the Source. That is what's behind the seeming paradox of "satisfying nothingness."

It is intuitively obvious that noticing vanishings might reverberate through your senses as a restful experience, that as the result of noticing the moment when a burst of talk comes to an end, it might be followed by some quiet. The relative rest states—a blank mental screen, a defocused external gaze, physical relaxation, emotional neutrality, physical silence, mental quiet—may begin to pervade your sensory experience as the result of noticing vanishings.

It's also intuitively obvious that if you're going through an uncomfortable experience, focusing on vanishings could bring microrelief. And it's not a big stretch to imagine that, if your ability to continuously focus on Goneness is high, those moments of microrelief might sum to significant relief, macrorelief.

It's not intuitively obvious that noting Gone would bring fulfillment, but many people over the ages have discovered this, hence the Sanskrit word nirvana. Are there any other counterintuitive "Gone goodies"? Indeed, yes. There is one more major one.

Noting Gone may lead to a spontaneous spirit of love and service (*bodhicitta*). As I've said, where sensory events go to is where sensory events arise from. Gone points to the Source of your own consciousness. As you come to know the Source of your own consciousness, you also come to know the Source of everyone's consciousness—the shared formless womb of all beings. Someone with whom you share a womb is referred to as brother or sister. So noting Gone can lead to a spontaneous sense of oneness with—and commitment to—all beings. Tibetan teachers like to emphasize the complementarity between emptiness and compassion.

Goneness, although seemingly cold and impersonal, is deeply connected to the issue of human fulfillment and human caring. This fact is the central mystery of world mysticism: *le coup du vide est l'Amour Pur*—the touch of the void is Love Itself.

Flow and Go

As you'll recall, Flow is the term I use for any detectable change in your sensory experience. Flow covers a wide range of phenomena. By definition, a given sensory event is either perfectly stable or it's flowing. Any increase or decrease in intensity, frequency, or spatial extent of a sensory event is Flow. Any waviness, swirling, or vibration within a sensory event is Flow. Some Flow is smooth. Some Flow is sudden. Some Flow is continuous. Some Flow is abrupt. Among the various flavors of Flow, expansion-contraction Flow and subtle vibratory Flow are especially significant. Subtle vibratory Flow is often quite pleasant. And expansion-contraction Flow is fundamental.

Subtle vibratory Flow is like a shower of effervescence or a puff of aerosol spray or a silky homogenous field of minute scintillations. Runner's high and lifter's pump, when viewed through the mindfulness microscope, turn out to be subtle vibratory Flow. Subtle vibratory Flow and Gone form a delicious contrast, light and smooth versus dramatic and abrupt. Sometimes a pattern develops wherein the two alternate: bubble spray/Gone; bubble spray/Gone; bubble spray/Gone.

At first, you'll probably be aware of where the subtle vibratory Flow is, what's flowing, and so forth. But you may reach a point where the different spaces begin to flow together and the distinctions are lost. You actually don't care and don't even know whether the subtle vibratory Flow is somatic, visual, or auditory. Those discriminations break down. The separation of subjective versus objective breaks down. The distinction between active states and restful states breaks down. All you're interested in is the bursts of subtle vibratory Flow and their vanishings. This homogenizing effect of subtle vibratory Flow is very pleasant, but you can't *make* it happen. It results from a dialectical process. Half of the process involves making discriminations in a healthy, empowering way, that is, separating inner versus outer, active versus restful, visual versus auditory versus somatic. The other half is destroying the discriminations in a healthy, empowering way, which we do in meditating on Flow in general and subtle vibratory Flow in specific.

Subtle vibratory Flow is a great leveler that destroys distinctions. An even greater leveler is expansion-contraction Flow. Smooth expansion-contraction Flow creates time and space. Abrupt contractive

Flow—Gone—destroys time and space. You can't have distinctions without time and space. With the subtle vibrations, you could still, in theory, distinguish the locations of that Flow. But the subtle vibratory Flow might become so pervasive that you don't know what it is or where it is, or who you are or where you are. When this happens, it means you're getting close to an important figure-ground reversal. You are about to *become* that subtle vibratory Flow. Good, go with that.

It's the same with Gone. With Gone, too, you may reach a point where you don't know what it is that's disappearing; you don't even know whether it is big or small, pleasant or unpleasant, simple or complex. You forget about all those things—you're just dominated by the vanishing-ness of things. It's just Gone, Gone, Gone. That, once again, leads to a figure-ground reversal. You are about to *become* Gone. Good, go with that.

As you become more sensitive to detecting Gone, you may come to a place where you note it so frequently that Goneness itself becomes an object of high concentration. The gaps between the Gones get shorter and shorter until a figure-ground reversal takes place. Self and world become fleeting figures, and Gone becomes the abiding ground. Needless to say, experiencing that will have a huge impact on how you relate to aging and death.

Dissolution

There is one possible negative effect from working with vanishing and the related themes of emptiness and no self. In extreme cases, the sense of Goneness, emptiness, and no self may be so intense that it creates disorientation, terror, paralysis, aversion, or hopelessness. Unpleasant reactions such as these are well documented in the classical literature of contemplation of both East and West. In the West, it is sometimes referred to as "the dark night of the soul." In the East, it is sometimes referred to as "the pit of the void" or *dukkhañana* (the unpleasant side of dissolution). This doesn't happen that often, but if it does, there are three interventions which you need to remember in order to transform the situation from problematic to blissful.

First, you *accentuate the good parts* of the dark night even though they may seem very subtle relative to the bad parts. For example, you may be able to glean some sense of tranquility within the nothingness. There may be some sense of inside and outside becoming one, leading to expanded identity. There may be some soothing, vibratory energy massaging you. There may be a springy, expanding-contracting energy animating you. Use your concentration power to focus on these positive aspects of the experience, and it may bring some relief and even enjoyment.

Second, *negate the negative parts* of the dark night by deconstructing them through noting with mindful awareness. Remember the divide-and-conquer strategy of vipassana. Experiences that are overwhelming become much less so when they are disentangled into their constituent parts. You simply notice which part of your void-triggered bum-out is emotional body sensation, which part is mental images, and which part is mental talk. Keep those clearly delineated. Another way to put this is: if everything is empty and that's bumming you out, then constantly remind yourself that the bum-out is empty. But you say, "That will leave me no place to stand." That's right. That's the whole point. You will become what Zen master Rinzai called "an authentic person with no fixed position."

Finally, you try to *affirm positive emotions, behaviors, and cognitions* in a sustained systematic way. Gradually, patiently, reconstruct a new, habitual self based on lovingkindness and related practices. Thinking positive, loving thoughts; seeing positive, loving images; and feeling love and positivity all help to palliate dukkhañana, the unpleasant perceptions caused by the dissolution.

In most cases, all three of these interventions must be practiced and maintained for however long it takes to get through the dark night. In the most extreme cases, it may require ongoing and intensive support from teachers and other practitioners to remind you to keep applying these interventions. The end result, though, will be a depth of joy and freedom beyond your wildest imagining. (You'll find a poetic Christian view of dissolution—and its challenges and rewards—in chapter 10.)

Primordial Feel

In my experience as a teacher, intense dark night problems are not very common. Usually, having everything just slipping away into nothingness over and over is tremendously restful and tranquil.

But in certain cases or at certain times, it can actually feel like the opposite of restful and peaceful. It can create emotional agitation. Even though this can be an unpleasant experience, it actually indicates something very powerful happening in your meditation. This emotional agitation is not the dramatic dark night described in the previous section—not at all. But it does have its own challenges and payoffs.

Vanishing points us to the most primordial, primitive experience that a human being can have: the ultimate grounding, which is a groundless grounding—Zero, the Source. It's so deep within you that it's no longer human, no longer personal. It's an inhuman experience that paradoxically nurtures, fulfills, and purifies all your human parts.

If Gone points us to the ultimately primordial experience that any human being can have—so primordial that it's not even human—there must also be the *second* most primordial experience. There is. And that experience is definitely a human experience; it's the experience of the chaotic emotion of the infant.

Gone may lead to contact with this state of primordial, chaotic body emotion. Each vanishing is like a little death. When you come back, it is like being born again. You come back as an infant, with an infant body, full of freaked out, chaotic body emotion, just like when you *were* an infant.

And that's really good. Because then you're working with the very first thing that separated you from your spiritual Source, the thing that split you off from the Source in the first hours and days and weeks of life. You're working with the normally subliminal limbic undercurrent of experience.

But back then, you were a helpless infant, and now you're an adult meditator. As an adult meditator, you're much better off than an ordinary adult; you're a super-adult because you have techniques you can apply to the situation. This allows you to work through that primordial level of infantile freak-out. And that original, primordial, infantile freak-out is at the core of all subsequent freak-out experiences a person has, as a child, as a teenager, as an adult, and as an aging senior. All emotional freak-out is based in this original, primordial freak-out of the infant, and you can work through it by loving it to death, knowing it to death. It's purgatorial. It unties some of the deepest knots in your soul.

The first thing that happens after Zero breaks apart is that expansion and contraction pull in opposite directions. This separation creates a cleft of pure space. But because expansion is pushing out and contraction is pulling in, that space vibrates. And it vibrates into the pure heat of *feel*. That pure heat of body emotion is the penultimate primordium of self.

The ultimate primordium of self is the space itself, born in the cleft between expansion and contraction. And the source of that space is spaceless—Zero. But the first thing that is in some sense personal is that pure heat of body emotion. If you can detect and complete it, then the part of it that came from the expansion goes back to expansion, and the part that came from contraction goes back to contraction. The freaked out infant *becomes* the activity of expansion and contraction. And when expansion and contraction reunite, mutually cancel, and vanish, you *are* that vanishing, that Zero, that Gone. If you participate in that enough times, you will completely re-parent yourself, and arise as a true super-adult, an enlightened adult.

CHAPTER TEN

Return to the Source

There's a famous story from the early history of Zen in China. Master Joshu was having a discussion with a monk, when a little puppy trotted up. The monk asked Joshu, "Does the dog have Buddha-nature?" Now, Zen is a form of Mahayana Buddhism and according to Mahayana philosophy, all beings have the Buddha-nature. So the correct academic answer is simply, "Yes, a dog has the Buddha-nature." But in the original Chinese, the monk's question is stated in a very dualistic way, connoting something like "Dog have Buddha-nature not have Buddha-nature, which is it?" Was the monk really asking a philosophical question about the Buddha-nature? I think not. I suspect what he was really asking was "How can one transcend the duality of existence and nonexistence?" Or more broadly, "How can one transcend all dualities, all conflicts—pleasure versus pain, inside versus outside, good versus evil, sense versus nonsense?"

So he put the question in a grammatical form that requires a dualistic response, requires taking sides—which is it, yes or no? The sly monk is setting a trap for the master, doing the Zen equivalent of trolling. Is the master worth his *mala*? How will he handle the sly monk's trap? Joshu was familiar with the customs of Zen, so he no doubt immediately saw the question for what it was, a set up.

Zen arose in China. In modern Chinese, the character for Zen is pronounced *chan*. Chan is the hybrid child of Indian Mahayana Buddhism and Chinese culture. From Confucianism, it got its work ethic and its ritualized daily schedule. From Taoism, it inherited several things: a model for nature based on the dialectical interplay of yang and yin, a paradigm for enlightenment based on oneness, and the custom of dialoging from a place of wisdom.

The Taoists called that custom "pure conversation." A pure conversation was an interaction in which people talked from the place of understanding the nature of nature. In the Taoist formulation, this meant to understand the interplay of yang and yin. In these pure conversations, they would speak from the wisdom mind. They would speak about the nature of nature *from* the nature of nature. Later, the Zen masters took over this Taoist tradition, and it turned into a distinctive style of dialogue called *mondo* in Japanese. The puppy mondo is one of the most famous. In the Rinzai Zen tradition, it's often the first koan (wisdom-generating conundrum) given to a student.

Such a Zen dialogue is basically a contest, but it's really an anti-contest. It's a kind of reverse or paradoxical contest. It works like this: two people talk, and the first one who speaks from the ego loses. The one who wants to win is certainly going to lose. That's why it's an anti-contest. The first one that fixates the self loses. Zen masters would have such dialogues as a playful thing. People who have seen the Buddha-nature can play and talk from the Buddha-nature.

When the monk asked Joshu whether the dog had the Buddha-nature, he was offering to play a game of spiritual tennis with the master, and the question was his opening serve, as it were.

If you were the master in this situation, what would you do? You have to return the ball, which means that, according to the rules of the game, you have to manifest the Buddha-nature in your answer. If you fail to return the ball, then you've lost, and the game is over. Remember that according to Mahayana Buddhism, all beings have the Buddha-nature. Thus the academic answer to the question is: "Yes, the dog has the Buddha-nature." Originally, the word Buddha-nature referred to a potential—all beings have the potential to become liberated. But later it came to refer to the fact that at a deep and subtle level, all beings, just as they are, already function in a liberated way. In other words, precisely because we are already there (subliminally), we can get there (explicitly). So the monk is posing a rich and interesting challenge: "Master Joshu, show me something regarding how our innate perfection allows for the transcendence of duality, and do so in a way that manifests that innate perfection."

What the monk probably expected was that Joshu would manifest the Buddha-nature as the dog-nature in a playful manner, perhaps as an uninhibited bark: woof, woof, woof! But Joshu didn't do that. He gave a very different answer. Instead of manifesting dog activity, he gave a seemingly incorrect and, hence, inscrutable response. He said, "Noooo."

In my opinion, Joshu brilliantly fulfilled the challenge presented to him. My purpose in this chapter is to address a different challenge. My challenge will be to explain Joshu's answer in a conceptually clear way. (I sometimes jokingly say that some Zen teachers don't say enough, and some mindfulness teachers say too much. Mea culpa.)

In Zen, initial enlightenment is called *kensho. Ken* means "to see" and *sho* means "nature." The nature that is seen is sometimes called *bussho* (Buddha-nature) or *shinsho* (the nature of consciousness) or *honrai no memmoku* (your original face). Many people who work in the Rinzai tradition of Zen get their first taste of kensho by working with Joshu's noooo. (This koan is sometimes called "Joshu's mu." *Mu* is the Sino-Japanese word that I'm translating as "noooo." It literally means not have, or not exist. In modern Chinese it's pronounced "*wu*.")

Which is the correct answer? Barking like a dog or noooo? I would suggest to you that both answers are correct. In order to pass the koan, you have to clearly understand why both answers are correct. You can't just play Zen. Anyone can intone *muuuu*.

It's important to understand the relationship between "woof, woof, woof" and "noooo." Each represents a way to transcend duality and therefore represents a way to become free from suffering. Either answer is correct if you clearly understand why it addresses the question, and if you can manifest the answer confidently. Fully giving yourself to "woof, woof, woof" is one way to transcend duality. You completely affirm dog—so completely that you become the activity called dog. As we shall see, this is a "yes!" that contains both yes *and* no (and hence is beyond yes *or* no). But how about Joshu's noooo? Well, that's a "no" that is neither yes *nor* no (and hence is also beyond yes *or* no).

How can you come to the experience of the "yes!" that contains both yes and no, and the noooo that's neither yes nor no? Lots of ways! In the Rinzai school of Zen, one typically does this through sustained equanimity with the confused state induced by an unanswerable question: What is the sound of one hand? What is your original face? What is mu? Questions like these are called koans. Koans can be used for various purposes, but initially, they're often used to stymie the conceptual mind. This induces a state of Don't Know. Learn to abide comfortably in that Don't Know long enough, and a new way of knowing will arise. That new way of knowing is called intuitive wisdom, prajna.

That's one approach. But personally, I prefer to work within the framework of mindfulness. So is there a way to use mindfulness-observing techniques to achieve the same goal? Sure. In fact, I already described half of it in the previous chapter when I explained how to note Gone. Joshu's mu is simply Gone experienced with great clarity. The noooo that is neither yes nor no, that transcends all duality, is present in each ordinary vanishing, although it may take a while to fully appreciate that fact.

> Not known, because not looked for
> But heard, half-heard, in the stillness
> Between two waves of the sea.
> T. S. ELIOT, "LITTLE GIDDING"

But how about the other half of the picture? The gush and gather of space, the sheer love that molds the activity called "dog," that molds the activity called "self," that molds the activity called "world"? For that, pay close attention to the very instant when things arise—just note "start." As soon as any inner or outer sensory event begins to arise, there's a spreading of activation. But right behind that activation, keeping perfect pace with it, there's a sequence of little Gones that sum together into the perception of space effortlessly collapsing. It's like you're dragging an eraser behind you all day long.

I once heard a Zen master say that a good doctor can cure your disease, but only a great doctor can show you that you were never sick.

Paradoxically, the effortless great perfection of things can sometimes show itself on occasions where you would least expect it, occasions when you find yourself in big trouble. There are two common expressions that we use to describe the experience of overwhelm. One is "I'm being flooded"—too much is happening in too many places at once. Mental images, mental talk, physical and emotional sensations, and perhaps also sights and sounds, pulling you in all directions at once. The other expression is "The rug is being pulled out from under me," meaning that your center has been ripped away, you've been decentered. But look carefully. Decentering creates a sequence of micro-Gones; the space of self collapses moment by moment. Metaphorically, we feel small, helpless, vulnerable. But it's not just that we feel small, we are literally shrinking, being contracted out of existence. Look carefully, really carefully. We're not helpless. Very much the opposite. That decentering, that shrinking of selfhood, can become something pleasant—like being gently squeezed. The flooding is your consciousness being stretched out into space in many directions at once. It's expansion, affirmation, yes. But each spreading engenders a collapse within. It's contraction, negation, no. Nature is constantly pointing us to freedom. The primordial perfection is always there. We just need to look at things in a different way.

Bring concentration, clarity, and equanimity to your experience. Do that consistently for a long time. At some point, you will hopefully notice an ordering principle that's so primordial that it can never be disordered.

No matter how uncomfortable your body might get, no matter how confused or negative your mind might become, that discomfort, confusion, or negativity is always surrounded by an effortless spontaneity. Once you notice this, you realize that you never needed to train, never needed to search, never needed to improve. But—and there's just no way around this one—it may require considerable training before you're able to notice this, *and* noticing it should give you an optimal place from which to improve yourself.

In terms of time, there's an absolute tranquility that precedes and follows each thing we see, hear, or feel and each thing we do, say, or think. In terms of space, there's an effortless spread and collapse that expands around and contracts within each thing we see, hear, or feel and each thing we do, say, or think. Indeed, each sensory or motor event is really just a cloud of effervescent foam churned up in the cleft that arises between this inward and outward motion. (Think of Hokusai's print *The Great Wave off Kanagawa*.) Each moment of life is born from the shearing forces that arise between those oppositely directed doings—each moment is molded by sheer love, molded by the shear of love. Absolute tranquility polarizes into simultaneous expansion-contraction, which briefly molds a moment of time, space, self, and world. When that expansion and contraction cancel into Gone, they carry with them all the richness of that sensory moment, leading to an even richer state of absolute tranquility.

One might be tempted to equate arising with expansion and passing with contraction, and indeed, from a superficial point of view, that's quite reasonable. But the unfixated standpoint of Zen asks for a deeper formulation. As soon as something begins to arise, it's *already beginning to pass*: "In my beginning is my end," as T. S. Eliot put it (riffing on Mary, Queen of Scots' motto). Realizing that arising entails simultaneous expansion *and* contraction is the deeper view that allows us to stay on the razor's edge of absolute now, to ride the Zen ox backward to the absolute rest of Gone. Gone occurs when expansion and contraction simultaneously cease, mutually cancel. Gone is the noooo that is neither yes nor no, neither good nor bad, neither sense nor nonsense.

But Gone is not a thing! It's what happens when all the yeses or noes needed to mold this world simultaneously cancel out, so it's incredibly rich, perhaps endlessly rich. The medieval Christian mystics called it *nihil per excellentiam* (nothing par excellence).

What's the difference between the *nihil* of the mystic, the successful practitioner, and the *nihil* of the nihilist, the cynical curmudgeon? They're both forms of nothing, yet their human significance couldn't be more different. The difference is in the *path* taken to get there. The nihilist has been wounded by the world, over and over again and, as a result, has come to an emptiness that's bleak and paralyzing. The mystic has seen the world arise from Nothing, over and over again. But equally important, the mystic has seen Nothing digest the world, over and over again. For the mystic the richness of the world is contained in that Nothing. Gone is not only a source of tranquility and safety, it's a source of fulfillment, empowerment, and love. To borrow a metaphor from thermodynamics, the human significance of nothingness is a path-dependent variable.

Because expansion and contraction pervade everything we sense and do, it seems reasonable to think of them as our nature. But how about a dog's nature? Observe a dog (or any other animal for that matter). It's obvious that everything the dog senses or does has an exuberant just-happening quality. That's why we enjoy having pets. So, clearly, the dog has the Buddha-nature. But what about a plant or a rock? Do they have the Buddha-nature? Is the Buddha-nature as described above in fact the nature of everything, the nature of nature?

Almost all the mystic masters of the past have claimed that the experiences they have in contemplation reveal directly the nature of the real world. But are such claims justified? The twentieth-century British philosopher Bertrand Russell wrote the classic essay "Mysticism and Logic." In Russell's view, such all-encompassing claims based on mystical experience are philosophically unjustified. The mystic may learn things about the nature of experience that are useful, important, and not known by most people, but the nature of objective reality is the purview of science and science only. In general, I tend to agree with Russell.

On the other hand, nature as described by mystics and nature as investigated by scientists have *some* sort of relationship. I don't think it's possible at this point in the history of our species to state with confidence what that relationship is. Indeed, arriving at a consensus regarding this issue is the central quest of the science of enlightenment. But if I had to shoot from the hip and make a wild-ass guess, it would be that the great primordial perfection discovered by the mystics is what happens when the human nervous system directly tastes the free energy principle that underlies its functioning (ΔG). But that's just a conjecture. What I *can* say with confidence is this primordial great perfection is not just a piece of esoterica, it's something useful for you to know about. The window could open for you at any time, perhaps when you least expect it or most need it. The Tibetans have an exclamatory cry reserved just for when that window opens. The cry is *Emaho!* which might be loosely rendered "Oh my God! Who would have thought it's this simple!"

Is the Buddha-nature as described above also the nature of everything, the nature of nature? I don't have a clue, but it can be fun to speculate as long as we don't take ourselves too seriously.

For starters, *if* indeed the primordial great perfection has something to do with the nervous system tasting free energy (and, hence, entropy), then the answer would be yes, because free energy and entropy are important variables in many areas of physical science. Thus, the Buddha-nature could turn out to be thermodynamics as experienced directly by the neurons themselves, as opposed to indirectly through physical reasoning and mathematical equations. Just a thought, not to be taken seriously at this point.

Another perspective might be to think of nature in dialectical terms. The Buddha-nature as described above entails a binary contrast: expansion versus contraction. The sensory experience of inner self (mental image, mental talk, and body emotion) and the sensory experience of outer scene (sight, sound, and physical body sensation) are born in between those forces. Furthermore, those forces can cancel into a rich nothing.

Do themes like binary contrast, born in-betweenness, and mutual cancellation reveal the nature of nature? Once again, I don't have a clue, but I do find the idea aesthetically pleasing. Recall that Zen inherited a dialectical philosophy from Chinese culture. Yang is expansion, yin is contraction. When they act together, it's called *taiji*—the great (*tai*) polarization (*ji*). When they mutually cancel, it's called *wuji*—the absence (*wu*) of polarity (*ji*). These notions underlie Asian martial arts and medical practices.

But it's not just an Eastern thing. Western philosophers from Heraclitus to Hegel have been fascinated by the notion of dialectical interplay.

Couples are things whole and not whole, what is drawn
together and what is drawn asunder, the harmonious
and discordant. The one is made up of all things, and all
things issue from the one.

HERACLITUS

The dialectic interplay is even found in Christianity; for example, in
the writings of the scholastic philosopher Nicholas of Cusa who spoke
of God as *coincidentia oppositorum*—"the falling together of opposites."

But perhaps most important of all, binary contrast, "born in-
betweenness," and mutual cancellation are fundamental to the mathematics we most commonly use to model the natural world—the
complex numbers system. The complex numbers are an intricate inter-
weaving involving *three* flavors of binary contrasts, each with its own
neutral canceled state. The first contrast is step forward versus step
back (complex addition). The second contrast is stretch out versus pull
in (the dilation aspect of complex multiplication). The third contrast
is turn right versus turn left (the rotational aspect of complex multiplication). The vast majority of functions that scientists use to describe
the physical world arise from the interplay of those contrasts. So they
are, in a sense, "born in between" those contrasts.

For another example, consider the genetic code. Tear the DNA apart,
and it basically contains a sequence of yeses and noes in a certain order.
DNA contains a code of yeses and noes that, when expressed in a body,
can genetically program a dog. Your computer operates by storing
yeses and noes as high and low voltages. The physicist John Wheeler
famously conjectured: "It [the cosmos] from bit [binary information]."
The noooo that is beyond yes and no is what happens when all the
yeses and all the noes line up and cancel out. A dog or any other particular activity of consciousness is what happens when the yeses and
noes polarize, when they push and pull to mold a dog into existence:
pushing out to create a nose, pulling in to open the nostrils, pushing
out to create ears, pulling in to make a mouth, stretching down and
back to form legs and a tail, puffing out plumply to manifest a belly,
and so on. This is the activity called (perceiving a) dog.

When this interplay of opposites comes to an end, when the wave reaches completeness, it flatlines into a moment of absolute nothing. This could be called Zero, or the Unborn. If you wanted to use the vocabulary of Patanjali's *Yoga Sutras,* it would be called *nirodha,* or cessation. This is how the *Yoga Sutras* begin: *"Yoga is the cessation of the fluctuations of consciousness. Then and only then does the true observer abide in its true nature."* This cessation of consciousness is called emptiness, *shunyata,* or zero in Buddhism.

But the best way to come to that cessation is to fully participate in each ordinary experience by quickly and loudly saying "Yes!" at the instant of its arising. For example, when you look at a flower or hear a bell or play with a dog, you so fully give your awareness to it that there is no time to fixate that awareness into a thing. When awareness is unfixated, you don't have nouns like flower, bell, or dog. You have the activity called flower, or the activity called bell, or the activity called dog. When that activity completes itself, watch where it goes. All the contrasts gather together and cancel out, and there is time out of time. Zero. Gone. A momentary cessation of the fluctuations of consciousness.

> At the still point of the turning world.
>   Neither flesh nor fleshless;
> Neither from nor towards; at the still point,
>   there the dance is,
> But neither arrest nor movement.
>   And do not call it fixity,
> Where past and future are gathered.
>   Neither movement from nor towards,
> Neither ascent nor decline. Except for the point,
>   the still point,
> There would be no dance, and there is only the dance.
>   T. S. ELIOT, "BURNT NORTON"

However, that cessation doesn't last. It's inherently unstable because it's made out of yes and no, expansion and contraction, yang and yin. At any instant, it can spontaneously repolarize.

If you are paying attention to your experiences, you'll begin to notice how experiences are molded by affirmation and negation, by pushing out and pulling in, by expansion and contraction. Give yourself to that pushing out and pulling in, totally and utterly until you become that pushing out and pulling in. Don't be afraid to let it tear you apart. Don't worry. It may kill you *as a noun,* but it will give you life as a verb. You become the doing of you, the activity called you.

When you are just the activity of you, everything you got from father-god you graciously return to father-god. Everything you got from mother-god you graciously return to mother-god. Now there is nothing in between to prevent the two halves of God from reuniting. The meditator disappears. The true observer, who doesn't exist inside time and space, appears. But the true observer doesn't need to observe or be observed. It's the ultimate simplicity, a kind of dimensionless, unfixated point that is the groundless ground. It's not any particular place because it gives rise to each particular place: the place of the dog, the place of the tree, the place of your room, the place of this book, and so on.

The two sides of this activity are the two right answers to the koan "Does the dog have the Buddha-nature?" To answer it, you have to be in contact with both sides of the Buddha-nature—the side that polarizes and manifests the activity of dog and the side that neutralizes and manifests Zero. The former is the "Yes" that involves both yes and no; the latter is the "No" that is neither yes nor no.

Impermanence

I know both from my own practice and from teaching others that this model of Buddha-nature fits well with the facts of experience and can bring you to an earthshaking sense of freedom and fulfillment. It is a kind of theory of everything, if we take everything to mean every experience that a human being can have.

Although this philosophy that sees the activity of the Source in terms of a pair of complementary doings is found all over the world, describing impermanence in terms of the two principles of expansion and contraction was not the way the Buddha himself taught. When you look carefully, however, you can see that it is implicitly there. Rather than expansion and contraction, early Buddhism uses the expression *udaya* ("arising") and *vyaya* ("passing"). And usually, in the vipassana tradition, that's how you get insight into impermanence—you watch things arise and pass, arise and pass.

Since the terms *arising* and *passing* already exist in Theravada Buddhism, you may wonder why I bother with expansion and contraction. The reason is that the terms *expansion* and *contraction* give us a broader, more general paradigm to work with because we can think of them as fundamental forces or qualities. This can be very helpful when we meditate on seemingly stable phenomena, things that don't seem to be arising or passing.

For example, when a sensation seems rock solid and, no matter how carefully we investigate it, doesn't seem to change at all, we might think that there is no impermanence there; there is absolutely no change whatsoever; there's no arising or passing; it's sitting still. But the expansion-contraction model allows us to analyze it in a different way.

Basically, there are two kinds of tensions or solidity that one encounters in meditation practice: tensions that we can intentionally relax, and tensions that we cannot intentionally relax. For the former, I recommend relaxing them and, if need be, continually re-relaxing them. The reason for my recommendation is that sustaining global relaxation represents a simple and tangible way to create equanimity.

But what about the other kinds of tensions, those that we cannot intentionally relax? They can be quite uncomfortable, but they do have a silver lining, so to speak. They represent, in an observable way, deeply held limiting forces within us. The trick is to welcome unrelaxable tensions with as much equanimity as possible. That will allow for optimal purification. The expansion and contraction paradigm can help here.

If a phenomenon is solid, unchanging, and uncomfortable, that's because there are pressure forces involved. Either there is a pressure force trying to push out, or a pressure force trying to pull in, or there is both a force moving out and a force moving in at exactly the same time. Even though the phenomenon doesn't change, you may still be able to detect the underlying polarized pressure forces of expansion and contraction within it.

In solidity, the two oppositely directed pressure forces bang against each other, causing coagulation and suffering. What to do? Bring equanimity to it! But how? Think of equanimity as giving the expansion permission to expand and giving the contraction permission to contract, *even though that may temporarily make the discomfort worse.* Expansion and contraction crash against each other over and over, but if you give each of them permission to "do its thing," at some point, they sort of interdigitate; that is, they pass through each other. Painful pressure turns into blissful gush and gather.

When things solidify, when there's pressure in body, mind, sight, or sound, people have a tendency to blame themselves: "*I'm* resisting." "*I* can't let go." Expansion and contraction give us a different way to think about pressure and solidity. It doesn't have to be about you at all; it's about two impersonal forces eventually learning how to mutually interpenetrate without mutually interfering. Relating to unrelaxable solidity in this way can help you to develop equanimity.

This paradigm allows you to contact impermanence even with phenomena that seem to be permanent. Things that don't move still show us anicca in disguise. If we look very carefully, we will see that the two elements of impermanence—expansion and contraction—are there, but they are there as *forces* rather than as movements.

So working with solidity is a practical application of the expansion-contraction paradigm. Far more important, however, is how this paradigm helps us avoid a classic potential pitfall in mindfulness practice—the "observer trap."

When we talk about observing arising and passing, it could imply that there is a separate observer who is watching the arising and passing. You, the fixated observer, sit over here, watching the arising and passing occurring over there. This sense of being an observer is good at first, because, initially, you need a meditating self to implement a technique. But in the end, it is a trap, because if the observer gets fixated, it becomes a kind of ego identity. The arising and passing is in a sense "flat" and objectified.

Expansion-contraction, on the other hand, is round and encompassing. It rips away your center of gravity, breaking down the sense of an observer fixated in some specific place. Expansion, the father, spreads out to the right, to the left, front and back, above and below. Wherever we might try to fixate our sense of self, it is going to be yanked away from us. Contraction, the mother, pulls in from the right, from the left, front and back, above and below, but not to any specific point. This unfixated center of gravity becomes a new ordering principle that holds us safe in a motherly embrace.

Our usual sense of order involves fixating some point as the center of our being and establishing a boundary to form the border of our being. But because expansion and contraction are all-pervasive, they won't let us fixate a center or maintain a border. We have to completely let go and get pulled into that Flow, then we become that Flow—we become father and mother.

From Sensation to Source

Now let's look at how to use this concept in actual meditation practice. Really experiencing it for yourself is the only way to pass the koan, to understand Joshu's noooo.

Let's say that you are meditating, and you become aware that you have a pain in your leg. You pay close attention to this pain, get a very clear sense of its shape, watch how its intensity may vary, let your awareness sort of float and circulate within it. At some point, you notice that sensation begins to soften a little and becomes more like a jellyfish, sort of puffing out here and pulling in there, like a two-dimensional surface that is waving in and out.

Then, as you penetrate more deeply into that, you realize that each time something puffs up or wells up, inside that welling up are small vibrations. The welling up is nothing but a whole bunch of tiny vibrations. Then those vibrations die down, that whole region of the sensation subsides, and this brings an insight. You get a very clear perception that two scales of impermanence are happening simultaneously: a stately undulatory movement, and within each undulation a more rapid vibratory movement.

As you pay even closer attention, you start to notice something that is quite subtle. When the upwelling takes place, there are actually two oppositely directed movements, one pushing out and one pulling in, and they arise at exactly the same time and with more or less equal strength—*simultaneous* and *equal* expansion and contraction. As these oppositely directed forces move, one at the core of the arising pulling in and one at the perimeter pushing out, they produce vibrations in between them. The vibrations come about because of the polarization of these two forces.

You can experience this quite tangibly in something as ordinary as your smile. If you really pay attention to what it feels like when you smile, you can feel the muscles contracting, while at the same time the quality of pleasure around the smile is expanding and spreading. You can feel a contractive core in the smile and an expansive perimeter simultaneously.

You can also detect this concurrent expansion-contraction in your breath. When you breathe in, the chest expands, but at the same time, the intercostal muscles are contracting. You can feel the expansion of your chest in terms of its volume, while all round there is a contraction of the muscles. When you breathe out, the chest collapses or contracts in volume, but you can feel it is expanding in the sense that all the muscles relax and stretch. You can actually feel those polarizations of expansion and contraction going on in everyday experiences like the breath and your smile. It's not something esoteric or remote; it's everywhere and in everything.

You can observe it in your thinking, too. When your mind is scattered, you sense your thoughts going in many directions at once. That scattering is expansive. At the same time, you feel an urge to somehow gather them together, to find the central point of those thoughts. This urge to "get to the point" is contractive. So thought is born in between the gushing and gathering of space.

Zen people say that the ordinary mind is the way, the ordinary mind is the Tao. What is the ordinary mind? The ordinary mind is constantly scattered in many directions and cannot hold a center. We think this monkey-mind experience is awful. People feel tormented by this ceaseless turning of the mind. But when you look beneath surface appearances, the scattering can be interpreted as space effortlessly spreading, and the inability to hold a center could be looked upon as contraction gobbling up the solid ground beneath you.

We are so preoccupied with determining the specific meaning of thought that we suffer because we can't look at it in terms of its universal movement. Because we somehow feel we have to extract meaning from this motion, we suffer. But if we are willing to just let the mind scatter and pull in at the same time, letting go of any need to make meaning, we reframe the situation. It's just another spontaneous space fountain, gushing and gathering. This puts us in contact with the universal meaning that underlies the meaning of every thought. It's the meaning of a flower, the meaning of a galaxy.

If you stay with that experience, you will notice that, at some point, the part that was pushing out isn't pushing out anymore, and the part that was pulling in isn't pulling in anymore. It's as if they commingle—the positive and the negative, the plus and the minus, the expansive and contractive—and mutually cancel, and that is when all the waves and little wavelets die away. They flatline, and in that cancellation is an experience of absolute rest—nirodha, a moment of nirvana, the peace of God's own heaven.

Then suddenly you become aware that the forces are pulling apart again. Expansion is pulling out; contraction is pulling in. Once again, vibration is born in between the two. This vibration came from the flatline breaking up. The canceled state of the universe has again polarized into a contrast of expansion and contraction, and absolute rest disappeared for a moment—it broke up its two halves: plus and minus, efflux and reflux.

Continue to observe. Once again, the half that is pushing out stops pushing out, and the half that is pulling in stops pulling in. The two come together, and there is another moment of earth-shattering tranquility, what in the Christian tradition is called the peace that passeth understanding.

And you come to realize that every experience is just another cycle of bliss. Even the sense of a material body experiencing pain goes away, and it is replaced by this rhythm of polarizing, vibrating, neutralizing peace, polarizing, vibrating, neutralizing peace, over and over again. It's effortless effervescence alternating with earthshaking peace. That's what the pain really was all along! This leads to a major shift in your understanding. Eventually, you switch from identifying with the *content* of experience to identifying with the *contour* of experience.

When you start to meditate, it seems like your mind and body are the abiding background, and within them, you are having various sensory experiences. But at some point, a striking figure-ground reversal takes place. Your mind and body become a transient figure, and the field of impermanence becomes the abiding ground. For a moment, you shift from identifying with the mind and body, which are the product of that field, to identifying with the field itself. For a period of time you un-become the product of impermanence, and you re-identify with impermanence itself. Impermanence viewed this way could also be called spirit or even soul.

That is a profound change in your fundamental perspective of things. It seems as if you are participating in the activity of the Source. You become the Source; you realize that you are the Source. You realize that you are not your mind and body, you are the Source of your mind and body, which is also the Source of all minds and all bodies.

You probably began meditation practice by learning to hold one thing, the in- and out-breath of your body, for example. Hopefully, at some point, you will experience being held by the Source of all things, the in- and out-breath of the universe.

When you have a complete thought—meaning that you pay close attention from beginning to end, allowing the thought to demonstrate its Flow qualities—that thought contains all the meanings in the universe. That may sound extreme, but since everything comes about through a polarization of expansion and contraction, any particular thing that you experience in these terms is linked to all things. The expansion and contraction in your thought is no different than the expansion and contraction that makes atoms vibrate, that makes stars pulsate. There are two forces that drive a star: the force of self-gravity that pulls the star inward, and the force of thermal pressure pushing outward. In between those two forces, the star lives its life, fusing new atomic elements into existence with each cycle of expansion and contraction.

As long as stars expand and contract, then you also will be expanding and contracting, because you too are this fundamental movement of the universe. The whole universe—your inner and outer sensory experience—comes from the Source and returns to the Source, moment by moment. Although your mind and body will someday pass away, once you have had this experience of returning to the Source, you'll identify somewhat less with that mind and body. Even though you are just a separate individual—who has certain thoughts and feelings, certain goals, certain bad habits, and certain desires—you realize that you are also none other than the activity of the entire universe.

As long as the fundamental forces of the universe act, as long as there is affirmation and negation, as long as anything breathes, as long as Zero polarizes and neutralizes, as long as matter and antimatter come out of nothing and return to nothing, the real you continues to live.

Zero

The ancient Taoists had the right idea with yang and yin, but they were missing a major piece, because ancient Chinese civilization didn't have the concept of the number zero. That was introduced later from India. The only way Joshu could express the cancellation of positive and negative, the mutual annihilation of yes and no, was to say "noooo." But with modern mathematics, we can call it zero instead.

Just as expansion and contraction have many other names, such as plus-minus and yang-yin, Gone can also be called by other names: the unborn, the witness, the true self, no self, emptiness, the peace of heaven. Some of these seem to contradict each other, but they are all referring to the same experience: the rich and fulfilling nothingness from which each something arises and to which it returns. Standard Buddhism calls it emptiness, but another possible name is zero. In English, the two terms are more related than they appear to be. In Sanskrit the mathematical number zero is called *shunya,* and in Mahayana philosophy, the word translated as "emptiness" is *shunyata* (literally "zero-ness").

People are often put off by the Buddhist philosophy of emptiness, but emptiness is not empty—it's rich and springy. It contains the entire universe, collapsed into a canceled state, zero. Because zero is made up of everything, it has the possibility to create anything.

You can arrive at zero in a lot of different ways, which in turn give different experiences. The experience of nothing is path dependent, so to speak. The path you take to zero can either be bleak and a bummer, or rich and vibrant. You can have an experience of emptiness just by ignoring things, but that is not a very rich experience. On the other hand, if you get to emptiness by the path of simplification, you understand why many mystics have chosen to describe God as a special kind of nothing. Mindfulness is the path of simplification.

In mindfulness, the complexity of sensory experience is reduced through progressively deeper unifications. No matter how big, complex, or overwhelming experiences may be, in mindfulness, we learn to break them down into the simplicity of the six senses (inner and outer visual, auditory, and somatic experience). In other words, by analyzing experience into its sensory components, we can reduce the ten trillion somethings of the world to combinations and subdivisions of just six sensory elements.

But that is by no means the ultimate simplification. Next, you further simplify the senses by experiencing them in terms of impermanence, or Flow. That is much simpler than six senses. But impermanence itself has many different guises or flavors—undulation, vibration, pixilation, scintillation, spiking, collapsing. Eventually, however, you realize that the various flavors of impermanence all arise from the interplay of just two flavors: expansion and contraction. So you've reduced everything down to just those two.

But things can become even further simplified. Sometimes you are primarily aware of expanding; sometimes you are primarily aware of contracting; sometimes you are aware that both are present at the same time. But if you look very carefully, you'll realize that any arising entails both. And at the point of vanishing, those Two *Doings* merge into the One Nothing, which is the simplest state of all: Zero, the Source, Joshu's noooo.

Then the cycle continues. The One Nothing breaks into the Two Doings, and the Two Doings give birth to the ten trillion somethings. But you realize that no matter what sorts of things arise between the two hands of God, they are always directly touched by those two hands. The Two Doings are a kind of umbilical cord that connect the ten trillion somethings of the world with the One Nothing that is the Source of the world. For a liberated person, that umbilical cord is never totally severed. This is true nondual awareness. It's not just the oneness of inside and outside, it's the oneness of form and formless, the direct contact of creation with creator. To experience this throughout the day, is to achieve what some Christians call the practice of the presence of God, and what the Jewish tradition calls *shiviti Hashem l'negdi tamid,* which might loosely be rendered as "be face-to-face with God all day."

But there is a further subtlety about zero. In point of fact, you never actually experience zero; you never experience emptiness; you never experience the cancellation of expansion and contraction. That would seem to contradict everything I just wrote, but this is where the subtlety lies. In the actual moment of cancellation, there is no self to know the Source. Thus, there is no experience there; it is nirodha, extinction. There's nobody there to have an experience.

However, in the very next instant, the self returns and looks back at the moment of Gone that just happened. It creates an image of that moment, and words to describe that moment, and it feels fulfillment, safety, peace, and love as the result of that moment. But that image and those words and those feelings are not zero itself, they are a sort of after-representation of zero. In fact, enlightenment is simply the ability to formulate a clear sensory representation of the formless state that immediately precedes each experience of form. Thus, enlightened wisdom is a kind of illusion, in the sense that it's composed of thought and feeling. It's just another conditioned event, not the unconditioned state itself. However, it's different from other conditioned events in that it *represents* something that is unconditioned. As your enlightenment deepens, you become clearer and clearer about what happens just before time, space, self, and world arise, and you come to a clearer and clearer realization that you *are* what happens just before time, space, self, and world arise.

It's important not to identify with wisdom mind. The actual moment of Gone is not experienced by anyone; what you experience is afterglow. You never directly experience God. You only experience the afterglow of God. That may sound like a letdown, but it's not, not at all. Each day is peppered with a holy glow.

More about Dissolution

In meditation practice, we learn to follow the senses back to where they come from, which reveals where we ourselves come from. With commitment to practice, and the guidance of competent instructors, most people can eventually have that experience. It's a good process, but it's not necessarily always a pleasant process. Sometimes it can be somewhat destabilizing.

Depending upon various factors—such as psychological disposition, early conditioning, genetics, random chance—some people experience significant instability along the journey from surface to Source.

For example, things might become quite chaotic, and it seems like you are literally being torn apart, like you are being ground up, like you are exploding and being crushed at the same time. Not everybody goes through this sense of utter chaos, but quite a few people do have to experience at least a little disorientation and fear before they get to primordial order. We call this process *bhanga*, the Sanskrit word for dissolution.

If it should happen that everything seems to be falling apart, that it seems like you are being torn apart, well, in fact you are. Your parents are tearing you apart. It sounds ghastly, I know—not a very politically correct way of talking. As offensive and inscrutable as this language is, when you find yourself being blown away and crushed, flooded and decentered, it can be helpful to know that these forces are in fact your parents in disguise. It is God, not the devil, that is tearing you apart. You can trust it.

There are two sides to bhanga: the pleasant side and the unpleasant side. The pleasant side feels like blissful bubbles and vibrations all over you. It's somewhat like runner's high, but more intense and pleasurable. After you're done exercising, you can have a runner's high that feels like your whole body is shimmering. If you have concentration power and great somatic resolution, and you tune in to this experience, you'll see that runner's high is actually a sort of subtle bubbly Flow, which is your body showing you its impermanent nature. Most people experience runner's high as a general state of euphoria. That's because they don't have the capacity to observe somatic sensations at high resolution. But if you really tune in, you can see that it's impermanence in the form of shimmering vibratory Flow. Some people pass through a stage in meditation where that vibratory Flow utterly inundates not only their body but also their mind. And then it spreads out into external sight and sound, and everything turns into this scintillating, bubbly field of energy. When it's like this, dissolution is a very blissful experience.

On the other hand, dissolution can be a very harsh and jarring experience, in which it seems like your mind can't make sense of anything. Your intellect is being torn from you. Your center of gravity is being ripped away. Your borders are being violated. There's no way you can be comfortable in the mind or the body. There are only two ways you can get any comfort at all. One is equanimity, meaning a kind of acceptance of the situation. The other is by contacting the underlying forces that are tearing you apart. You are being blown away and crushed. Blown away means expansion, crushed means contraction. If you know what to look for and are able to give yourself simultaneously to father and mother, surrender to the forces of ripping and pounding. Those forces eventually evolve into a delicious, gentle stretching and squeezing.

If it seems like you are dropping into scary states of chaos as you are meditating, understand that that's a stage some people have to go through. Take equanimity and impermanence as your refuge and try to get with the program. Understand that your ordinary ordering principle is being ripped away—the body cannot get comfortable, the mind cannot get answers—but a new ordering principle, which is much deeper, is in the process of revealing itself.

To repeat, not everybody goes through dramatic bhanga experiences. Some people do this path with blissful dissolutions. For some people, this path is composed of a mixture of blissful and not-so-blissful dissolution. Many people never go through a bhanga stage; they just drop into freedom.

In 1948, the Anglo-American T. S. Eliot was awarded a Nobel Prize in Literature for his contribution to modern-day poetry, including a relatively short poetic work entitled *Four Quartets*. Although it covers a range of topics, the main theme is what I refer to as the "awkward intermediate zone."

The awkward intermediate zone is a stage that some meditators pass through wherein the old coping mechanism (tighten up and turn away) is in the process of being shed, but the new coping mechanism (open up and turn toward) is not yet strong enough to provide abiding safety and fulfillment. Here's a poetic description of that from Eliot's "Little Gidding":

> Midwinter spring is its own season
> Sempiternal though sodden towards sundown,
> Suspended in time, between pole and tropic.
> When the short day is brightest, with frost and fire,
> The brief sun flames the ice, on pond and ditches,
> In windless cold that is the heart's heat,
> Reflecting in a watery mirror
> A glare that is blindness in the early afternoon.
> And glow more intense than blaze of branch, or brazier,
> Stirs the dumb spirit: no wind, but pentecostal fire
> In the dark time of the year. Between melting and freezing
> The soul's sap quivers. . . .
>
> Where is the summer, the unimaginable
> Zero summer?

"Between melting and freezing / The soul's sap quivers" nicely describes the alternating cycle of solidification and flow that some people go through in the intermediate stages of their practice. When that happens, the student is encouraged to greet both the rocky tension and the luscious bliss with the same response—equanimity. This optimizes progress.

Although influenced by Buddhism and Hinduism, Eliot's primary allegiance was to Christianity. In the *Four Quartets,* Eliot describes dissolution by way of poignant Christian symbolism: he compares it to being in a hospital staffed by the Holy Trinity. The Three Persons operate on the patient's soul, excising the sin, removing the blocks to beatitude. Eliot's view of Christianity was essentially medieval, a view I share: the mystic is anyone who is willing to experience purgatory in this life. The reward is a direct and abiding glimpse of heaven in this life. Here's how he describes God's hospital.

> The wounded surgeon plies the steel
> That questions the distempered part;
> Beneath the bleeding hands we feel
> The sharp compassion of the healer's art
> Resolving the enigma of the fever chart.
>
> Our only health is the disease
> If we obey the dying nurse
> Whose constant care is not to please
> But to remind of our, and Adam's curse,
> And that, to be restored, our sickness must grow worse.
>
> The whole earth is our hospital
> Endowed by the ruined millionaire,
> Wherein, if we do well, we shall
> Die of the absolute paternal care
> That will not leave us, but prevents us everywhere.
>
> The chill ascends from feet to knees,
> The fever sings in mental wires.
> If to be warmed, then I must freeze
> And quake in frigid purgatorial fires
> Of which the flame is roses, and the smoke is briars.

"Flame is roses, and the smoke is briars" nicely summarizes the mix of agony and ecstasy that some practitioners experience during the dissolution process.

The Source of Us All

Does the dog have the Buddha-nature? What is your answer to this koan? The answer is to participate in the activity of your Source. But your Source is also everyone's Source. To the extent that you contact your Source, you contact everybody's Source, the formless womb which expands and contracts, loving self and other into and out of being.

What do we call someone with whom we shared a womb? We call them a sibling. In Greek, the word for sibling is *adelphos,* which means literally "from the same womb." We have all been birthed into existence by the same formless womb, and therefore, we are all siblings. When you allow yourself to be pulled back to the Source, to drop to the groundless ground, your happiness is no longer dependent on the vagaries of conditions. But returning to the Source is not *just* for that. It's not only something we do for ourselves. When you realize your Source, you have no choice but to see everyone as a close relative. Each time you interact with another person, you experience both yourself and that person being loved into existence by the Source. It's not a belief or an emotion, but a direct sensory experience that's always there. So it's easy and natural to care for others. In the end, Master Joshu's noooo calls us to a life of spontaneous service.

CHAPTER ELEVEN

My Happiest Thought

It is quite possible that in contact with western science,
and inspired by the spirit of history, the original
teaching of Gautama, revived and purified, may yet play
a large part in the direction of human destiny.

H. G. WELLS

H. G. Wells wrote those words in 1920 in his classic opus *The Outline of History*. Eighty-five years later, in 2005, the Society for Neuroscience made an unprecedented invitation. They asked the Dalai Lama of Tibet to be the keynote speaker at their annual meeting. The Dalai Lama's participation ignited a firestorm of controversy, some of which was motivated by political concerns outside the scope of science, but some of which involved the legitimate issue of whether someone representing a spiritual philosophy should be anointed with an aura of credibility by the scientific establishment. Although I was not there myself, I have been told that the Dalai Lama charmed many of the thousands of hard-nosed scientists who participated. During one of the question and answer sessions, one of them pointedly asked the Dalai Lama something like: "If I developed a purely physical surgical procedure that would result in spiritual awakening, as a Buddhist spokesperson, what would be your position on that?" The Dalai Lama replied, "I would want to be the first person in line to receive that surgery!"

When I returned to the United States from Japan, I set for myself a sequence of three goals for the rest of my life, with each goal more ambitious than its predecessor. Goal number one was to reformulate the path to enlightenment in a modern, secular, and science-based vocabulary. I wanted to create a system completely free from the cultural trappings and doctrinal preconceptions of traditional Buddhism yet capable of bringing people to classical enlightenment. In my opinion, I have made significant strides toward creating such a system. (You can find a detailed description of it at unifiedmindfulness.com.) What you've been reading here *reflects* that system but is still somewhat framed in the traditional language of Buddhism.

My second goal was to develop a fully modern delivery system that would make the practice of that path available to any person in the world, regardless of where they may live, what their work or familial responsibilities may be, what their health situation may be, or what their financial situation may be. I believe my monthly conference call–based home practice program has made that feasible. (It can also be accessed at unifiedmindfulness.com.)

My third goal was to help develop a technology of enlightenment—a science-based intervention powerful enough to make enlightenment readily available to the majority of humanity. Such a science-based technology is yet to be developed and most likely will not be developed in my lifetime. My "happiest thought" is the key concept that makes that goal feasible.

I got the phrase "happiest thought" from Albert Einstein. His happiest thought was a conceptual breakthrough that allowed him to develop the theory of general relativity. The thought was this: gravitational fields and accelerating frames are essentially the same thing. An example of an accelerating frame would be an elevator as it begins to lift you. When it's gaining speed, for a few seconds you experience yourself getting heavier as if the force of earth's gravity were increasing. That effect goes away when the elevator attains a constant speed—when the frame is no longer accelerating. The opposite effect occurs when you taste a bit of weightlessness as the elevator initially descends.

The significance of this insight—gravitational fields are equivalent to accelerating frames—may not be immediately evident to the nonspecialist, but for Einstein, the implications were earthshaking. It allowed him to apply the results of special relativity to issues regarding the nature of gravity. For example, to correctly predict that the presence of a gravitational field will affect the rate at which a clock ticks. This broader paradigm is referred to as general relativity. According to general relativity, matter and space are linked in a nonlinear dance: space is curved by matter, but matter flows along the curve of space. Einstein's happiest thought allowed him to create a revolutionary new science that fundamentally changed humanity's perspective on the nature of physical reality. If correct, my happiest thought will fundamentally change humanity's perspective on the nature of spiritual reality.

Here's my happiest thought: *most likely, there are things that are true and important about enlightenment that neither the Buddha nor any of the great masters of the past knew, because to know them requires an understanding of modern science.*

Enlightenment and Innovation

Buddhist tradition has long held that Prince Siddhartha Gautama was not the only Buddha. Prior to him, there had been Buddhas, and in later ages, there will be other Buddhas. Buddhist mythology tells us that the next Buddha will be named Maitreya. It is said that he now abides in one of the heavenly realms known as the Tushita Heaven, from which he contemplates the world, trying to figure out the best way to enlighten all beings.

Interestingly, Maitreya is the only Buddhist archetype who demonstrates what might be considered a somewhat Western body language. Traditionally, he is portrayed sitting in a chair with one elbow on his knee, one leg crossed on the other, one leg dangling from the chair, his cheek supported by one hand, as if engaged in discursive thought. His eyes are depicted as looking down, as if surveying the condition of the world below the heaven where he resides. The iconography is in striking contrast to the standard yogic representation of Buddhist archetypes, who sit in full or half lotus, hands joined in a symmetric gesture, and consciousness withdrawn into nondiscursive, formless states. If anything, the traditional iconography of Maitreya is reminiscent of Rodin's famous sculpture *The Thinker*. The difference is that Maitreya has better posture, and his eyes are open looking at the world, because he is thinking about the next way to bring enlightenment to humanity.

Maitreya could be thought of as the next great friend to humanity, as his name indicates. Maitreya literally means "the friendly one," derived from the Sanskrit stem *mitra* ("friend"). This word is also the basis for the word *metta,* which is usually translated as lovingkindness but literally means "friendliness."

Buddhist tradition also states that there are individuals whose enlightenment is the equal of a Buddha in terms of depth of wisdom (prajna), depth of purification (vishuddhi), and impeccability of behavior (*sila*). A person who is equal to a Buddha in regard to wisdom, purification, and conduct is called a "worthy," which in Sanskrit is *arhat* (if he is a man) or *arhati* (if she is a woman). Among the disciples of the historical Buddha were numerous arhats and arhatis. It would seem then that a Buddha is a special case of a "worthy." So a natural question is, given that their enlightenment, purification, and conduct are on the same level, what is the difference between a Buddha and a "mere" arhat?

According to the Buddhist tradition, the Buddha was a *creative* arhat—an arhat whose creativity was of such power and relevance that the whole world changed as the result of his spiritual discoveries. Put in other terms, a Buddha is a deeply enlightened being who discovers something new about the nature of enlightenment and whose discovery leads to a dramatic increase in enlightenment in the world.

Certainly, this was true of Prince Siddhartha Gautama, the historical person who became known as the Buddha. Prior to his time, people in India had gotten enlightenment through some combination of high concentrative practices and ascetical practices. The Buddha took the spiritual technology that existed in his time, reformulated it and refined it, and added new elements. He discovered that you could use sensory clarity to analyze I-am-ness into its components and that this leads to freedom from the limited identity. This was definitely an innovative notion and formed the basis of mindfulness practice. He also reformulated the ascetic paradigm of "the more it hurts, the more it purifies" to "the more equanimity you apply, the more it purifies." He referred to this distinctive approach as the Middle Way. These and other innovations of the Buddha propagated throughout India and the rest of Asia, profoundly altering the course of human history.

The idea that sometime in the future someone like Maitreya will appear in the human realm and revitalize the dharma seems reasonable to me. *However, my view of how it might happen differs from the traditional view in several significant ways.* The traditional view is that the teachings of each Buddha are new, but not revolutionary. They are essentially similar to the teachings of the last Buddha and all preceding Buddhas, because there is only one perennial truth that needs to be rediscovered from time to time. But my view is somewhat different. My view is that the teachings of the next Buddha will indeed harmonize with those of the Buddhas and masters of the past, but may in fact be radically innovative.

This view is based on how science grows with time. Einstein's formulation of physics harmonizes with that of Newton, but reframes Newton's discoveries within a broader, deeper, and more accurate paradigm. The jump from Newtonian physics to modern physics is huge. If we imagine a dialogue between Newton and Einstein, no doubt Newton would, at first, be shocked by Einstein's claims, but after sufficiently deep and patient dialoging, he would realize that Einstein's view harmonized with and built upon his own.

I imagine that the Buddha of the future, Maitreya, may discover a paradigm that on the surface appears to be quite different from traditional Buddhist teachings, but after sufficiently deep and patient dialoging would be revealed to be both in harmony with and building upon Siddhartha Gautama's discoveries. The teachings of the next Buddha will also probably be based not merely upon looking from within (first-person perspective), but on some combination of looking from within *and* looking from without (combined first- and third-person perspectives). In other words, the next Buddha will have an internal practice, but will also utilize the discoveries of external, objective science.

Finally, there is a third way in which my concept of Maitreya differs from the traditional one. Traditionally, it is assumed that the Buddha-to-come will be an individual. I imagine that Maitreya will not be an individual enlightened being, but a *team* of enlightened beings, most of whom will be scientists, specifically neuroscientists. This team would use the power of post-twentieth-century science, combined with the depth of their personal experiences, to formulate a radically innovative paradigm for what enlightenment is and how to get there.

That new paradigm should have two characteristics. First, it should harmonize with the discoveries of the Buddha and other masters of the past. Second, the innovative part should be powerful enough to alter the course of human history. Here's what I mean: along with a new, neuroscience-based model of enlightenment would presumably come new neuroscience-based technologies that could accelerate the practice of meditation, making classical enlightenment available to a significant percentage of the world's population.

Objections

Sometimes, my happiest thought causes people to freak out. It's not hard to come up with a series of "yeah, but" objections.

One objection that might come from very traditional Buddhists is to remind me that the role of Maitreya is not to create a new version of the dharma, but merely to revive the forgotten truth of the former Buddhas. This objection is interesting and deserves some careful attention. It is based on an assumption about how history works. The assumption is that conditions in the world only deteriorate as time goes on. Conditions started out very good, over time they have slowly gotten bad, and in the future they will get even worse. This notion pervades traditional Indian thinking and also impacts cultures influenced by India through Buddhism.

The idea that the process of history is essentially a process of devolution is of course not unique to India. It was also held by some thinkers in classical Greece. In China, Confucius voiced the same idea. Within the context of Hinduism, this notion takes the form of a belief that history moves through four successive *yugas* (eons), each characterized by the deterioration in the quality of human life. Because Buddhism comes from India, it inherits the traditional Indic view of history: The one true dharma is delivered by a perfect and complete master. Then, as the world situation deteriorates over subsequent centuries and millennia, the dharma deteriorates in three stages. During the last stage, human nature becomes so degenerate that no one can achieve enlightenment anymore, and the dharma is eventually forgotten until the next perfect expositor appears.

The assumption that the march of history can only run downhill is unsupported by evidence. Of course sometimes things do get worse—for example, Europe in the Dark Ages. But modern historiographers recognize that things can also improve. There can be evolution as well as devolution. In fact, futurists assume the exact opposite of the traditional Indic view, namely that, globally, things can only get better and better. Personally, I don't see any strong proof of that either, although I would rather believe the futurist scenario than the "things can only get worse" scenario. Based on history, we can say for sure that sometimes the quality of human life progresses and sometimes it regresses. (Our old friends expansion and contraction again!)

It is true that by the ninth century, European civilization had experienced a catastrophic decline relative to the classical period. However, it is also true that while that was happening in Europe, Islamic civilization was flowering. Furthermore, after a thousand years of backwardness, European civilization experienced a renaissance, the likes of which the world had never seen. And although there is at present an unacceptable disparity in the quality of life among human beings worldwide, it is also true that thanks to post-Renaissance advances in science, medicine, sanitation, agriculture, and so forth, hundreds of millions of human beings are able to enjoy a level of knowledge, power, and convenience that would have been the envy of the kings and emperors of yore. From that perspective, we seem to be in a period of expansive progress. Clearly, the quality of human life does not just go downhill.

So if we look upon the Buddha as an innovator in the technology of enlightenment, then it is certainly reasonable to think that future

Buddhas might do the same thing: take everything known from the past, the approaches to enlightenment that have come down to us from the contemplative traditions of the world, in addition to what modern science knows about the brain, and come up with something radically new and powerful—hopefully something powerful enough to *democratize* enlightenment, making it available to hundreds of millions of human beings instead of the purview of a handful of dedicated adepts.

When I give voice to my happiest thought, people often assume that I am advocating some process that automatically zaps you with enlightenment, circumventing any need for study or practice. There is nothing in my happiest thought that implies that. Even if a new technology-assisted path to enlightenment is developed, it is highly probable that there will still be a need for study and practice. But the amount of study and practice may be reduced to a level that is doable by just about anyone. Perhaps something like a yearlong course at any community college. During that time, a person would study and do focus techniques, in addition to receiving some sort of technology-based aid to their practice. The technologically boosted experience of liberation would be carefully integrated into that person's life.

But even if it were possible to do what I am advocating, would that not cheapen the experience of enlightenment? Isn't it better to do it the old-fashioned way? Indeed a technology-assisted spiritual practice could conceivably cheapen enlightenment, making it in some ways a secular product, like a LASIK surgery for consciousness. However, we have to weigh this undesirable effect against some important considerations. If hundreds of millions of people are able to live their lives ten times larger, I think it is worth the price of a little cheapening and secularizing, or even trivializing. Flying in an airplane is not nearly as graceful, spiritual, or natural as the flight of a bird. It destroys the charm of distance, does away with the richness of land journey—in a sense trivializing travel. But most people would agree that its practical consequences more than compensate for those losses.

I find that many people are quite pessimistic regarding the future: the degradation of the environment, acts of senseless violence, depletion of natural resources, and economic chaos all seem to bode ill for humanity in this century. It is impossible to predict the future, but if the forces of negativity are as deep and widespread as many believe, then it may be the case that humanity's main hope lies in something new and fundamentally different, like a way to democratize enlightenment. If the patient's medical condition is dire, the doctors must consider radical interventions.

Another objection to my happiest thought is that I am advocating something unnatural. But what's unnatural depends on what you choose to call natural. There is a trend of thought in Buddhism, and in many other contemplative traditions, to speak of the enlightened state as natural. This means that the unenlightened state is the unnatural one. What prevents the natural state of enlightenment from being evident are "adventitious impurities" (*agantukakilesa*). The word *adventitious* literally means "coming from the outside," that is, not intrinsic to the system itself.

If I had to make a guess about the nature of a technology that could facilitate the attainment of classical enlightenment, it would be that the technology would *not* somehow zap you with enlightenment. Rather, if anything got zapped, it would be what *gets in the way* of the enlightenment that's already there. If indeed enlightenment is natural and just waiting to happen, then using a technological intervention to restore a natural condition is a natural solution. A technology that eliminates an unnatural condition is, by definition, in harmony with nature.

Possible Directions

When I describe my happiest thought to people, they often ask me if I have any guesses about what kinds of new interventions might arise from the cross-fertilization of science and meditation. I certainly would never claim to make predictions in this regard. However, there are a few directions of research that I think might be promising.

When scientists first began to research which parts of the brain are associated with what functions, they did this largely through studying the effects of brain injuries. The field of functional neuroanatomy experienced a huge leap forward right after World War I because there were so many people with personally tragic but scientifically useful brain injuries. In some cases, scientists were able to figure out what part of the brain performs what job by studying what functions got knocked out when a particular part of the brain was damaged.

It turns out that certain very specific kinds of brain injury seem to knock out the sense of "self as thing." Investigating the mechanism by which this happens might give us insight into the nature of enlightenment. Don't get me wrong here. These traumas are pathologies. Such dysfunctional conditions are certainly *not* an enlightened state. However, some aspects of these conditions seem to imitate or emulate aspects of enlightenment. Since these conditions can be studied neuroanatomically and neurochemically, they may perhaps provide a hint of a direction in which to look in order to find the neurocorrolates of no self.

In her book *My Stroke of Insight,* neuroscientist Jill Bolte Taylor gives a vivid and moving description of how a hemorrhaging in her brain's left hemisphere caused a radical and permanent shift in her state of consciousness. Her description of that shift sounds remarkably similar to the classical mystical experience where inside and outside merge, leading to a sense of freedom from the limited, egoic perspective. After her stroke, Dr. Taylor found herself facing two challenges. The first challenge was to reestablish her ability to function: walking, talking, thinking, and so forth. Her second challenge was to attempt to understand, as a scientist, how this particular form of trauma to the brain could produce such positive results. Some people believe that by diminishing the function of the left hemisphere, the right hemisphere is freed up to present its perspective on reality. Although that might be true, I suspect that the actual situation is more complicated than that. What is important about her case, however, is that it represents a clear example of an enlightenment-like experience arising due to *losing* something at the neuroanatomical level.

Recall my remark about the naturalness of artificial enlightenment. The point I made was that enlightenment will just happen automatically as soon as we eliminate what gets in its way. So perhaps, if you knock out just the correct portion of the brain, it can neuroanatomically eliminate something that is preventing enlightenment.

Dr. Taylor's case involved the left hemisphere. The stroke condition that Dr. Taylor reports would seem in some ways to emulate "stream entry" (also known as kensho, or the initial experience of no self). There is a post-stroke condition that occurs in a different part of the brain, which leads to a condition that produces an even more stunning version of pseudo-enlightenment. This condition seems to emulate the completely selfless state of an arhat! As a meditation teacher, I can tell you that the experience of stream entry is relatively common. You probably know or have met someone who is a stream enterer. On the other hand, arhats—people who have *completely* worked through the egoic perspective—are exceedingly rare. In my entire career, I have met three or four masters who were *perhaps* arhats. I am utterly fascinated by the fact that there is a relatively well-understood form of stroke that induces a sort of a weird caricature of that attainment.

The condition I am referring to is known as athymhormia. Medically it comes about due to tiny and precisely placed bilateral lesions to the basal ganglia of the brain. For example, at the anterior tip of the caudate nuclei. The effects of this condition are both dramatic and strange. The victim essentially loses the ability to bootstrap selfhood from the inside. They just sit hour after hour, day after day, with their eyes open, fully conscious of their surroundings, apparently without any thoughts or desires or sense of suffering. If you activate their sense of self *from the outside* by engaging them in a conversation, they can often respond normally, without cognitive impairment. Furthermore, if you ask them to perform a task they may be able to do so without difficulty at least for a while. But if you don't continually engage them from the outside, they will soon return to a default state of pseudo no self. Doctors find this condition mystifying. When they ask the victims what they think about all day, the answer is nothing. Their mind is simply blank all the time, even when their eyes are open. The other strange thing is that the victims usually don't complain about their situation, or about anything at all for that matter. They do not perceive their obvious dysfunction as problematic. No self, no problem.

I originally read about this condition in an April 2005 *Scientific American* article entitled "Drowning Mr. M." The article contains some remarkable stories. It starts with the description of a man swimming in his pool who suddenly loses all motivation to keep swimming. He is aware that he is sinking to the bottom of the pool, aware that he is breathing water, but has no sense that there is a problem. Then he hears his daughter screaming his name, at which point the notion of self-preservation kicks in again, and he swims his way to the surface. A second story in that article describes a French woman who went to the beach one morning and, as she was sitting in the sun, lost all desire to move to shade. She simply sat in one spot as the sun gradually burnt away several layers of her skin, resulting in massive burns. When asked if she felt the pain of the burning, she said that she felt it all poignantly and intensely, but did not perceive it as a problem!

Clearly, something very dramatic took place within the perceptual mechanism of these patients. A couple of tiny but strategically positioned regions of tissue damage apparently resulted in the elimination of all drivenness and suffering, whether physical or emotional. Once again, don't get me wrong. I'm not saying that these people are enlightened in any sense of that word. Enlightened people are functioning humans who can bootstrap the activity of self from the inside. Arhatship is not a pathology. But the fact that a tiny lesion in the brain can create a state that in some way mimics arhatship, I find utterly fascinating.

It is not hard to imagine that there may be many regions in the brain that play a crucial role in maintaining the limited perspective on identity. Dr. Taylor's stroke and the strokes that underlie athymhormia represent irreversible trauma to cerebral tissue and consequently result in varying degrees of dysfunction. However, it may be possible to *temporarily* and noninvasively suspend the function of such regions, perhaps for a few hours or a few days, allowing a person to get a glimpse of what the non-egoic perspective is like. If such an intervention were preceded by a certain amount of training in concentration skills, it is conceivable that the person could hold on to the non-egoic framework even after the temporary suspension wore off. But, you ask, how would it be possible to safely and reversibly suspend the function of a certain region of the brain for a period of time? Actually, scientists are currently pursuing a wide spectrum of approaches that will make it possible to do precisely that.

Many years ago, a retreat participant left me a note requesting some private meeting time. When we got together, he explained that he was a retired neuroscientist who had been part of the team that had first successfully recorded the electrical activity from within individual neurons. His name was David Stoney, and he had in fact built the glass microelectrodes that were first inserted into a living neuron. When I asked him why he had requested special time to talk, he drew my attention to an article that had recently been published about what was, at that time, a little-known process—transcranial magnetic stimulation (TMS).

TMS involves placing a rather small magnetic coil an inch or so away from a person's head, and then causing a high amperage current to switch directions very rapidly within the coil. A well-known result of basic physics is that a rapidly changing electrical current will create a strong magnetic field around its conductor. That magnetic field can in turn generate a current in any other conductor that happens to be nearby. This is the principle behind microphones, loudspeakers, and adapters. So a precisely placed changing magnetic field can create a pulse of current in a person's brain, causing the functioning of that region of the brain to be temporarily impeded. That's how TMS works.

The scientific article that Dr. Stoney showed me was about treating schizophrenics using TMS. One common symptom of schizophrenia is "hearing voices." Various medications are routinely used to reduce that symptom, but for a certain percentage of schizophrenic patients, those medications do not work. The article discussed an extremely brief TMS stimulation that was done over the part of the left hemisphere known to control external and internal talk. The experimenters claimed that the stimulation resulted in week-long suspension of the "voice in the head" phenomenon for the schizophrenic patients. A single, isolated piece of research like that means relatively little unless it can be reproduced, but as a preliminary result, it was intriguing.

He reminded me that one of the main difficulties for beginning meditators was that they are constantly bombarded by and lost in internal conversations. He wondered if a TMS stimulus might be used to temporarily suspend the talk center in normal people, allowing them to experience what it is like to meditate without all that internal palaver. It occurred to me, though, that something like TMS might be used not just to temporarily cool out mental talk, but to cool out a person's entire sense of self as thing. Perhaps there exists one or several sweet spots in the brain that function as switches to turn on limited identity. If so, a carefully aimed physical stimulus might temporarily turn the switch off. Another possibility would be to have three simultaneous stimuli: one to suspend mental image activity, one to suspend mental talk activity, and a third to cool out the emotional body. Such were some ideas that initially occurred to me during my conversations with Dr. Stoney.

Over the years, I have watched with fascination as interest in TMS research has grown exponentially. The problem with TMS is that it is very difficult to focus the magnetic field narrowly enough to aim it tightly at pivotal structures. But perhaps at some time in the future, it may be possible to temporarily and reversibly induce effects like those reported by Dr. Taylor or the victims of athymhormia, using other more easily aimed modalities: transcranial direct current stimulation (tDCS), focused ultrasound, fine-grained neurofeedback, and such.

The Buddha formulated his path to enlightenment in terms of the four noble truths. Suffering has a necessary cause, meaning that there is a factor whose elimination will eliminate suffering. The Buddha named that factor *trishna,* usually translated as "grasping." He claimed that he had found an intervention which would eliminate trishna, and he called that intervention the Path. The Path consists of sila (ethics), samadhi (concentration power), and prajna (insight). In other words, because the Path is *sufficient* for the elimination of grasping, and because grasping is *required* for there to be suffering, the Path is sufficient for elimination of suffering. Trishna is a characteristic of consciousness, but consciousness arises in the physical matrix of the brain. *Is there a necessary physical condition in the brain that in turn is a necessary condition for the existence of trishna in consciousness?* If so, then there may be a technological intervention that could eliminate the necessary physiological condition in the brain that gives rise to the necessary condition for suffering in general—any and all suffering.

A few years ago, the director of the National Institute on Drug Abuse publicly advocated intensive research on a region of the brain known as the anterior insular cortex. Some believe that this region plays a pivotal role in many, if not all, addictive processes. In other words, it may represent a physical center for trishna. And the director specifically suggested that TMS be used on that region as a general treatment for addiction. If it were to turn out that, instead of being an intervention for addiction, TMS ends up being a general intervention for trishna, then the consequences of this line of research could end up being scientific validation of the Buddhist four noble truths.

The four noble truths are the centerpiece of the historical Buddha's teaching. If we look at the logic structure, it runs something like this: In order for suffering of any type to occur there must be grasping. There is a way to eliminate grasping; therefore, there is a way to eliminate suffering. When suffering is eliminated, a state of non-suffering arises, which the Buddha referred to as nirvana. It is clear from the Buddha's description that nirvana is not just an absence of suffering in the sense of being anesthetized, unconscious, or dead. It is described as a highly positive state of deep fulfillment, empowerment, and freedom from limitation. The implication here is that the elimination of grasping reveals a state of primordial well-being that is always present, albeit hidden to most people.

Thus, if we unfold the logical structure of the four noble truths, the Buddha is, in essence, saying: There is a primordial well-being just waiting to show itself, but it is blocked by a habit of consciousness. There is something you can do to change that habit of consciousness. As soon as you do that, the primordial perfection presents itself automatically.

I find this logical structure very interesting. One of the major themes in science and mathematics is what is known as generalization. Within the context of mathematics and science, generalization does not mean "vagueness," but rather the process by which one goes from a single instance of a truth to a broad perspective that contains that truth as a special case. In the historical Buddha's model, what needs to be eliminated in order for the primordial well-being to appear is specified as "grasping." But in order for grasping to occur, certain neurophysiological events may be required. In other words, if we assume grasping is a necessary condition for suffering, then there may be one or several physiological conditions in the nervous system that are themselves necessary conditions for grasping. If that is indeed the case, then medical or technological interventions become relevant to the Path of Enlightenment.

Viscosity

Let's review. In the traditional Buddhist formulation, trishna is looked upon as a necessary cause for suffering. In a sense, it's the opposite of equanimity. The corresponding word in Japanese is *shujaku,* which literally means "attachment." Sometimes in the context of Japanese Zen, one hears an interesting re-languaging. Some Zen masters substitute the word *kotei* for shujaku. *Kotei* means "fixation" or "coagulation." In this formulation, as soon as one stops fixating the self, suffering and incompleteness go away. Although coagulation sounds similar to the traditional Buddhist notion of grasping, it is not quite the same thing. To me, coagulation sounds a bit more like a physical parameter of the central nervous system, perhaps in some way analogous to friction in a mechanical system, or viscosity in a hydrodynamic system, or resistance in an electrical circuit.

When you look at senior Zen masters or some of the reputed arhats from Southeast Asia, you are immediately struck by their distinctive body language. There is a kind of graceful, "it just happens" quality to their movements, their gaze, and their speech.

All of the great masters that I have ever met had this same distinctive quality. It's so distinctive that you can even spot it at a distance. Once, I was waiting in an airport when I noticed someone in one of the security lines. The person was so far away that I could not identify their race or gender, but I could detect the unfixated quality in the way that they were placing their luggage on the scanner. As I got closer, I noticed he was Asian, probably Chinese. I don't know what got into me, but throwing caution to the wind, I initiated a conversation in Mandarin. Sure enough, it turned out that he was a senior Taoist master from mainland China.

Clearly, something has taken place on a neurophysiological level in such people. Something dramatic has occurred in the way *all* information flows into and the way *all* motor activity flows out of their central nervous system. It's a global change. A dramatic global change such as that should have neural correlates. If we can identify those, we may be able to characterize the "unfixated self" with a mathematical model involving something like a quantifiable coefficient of fixation, analogous to physical coefficients, such as those of turbulence, viscosity, or friction.

How does microfixation arise at the neurophysiological level? I'm not aware of any breakthrough research on this question, but I suspect that the answer could lead to significant practical consequences. Perhaps microfixation has something to do with the delicate timing mechanisms that control the flow of data in and out of the central nervous system. Or perhaps it's related to phase relationships within the thalamic system clocks at the center of the brain. If so, there may be highly sophisticated forms of biofeedback that reset those phase relationships and, thus, eliminate fixation at the deepest level and broadest scope. Or it may have something to do with the brain's ability to erase a data wave quickly, so as not to interfere with the next propagation of data. In other words, in the unenlightened person, the "blackboard" isn't erased quickly enough, and so the brain is constantly microscopically jamming at the millisecond level, creating viscosity.

Recently, neuroscientists have come to identify a physical parameter they call "stickiness," which essentially refers to how long the brain hangs on to an experience before moving on to the next. This quality is related to a phenomenon called the "attentional blink." Perhaps the base level of stickiness in a person's nervous system can be radically reduced through biofeedback or direct intervention. Stickiness is a well-defined physical phenomenon that can be monitored by analyzing a person's EEG signal. Perhaps stickiness is a necessary condition for grasping and, hence, a necessary condition for limited identity and suffering.

Some people say that the four noble truths represent a pessimistic view of things, but I derive a lot of optimism from them. On the surface, the formulation would seem to imply that life sucks, but the deeper implication is that enlightenment, unconditional well-being, is the natural state, just waiting to happen. All we have to do is negate that which is negating it. In other words, you don't have to get enlightenment, all you have to do is *get rid* of what's keeping you from enlightenment. Moreover, it is entirely possible that the unenlightened state requires *many* necessary conditions, and some of them are physiological. All we have to do is eliminate just one of those, *any* of those, and enlightenment will spontaneously show itself. This point of view could be seen as expanding the Buddha's four noble truths into a more general paradigm.

If we were to give scientists the task of creating liberation, it would be a daunting project indeed. On the other hand, if it is true that liberation happens automatically as soon as some necessary condition such as fixation has been eliminated, the project now becomes tractable. All the scientists need to do is identify what's getting in the way and then devise a process to neutralize it.

Perhaps a simple physical example will serve to make the contrast tangible. Creating a house of cards is difficult because one has to go *against* entropy to do so. Eliminating a house of cards is simple: just remove *any one* of the base cards and the house of cards spontaneously tumbles. That's because the tumbling of the house of cards flows *with* entropy. Natural events tend to flow with entropy. If enlightenment is natural, it's reasonable to assume that it flows with entropy. It's more like collapsing a house of cards, less like having to build one.

Another reason people sometimes get upset when I talk about my happiest thought is because they assume I'm claiming more than I actually am. In the field of consciousness studies, it's become common to speak of easy problems and the hard problem. Easy problems are the ones we can settle with the standard methods of science—mapping out neural circuits, monitoring neurotransmitter levels, modeling certain aspects of attention, and so forth. The hard problem is to figure out what consciousness is and how it relates those biophysical processes. Among the so-called easy tasks, the holy grail is to create a complete simulation of the human nervous system as it processes sensory information (including thought) and responds motorically. "Complete" in this case means that the simulation's temporal and spatial resolutions reach down to the finest relevant levels. We might refer to this task as the "hardest easy task." Most neuroscientists are confident that the hardest easy task can be successfully tackled; it's just a matter of time, given how quickly the relevant technology is growing. I suspect that the science of enlightenment I dream of will only arise after the hardest easy task has been resolved. It will probably require that level of biophysical knowledge. Conversely, I strongly suspect that once the hardest easy task has been completed, the biophysical markers of enlightened brains will be clearly evident, and our species will be able to use that information to develop powerful new ways to facilitate freedom. When I say freedom, here I'm referring to the "liberated from mind-body" aspect of the Path. As far as the "be-a-good-person" aspect of the Path goes, well, that's a whole other question—which brings me to my next point of clarification.

When I describe my happiest thought, some people assume that I'm saying that science will explain (or even explain away) enlightenment—"Oh, it's all just electricity and chemicals." But that's not what I'm claiming—not at all. The question of what enlightenment *is* is similar to questions like what the experience of blue is or what the experience of love is or what consciousness is. All of those are part of the other problem, the so-called "hard problem." I don't have a clue as to whether science will solve the hard problem. Fortunately, I don't think we need to solve the hard problem in order to create a science of enlightenment. Solving the hardest of the easy problems will probably be sufficient to give us the spatial and temporal resolutions we need in order to say to the world "Just look! Here's your brain on self. Here's your brain on no self. Get it?!"

Will this then cause all our big global problems to go away? No. But certainly many of them will be solved more effectively and quickly, and problems that seem at this point to be utterly intractable may well turn out to have feasible solutions within a few generations, certainly within a few centuries—which, by Darwinian standards, is a mere wink.

But how about the technology itself? Solving the hardest easy problem might lead to technologies that can effectively enslave people, in addition to possibly setting them free. That's certainly a legitimate concern, but it's part of a different discussion. It's unlikely that anyone is going to prevent neuroscientists from completing the hardest easy task. The new field of neuroethics seeks to address the consequences of this and related developments. A lifetime of meditation has made me an optimist, so I tend to think this powerful knowledge will, in the end, be put to good use—indeed, the best use.

In science, there is a dialectical interplay between fundamental research and practical application. When scientists seek funding from governments, the politicians will often ask what the practical application of their research is. This can be a frustrating experience for the scientist, because politicians may find it hard to understand that numerous powerful but unpredictable applications will arise from a single fundamental breakthrough. There's a parallel here. Enlightenment is to the specific issues of a person's life as fundamental science is to practical applications. If science were to make enlightenment massively available to humanity, we should expect to see numerous and stunning positive improvements in the human situation: dramatic reduction in conflict and violence from the interpersonal level to the international level, reduction in crime and substance addiction, vast improvement in the global baseline of physical and mental health, and probably even a general elevation of human intelligence.

Will hard-nosed science and contemplative-based spirituality in fact cross-fertilize to create new understandings and technologies that accelerate classical enlightenment on this planet? I don't know. But I do know that there is plenty of evidence that suggests this could happen; it's not a ridiculously impossible prospect.

Some people claim that there are currently known technologies that significantly accelerate enlightenment. I disagree. Although it's true that some of the brain hacks currently available seem to marginally help some people do better in meditation, they still fall far short of reliably and effectively fostering classical enlightenment. The breakthroughs I'm envisioning are planet-changing. Anything short of that cannot claim to be a science-based technology of enlightenment. Does any currently available process provide that level of clout? I sincerely doubt it. Might we develop something in the next century that carries that level of clout? I sincerely wish it.

Good, new technology typically requires good, new basic science. Our current imaging technology is probably woefully insufficient to capture the biophysiology of enlightenment, and our neuromodeling methods are probably far too crude.

My happiest thought involves two steps. First, discover a biophysical model for enlightenment (assuming one exists). Then, create technological boosts that reliably facilitate it (if that's possible). Anything short of that is, in my way of thinking, insufficient—indeed, trivial. Causes have consequences. If my happiest thought is correct, the entire course of human history could dramatically change for the better. Enlightenment could go viral.

Neuroscience is progressing rapidly, and thanks to organizations like the Mind and Life Institute, many young neuroscientists—perhaps even most—have been exposed to meditation. If we can hold out for another century or so, we may well create the kind of science I dream of. A pessimistic person might say that a technology powerful enough to liberate the planet will also be powerful enough to enslave it. That may be so. Perhaps the devils and the angels of our species will run neck and neck to the end. My gut tells me that the angels will win. A happy thought indeed.

Of course, I'm not claiming that this hopeful scenario *will* inevitably unfold, only that it's not ludicrous or far-fetched. Knowing that this research program *could* be successful helps me cope with the senseless litany of horrors that is the news I watch each evening. And knowing that I am in a small way part of this research energizes this aging body when I get up each morning.

I began this chapter with a quote from H. G. Wells, who is credited with an impressive string of accurate predictions. In his nineteenth- and early twentieth-century works, he describes things like the

Internet, Wikipedia, and role-playing war games. He accurately predicted when World War II would begin and that it would be aerial in nature. Most famously, he described a then-fictional mechanism whereby splitting atoms propagate in a chain reaction releasing huge amounts of energy for use in war and peace. Leo Szilard, a key figure in the early development of atomic energy, explicitly acknowledged that the fictional writings of Wells had influenced his real-world research.

Will Wells turn out to be right about the Buddha and humanity's future? Let's look again at what he said nearly a century ago.

> It is quite possible that in contact with western science, and inspired by the spirit of history, the original teaching of Gautama, revived and purified, may yet play a large part in the direction of human destiny.
>
> H. G. WELLS, 1920

I would rephrase this slightly with a twist:

> It is not *unreasonable* that in contact with *modern* science, and inspired by the spirit of history, the original *discoveries* of Gautama, *rigorized* and *extended, will* play a large part in the direction of human destiny.
>
> SHINZEN YOUNG, 2015

Index

About the Author

Shinzen Young became fascinated with Asian culture while a teenager in Los Angeles. Later he enrolled in a PhD program in Buddhist Studies at the University of Wisconsin. Eventually, he went to Asia and did extensive training in each of the three major Buddhist traditions: Vajrayana, Zen, and Vipassana. Upon returning to the United States, his academic interests shifted to the burgeoning dialogue between Eastern meditation and Western science.

Shinzen is known for his innovative "interactive, algorithmic approach" to mindfulness, a system specifically designed for use in pain management, recovery support, and as an adjunct to psychotherapy. He leads meditation retreats throughout North America and has helped establish numerous mindfulness centers and programs. He also consults widely on meditation-related research, in both the clinical and the basic science domains.

Shinzen often says, "My life's passion lies in exploring what may arise from the cross-fertilization of the best of the East with the best of the West."

About Unified Mindfulness

Many people experience immediate positive effects from mindfulness, but its real power to foster broad and deep psycho-spiritual transformation only becomes evident through ongoing practice. The problem is that most people are not able to get away on a regular basis to do extended retreats. Without regular retreats it is usually difficult to realize the exponential growth potential of the practice. Family and work responsibilities, the expenses involved, and the travel required prevent the vast majority of those ready to take on a regular practice from doing so.

To overcome these barriers, Shinzen Young has developed a unique program of monthly phone-based "mini retreats." These retreats involve guided practice, self practice, group discussion, and a chance for one-on-one private interviews with a teacher—just like onsite retreats do.

Shinzen's approach is not so much a specific system of practice, but rather a general way of thinking about any system of practice. In the past, Shinzen has called this perspective "Basic Mindfulness," but he also has characterized it as "Unified Mindfulness." He chose the word *basic* not to indicate simple, but rather as a reminder of what he considers to be the core principle that underlies most successful scientific theories. Shinzen takes each aspect of practice and analyzes it into its basic dimensions, what a mathematician would refer to as its "basis vectors."

Shinzen's hope is that students will use that perspective to appreciate all approaches to practice and to feel comfortable at anyone's retreat regardless of lineage or the personal style of the teacher, hence *unified* mindfulness. If you find this perspective appealing and would like to go deeper, you can check out the following sites:

- shinzen.org
- unifiedmindfulness.com
- unifiedmindfulness.org

About Sounds True

Sounds True is a multimedia publisher whose mission is to inspire and support personal transformation and spiritual awakening. Founded in 1985 and located in Boulder, Colorado, we work with many of the leading spiritual teachers, thinkers, healers, and visionary artists of our time. We strive with every title to preserve the essential "living wisdom" of the author or artist. It is our goal to create products that not only provide information to a reader or listener, but that also embody the quality of a wisdom transmission.

For those seeking genuine transformation, Sounds True is your trusted partner. At SoundsTrue.com you will find a wealth of free resources to support your journey, including exclusive weekly audio interviews, free downloads, interactive learning tools, and other special savings on all our titles.

To learn more, please visit SoundsTrue.com/freegifts or call us toll-free at 800.333.9185.

SOUNDS TRUE
many voices, one journey

T S Eliot
Wm Blake